D1881579

THE SACRED BOOKS OF THE EAST

F. MAX MULLER (ED.)

LIST OF THE 50 VOLUMES

1. Upanishads.
2. Sacred Laws of Aryas.
3. Texts of Confucianism.
4. Zend-Avesta.
5. Pahlavi Texts.
6. Qur'an.
7. Institutes of Vishnu.
8. Bhagavadgita, & c.
9. Qur'an.
10. (i) Dhammapada.
10. (ii) Sutta-Nipata.
11. Buddhist Suttas.
12. Satapatha-Brahmana.
13. Vinaya Texts.
14. Sacred Laws of Aryas.
15. Upanishads.
16. Texts of Confucianism.
17. Vinaya Texts.
18. Pahlavi Texts.
19. Fo-sho-hing-tsanking.
20. Vinaya Texts.
21. Saddharma Pundarika.
22. Gaina-Sutras.
23. Zend-Avesta.
24. Pahlavi Texts.
25. Laws of Manu.
26. Satapatha-Brahmana.
27. Texts of Confucianism (Li Ki).
28. Texts of Confucianism (Li Ki).
29. Grihya-Sutras.
30 Grihya-Sutras.
31. Zend-Avesta.
32. Vedic Hymns.
33. Minor Law-Books.
34. Vedanta-Sutras.
35. Milinda.
36. Milinda.
37. Pahlavi Texts.
38. Vedanta-Sutras.
39. Texts of Taoism
40. Texts of Taoism
41. Satapatha-Brahmana
42. Atharva-veda.
43. Satapatha-Brahmana.
44. Satapatha-Brahmana.
45. Gaina-Sutras.
46. Vedic Hymns.
47. Pahlavi Texts.
48. Vedanta-Sutras.
49. (i) Buddhakarita.
49. (ii) Mahayana Texts.
50. A General Index

The Sacred Books of the East (China) Vol. 40

THE TEXTS OF TAOISM

Edited by

F. MAX MULLER

Translated by

JAMES LEGGE

PART II

THE WRITINGS OF KWANG-3ZE
BOOKS XVIII–XXXIII

THE THAI-SHANG TRACTATE OF ACTIONS AND THEIR RETRIBUTIONS

APPENDICES I-VIII

GYAN

Published by

Gyan Publishing House
5, Ansari Road
Daryaganj, New Delhi-110002
Phone: 011-47034999, 9811692060
E-mail: books@gyanbooks.com

Distribution Network
gyanbooks.com
India, USA, Canada, UK, Australia, France

ISBN : 978-81-212-2937-1 (Set)
ISBN : 978-81-212-2765-0 (PB)
First Published, 1891

2nd Impression 2021

Printed at: Gyan Press, Delhi.

The Sacred Books of the East (China) Vol. 40

The Texts of Taoism, Part-II
Edited by: F. Max Muller, Translated by: James Legge

THE

SACRED BOOKS OF THE EAST

TRANSLATED

BY VARIOUS ORIENTAL SCHOLARS

AND EDITED BY

F. MAX MÜLLER

VOL. XL

Oxford

AT THE CLARENDON PRESS

1891

THE

SACRED BOOKS OF CHINA

THE TEXTS OF TÂOISM

TRANSLATED BY

JAMES LEGGE

PART II

THE WRITINGS OF *K*WANG-ȜZE

BOOKS XVIII—XXXIII

THE THÂI-SHANG TRACTATE OF ACTIONS AND THEIR RETRIBUTIONS

APPENDIXES I-VIII

Oxford

AT THE CLARENDON PRESS

1891

CONTENTS.

THE WRITINGS OF *K*WANG-3ZE.

PART II.

PART III.

THE THÂI-SHANG TRACTATE OF ACTIONS AND THEIR RETRIBUTIONS.

APPENDIXES.

THE TEXTS OF TÂOISM.

BOOK XVIII.

PART II. SECTION XI.

*K*ih Lo, or 'Perfect Enjoyment[1].'

1. Under the sky is perfect enjoyment to be found or not? Are there any who can preserve themselves alive or not? If there be, what do they do? What do they maintain? What do they avoid? What do they attend to? Where do they resort to? Where do they keep from? What do they delight in? What do they dislike?

What the world honours is riches, dignities, longevity, and being deemed able. What it delights in is rest for the body, rich flavours, fine garments, beautiful colours, and pleasant music. What it looks down on are poverty and mean condition, short life and being deemed feeble[2]. What men consider bitter experiences are that their bodies do not get rest and ease, that their mouths do not get food of rich flavour, that their persons are not finely clothed, that their eyes do not see beautiful colours, and that their ears do not listen to pleasant music. If they do not

---

[1] See vol. xxxix, pp. 149, 150.

[2] Of riches, dignities, longevity, and their opposites, enough is said, while the other two qualities are lightly passed over, and referred to only in connexion with 'meritorious officers.' I can only understand them as in the translation.

get these things, they are very sorrowful, and go on to be troubled with fears. Their thoughts are all about the body;—are they not silly?

Now the rich embitter their lives by their incessant labours; they accumulate more wealth than they can use:—while they act thus for the body, they make it external to themselves[1]. Those who seek for honours carry their pursuit of them from the day into the night, full of anxiety about their methods whether they are skilful or not:—while they act thus for the body they treat it as if it were indifferent to them[2]. The birth of man is at the same time the birth of his sorrow; and if he live long he becomes more and more stupid, and the longer is his anxiety that he may not die; how great is his bitterness!—while he thus acts for his body, it is for a distant result. Meritorious officers are regarded by the world as good; but (their goodness) is not sufficient to keep their persons alive. I do not know whether the goodness ascribed to them be really good or really not good. If indeed it be considered good, it is not sufficient to preserve their persons alive; if it be deemed not good, it is sufficient to preserve other men alive. Hence it is said, 'When faithful remonstrances are not listened to, (the remonstrant) should sit still, let (his ruler) take his course, and not strive with him.' Therefore when 3ze-hsü[3] strove with (his ruler), he brought on him-

[1] If they did not do so, they would be content when they had enough.

[2] Wishing to attach it more closely to them.

[3] Wû 3ze-hsü, the scourge of *Kh*û; and who perished miserably at last, when the king of Wû would no longer listen to his remonstrances;—in about B.C. 475.

self the mutilation of his body. If he had not so striven, he would not have acquired his fame:—was such (goodness) really good or was it not?

As to what the common people now do, and what they find their enjoyment in, I do not know whether the enjoyment be really enjoyment or really not. I see them in their pursuit of it following after all their aims as if with the determination of death, and as if they could not stop in their course; but what they call enjoyment would not be so to me, while yet I do not say that there is no enjoyment in it. Is there indeed such enjoyment, or is there not? I consider doing nothing (to obtain it) to be the great enjoyment[1], while ordinarily people consider it to be a great evil. Hence it is said, 'Perfect enjoyment is to be without enjoyment; the highest praise is to be without praise[2].' The right and the wrong (on this point of enjoyment) cannot indeed be determined according to (the view of) the world; nevertheless, this doing nothing (to obtain it) may determine the right and the wrong. Since perfect enjoyment is (held to be) the keeping the body alive, it is only by this doing nothing that that end is likely to be secured. Allow me to try and explain this (more fully):—Heaven does nothing, and thence comes its serenity; Earth does nothing, and thence comes its rest. By the union of these two inactivities, all things are produced. How vast and imperceptible is the process!—they seem to come from

[1] This is the secret of the Tâo.

[2] The last member of this sentence is the reading adopted by Wû *Kh*ăng towards the conclusion of the thirty-ninth chapter of the Tâo Teh *K*ing, instead of the common 致數車無車.

nowhere! How imperceptible and vast!—there is no visible image of it! All things in all their variety grow from this Inaction. Hence it is said, 'Heaven and Earth do nothing, and yet there is nothing that they do not do[1].' But what man is there that can attain to this inaction?

2. When *K*wang-ȝze's wife died, Hui-ȝze went to condole with him, and, finding him squatted on the ground, drumming on the basin[2], and singing, said to him, 'When a wife has lived with her husband, and brought up children, and then dies in her old age, not to wail for her is enough. When you go on to drum on this basin and sing, is it not an excessive (and strange) demonstration?' *K*wang-ȝze replied, 'It is not so. When she first died, was it possible for me to be singular and not affected by the event? But I reflected on the commencement of her being[3]. She had not yet been born to life; not only had she no life, but she had no bodily form; not only had she no bodily form, but she had no breath. During the intermingling of the waste and dark chaos[3], there ensued a change, and there was breath; another change, and there was the bodily form; another change, and there came birth

[1] Compare similar statements in the Tâo Teh *K*ing, ch. 48, et al.

[2] The basin or tub, not 'a basin.' The reference is, no doubt, to the basin of ice put down near or under the couch on which the body was laid. I suppose that *K*wang-ȝze was squatting so as to have this between his legs.

[3] Is the writer referring to the primal creation as we may call it, or development of things out of the chaos, or to some analogous process at the birth of his wife? However that be, birth and death appear to him to be merely changes of the same kind in the perpetual process of evolution.

and life. There is now a change again, and she is dead. The relation between these things is like the procession of the four seasons from spring to autumn, from winter to summer. There now she lies with her face up, sleeping in the Great Chamber[1]; and if I were to fall sobbing and going on to wail for her, I should think that I did not understand what was appointed (for all). I therefore restrained myself[2]!'

3. Mr. Deformed[3] and Mr. One-foot[3] were looking at the mound-graves of the departed in the wild of Khwăn-lun, where Hwang-Tî had entered into his rest. Suddenly a tumour began to grow on their left wrists, which made them look distressed as if they disliked it. The former said to the other, 'Do

---

[1] Between heaven and earth.

[2] Was it necessary he should fall singing to his drumming on the basin? But I subjoin a note here, suggested by the paragraph, which might have found, perhaps, a more appropriate place in the notice of this Book in vol. xxxix, pp. 149, 150.

In Sir John F. Davis' 'Description of the Empire of China and its Inhabitants (edition of 1857),' vol. ii, pp. 74–90, we have the amusing story of 'The Philosopher and his Wife.' The philosopher is *K*wang-ȝze, who plays the part of a magician; and of his wife it might be said, 'Frailty! thy name is woman!' Sir John Davis says, 'The story was translated into French by Père d'Entrecolles, and supplied the materials of Voltaire's Zadig.' I have not met in Chinese with Father d'Entrecolles' original. All of Zadig which can be supposed to have been borrowed from his translator is only a few sentences. The whole story is inconsistent with the account in paragraph 2 of the death of *K*wang-ȝze's wife, and with all which we learn from his writings of his character.

[3] We know nothing of these parties but what we are told here. They are called Shû, meaning 'uncle,' often equivalent in China to our 'Mr.' The lesson taught by them is that of submission to pain and death as merely phenomena in the sphere of change. For the phraseology of their names, see Bk. III, par. 3, and Bk. IV, par. 8.

you dread it?' 'No,' replied he, 'why should I dread it? Life is a borrowed thing. The living frame thus borrowed is but so much dust. Life and death are like day and night. And you and I were looking at (the graves of) those who have undergone their change. If my change is coming to me, why should I dislike it?'

4. When *K*wang-ȝze went to *Kh*û, he saw an empty skull, bleached indeed, but still retaining its shape. Tapping it with his horse-switch, he asked it, saying, 'Did you, Sir, in your greed of life, fail in the lessons of reason, and come to this? Or did you do so, in the service of a perishing state, by the punishment of the axe? Or was it through your evil conduct, reflecting disgrace on your parents and on your wife and children? Or was it through your hard endurances of cold and hunger? Or was it that you had completed your term of life?'

Having given expression to these questions, he took up the skull, and made a pillow of it when he went to sleep. At midnight the skull appeared to him in a dream, and said, 'What you said to me was after the fashion of an orator. All your words were about the entanglements of men in their lifetime. There are none of those things after death. Would you like to hear me, Sir, tell you about death?' 'I should,' said *K*wang-ȝze, and the skull resumed: 'In death there are not (the distinctions of) ruler above and minister below. There are none of the phenomena of the four seasons. Tranquil and at ease, our years are those of heaven and earth. No king in his court has greater enjoyment than we have.' *K*wang-ȝze did not believe it, and said, 'If I could get the Ruler of our Destiny[1] to restore your body to life with its bones and flesh and skin, and to give you back your father and mother, your wife and children, and all your village acquaintances, would you wish me to do so?' The skull stared fixedly at him, knitted its brows, and said, 'How should I cast away the enjoyment of my royal court, and undertake again the toils of life among mankind?'

5. When Yen Yüan went eastwards to *Kh*î, Confucius wore a look of sorrow[2]. Ȝze-kung left his mat, and asked him, saying, 'Your humble disciple ventures to ask how it is that the going eastwards of Hui to *Kh*î has given you such a look of sadness.' Confucius said, 'Your question is good. Formerly Kwan-ȝze[3] used words of which I very much approve. He said, "A small bag cannot be made to contain what is large; a short rope cannot be used to draw water from a deep well[3]." So it is, and man's appointed lot is definitely determined, and his body is adapted for definite ends, so that neither the one nor the other can be augmented or diminished. I am afraid that Hui will talk with the marquis of *Kh*î about the ways of Hwang-Tî, Yâo, and Shun, and go on to relate the words of Sui-*z*ăn and Shăn Năng. The marquis will seek (for the correspondence of what he is told) in himself; and, not finding

[1] I suppose the Tâo; but none of the commentators, so far as I have seen, say anything about the expression.

[2] Compare the long discourse of Confucius with Yen Hui, on the latter's proposing to go to Wei, in Bk. IV.

[3] Kwan Î-wû or Kwan *K*ung, the chief minister of duke Hwan of *Kh*î, whom he is supposed to have in view in his 'small bag and short rope.'

it there, will suspect the speaker; and that speaker, being suspected, will be put to death. And have you not heard this?—Formerly a sea-bird alighted in the suburban country of Lû[1]. The marquis went out to meet it, (brought it) to the ancestral temple, and prepared to banquet it there. The *K*iû-shâo[2] was performed to afford it music; an ox, a sheep, and a pig were killed to supply the food. The bird, however, looked at everything with dim eyes, and was very sad. It did not venture to eat a single bit of flesh, nor to drink a single cupful; and in three days it died.

'The marquis was trying to nourish the bird with what he used for himself, and not with the nourishment proper for a bird. They who would nourish birds as they ought to be nourished should let them perch in the deep forests, or roam over sandy plains; float on the rivers and lakes; feed on the eels and small fish; wing their flight in regular order and then stop; and be free and at ease in their resting-places. It was a distress to that bird to hear men speak; what did it care for all the noise and hubbub made about it? If the music of the *K*iû-shâo[3] or the Hsien-*kh*ih[4] were performed in the wild of the Thung-thing[4] lake, birds would fly away, and beasts would run off when they heard it, and fishes would dive down to the bottom of the water; while men, when they hear it, would come all round to-

[1] Perhaps another and more ridiculous version of the story told in 'the Narratives of the States,' II, i, art. 7.

[2] The name of Shun's music;—see the Shû (in vol. iii), par. 2.

[3] Called also Tâ Shâo, in Book XXXIII, par. 2.

[4] Hwang-Tî's music;—see Bk. XIV, par. 3.—But the genuineness of the whole paragraph is called in question.

gether, and look on. Fishes live and men die in the water. They are different in constitution, and therefore differ in their likes and dislikes. Hence it was that the ancient sages did not require (from all) the same ability, nor demand the same performances. They gave names according to the reality of what was done, and gave their approbation where it was specially suitable. This was what was called the method of universal adaptation and of sure success.'

6. Lieh-ȝze (once) upon a journey took a meal by the road-side. There he saw a skull a hundred years old, and, pulling away the bush (under which it lay), he pointed to it and said, 'It is only you and I who know that you are not dead, and that (aforetime) you were not alive. Do you indeed really find (in death) the nourishment (which you like)? Do I really find (in life my proper) enjoyment? The seeds (of things) are multitudinous and minute. On the surface of the water they form a membranous texture. When they reach to where the land and water join they become the (lichens which we call the) clothes of frogs and oysters. Coming to life on mounds and heights, they become the plantain; and, receiving manure, appear as crows' feet. The roots of the crow's foot become grubs, and its leaves, butterflies. This butterfly, known by the name of hsü, is changed into an insect, and comes to life under a furnace. Then it has the form of a moth, and is named the *kh*ü-to. The *kh*ü-to after a thousand days becomes a bird, called the *k*an-yü-kû. Its saliva becomes the sȝe-mî, and this again the shih-hsî (or pickle-eater). The î-lo is produced from the pickle-eater; the hwang-kwang from the

*k*iû-yû; the mâu-zui from the pû-khwan. The ying-hsî uniting with a bamboo, which has long ceased to put forth sprouts, produces the *kh*ing-ning; the *kh*ing-ning, the panther; the panther, the horse; and the horse, the man. Man then again enters into the great Machinery (of Evolution), from which all things come forth (at birth), and which they enter at death[1].'

---

[1] A much larger paragraph from which this must have been abbreviated, or which must have been enlarged from this, is found in the first Book of Lieh-ȝze's works (pp. 4, 5). In no Buddhist treatise is the transrotation of births more fully, and, I must add, absurdly stated.

BOOK XIX.

PART II. SECTION XII.

Tâ Shăng, or 'The Full Understanding of Life[1].'

1. He who understands the conditions of Life does not strive after what is of no use to life; and he who understands the conditions of Destiny does not strive after what is beyond the reach of knowledge. In nourishing the body it is necessary to have beforehand the things (appropriate to its support)[2]; but there are cases where there is a superabundance of such things, and yet the body is not nourished[2]. In order to have life it is necessary that it do not have left the body; but there are cases when the body has not been left by it, and yet the life has perished[3].

When life comes, it cannot be declined; when it goes, it cannot be detained. Alas! the men of the world think that to nourish the body is sufficient to preserve life; and when such nourishment is not sufficient to preserve the life, what can be done in the world that will be sufficient? Though (all that men can do) will be insufficient, yet there are things which they feel they ought to do, and they do not try to avoid doing them. For those who wish to

[1] See vol. xxxix, pp. 150, 151.

[2] Wealth will supply abundantly the things that are necessary and fit for the nourishment of the body, but sudden death may render them unavailing.

[3] That is, the higher life of the spirit has perished.

avoid caring for the body, their best plan is to abandon the world. Abandoning the world, they are free from its entanglements. Free from its entanglements, their (minds) are correct and their (temperament) is equable. Thus correct and equable, they succeed in securing a renewal of life, as some have done[1]. In securing a renewal of life, they are not far from the True (Secret of their being). But how is it sufficient to abandon worldly affairs? and how is it sufficient to forget the (business of) life? Through the renouncing of (worldly) affairs, the body has no more toil; through forgetting the (business of) life, the vital power suffers no diminution. When the body is completed and the vital power is restored (to its original vigour), the man is one with Heaven. Heaven and Earth are the father and mother of all things. It is by their union that the body is formed; it is by their separation that a (new) beginning is brought about. When the body and vital power suffer no diminution, we have what may be called the transference of power. From the vital force there comes another more vital, and man returns to be the assistant of Heaven.

2. My master[2] Lieh-ȝze[2] asked Yin, (the warden) of the gate[2], saying, 'The perfect man walks under

[1] I think I have caught the meaning. The phrase signifying 'the renewal of life' has been used to translate 'being born again' in John's Gospel, ch. 3.

[2] We find here Lieh-ȝze (whose name has already occurred several times) in communication with the warden Yin, who was a contemporary of Lâo-ȝze, and we must refer him therefore to the sixth century B.C. He could not therefore be contemporary with our author, and yet the three characters of the text mean 'My Master, Lieh-ȝze;' and the whole of the paragraph is found in Lieh-ȝze's second Book (4^a–5^a) with a good many variants in the text.

water without encountering any obstruction, treads on fire without being burned, and walks on high above all things without any fear; let me ask how he attains to do this[1]?' The warden Yin replied, 'It is by his keeping of the pure breath (of life); it is not to be described as an achievement of his skill or daring. Sit down, and I will explain it to you. Whatever has form, semblance, sound, and colour is a thing; how can one thing come to be different from another? But it is not competent for any of these things to reach to what preceded them all;—they are but (form and) visibility. But (the perfect man) attains to be (as it were) without form, and beyond the capability of being transformed. Now when one attains to this and carries it out to the highest degree, how can other things come into his way to stop him? He will occupy the place assigned to him without going beyond it, and lie concealed in the clue which has no end. He will study with delight the process which gives their beginning and ending to all things. By gathering his nature into a unity, by nourishing his vital power, by concentrating his virtue, he will penetrate to the making of things. In this condition, with his heavenly constitution kept entire, and with no crevice in his spirit, how can things enter (and disturb his serenity)?

'Take the case of a drunken man falling from his carriage;—though he may suffer injury, he will not

---

The gate was at the passage leading from the Royal Domain of those days into the great feudal territory of Ȝin;—from the north-west of the present province of Ho-nan into Shen-hsî.

[1] Lieh-ȝze puts an absurd question to the warden, which is replied to at length, and unsatisfactorily. We need not discuss either the question or the answer in this place.

die. His bones and joints are the same as those of other men, but the injury which he receives is different:—his spirit is entire. He knew nothing about his getting into the carriage, and knew nothing about his falling from it. The thought of death or life, or of any alarm or affright, does not enter his breast; and therefore he encounters danger without any shrinking from it. Completely under the influence of the liquor he has drunk, it is thus with him;—how much more would it be so, if he were under the influence of his Heavenly constitution! The sagely man is kept hid in his Heavenly constitution, and therefore nothing can injure him.

'A man in the pursuit of vengeance would not break the (sword) Mo-yê or Yü-*k*iang (which had done the deed); nor would one, however easily made wrathful, wreak his resentment on the fallen brick. In this way all under heaven there would be peace, without the disorder of assaults and fighting, without the punishments of death and slaughter:—such would be the issue of the course (which I have described). If the disposition that is of human origin be not developed, but that which is the gift of Heaven, the development of the latter will produce goodness, while that of the former would produce hurt. If the latter were not wearied of, and the former not slighted, the people would be brought nearly to their True nature.'

3. When *K*ung-nî was on his way to *Kh*û, as he issued from a forest, he saw a hunchback receiving cicadas (on the point of a rod), as if he were picking them up with his hand[1]. 'You are clever!' said he

[1] This paragraph is also found with variations in Lieh-ȝze,

to the man. 'Is there any method in it?' The hunchback replied, 'There is. For five or six months, I practised with two pellets, till they never fell down, and then I only failed with a small fraction[1] of the cicadas (which I tried to catch). Having succeeded in the same way with three (pellets), I missed only one cicada in ten. Having succeeded with five, I caught the cicadas as if I were gathering them. My body is to me no more than the stump of a broken trunk, and my shoulder no more than the branch of a rotten tree. Great as heaven and earth are, and multitudinous as things are, I take no notice of them, but only of the wings of my cicadas; neither turning nor inclining to one side. I would not for them all exchange the wings of my cicadas;—how should I not succeed in taking them?' Confucius looked round, and said to his disciples, '"Where the will is not diverted from its object, the spirit is concentrated;"—this might have been spoken of this hunchback gentleman.'

4. Yen Yüan asked *K*ung-nî, saying, 'When I was crossing the gulf of *Kh*ang-shăn[2], the ferryman handled the boat like a spirit. I asked him whether such management of a boat could be learned, and he replied, "It may. Good swimmers can learn it quickly; but as for divers, without having seen a boat, they can manage it at once." He did not

Bk. II (9ᵃ). The dexterity of the hunchback in catching the cicadas will remind some readers of the account given by the butcher in Book III of his dexterity in cutting up his oxen.

[1] The names of two small weights, used anciently for 'a fraction,' 'a small proportion.'

[2] This is another paragraph common both to our author and Lieh-ȝze, but in neither is there any intimation of the place.

directly tell me what I asked;—I venture to ask you what he meant.' *K*ung-nî replied, 'Good swimmers acquire the ability quickly;—they forget the water (and its dangers). As to those who are able to dive, and without having seen a boat are able to manage it at once, they look on the watery gulf as if it were a hill-side, and the upsetting of a boat as the going back of a carriage. Such upsettings and goings back have occurred before them multitudes of times, and have not seriously affected their minds. Wherever they go, they feel at ease on their occurrence.

'He who is contending for a piece of earthenware puts forth all his skill[1]. If the prize be a buckle of brass, he shoots timorously; if it be for an article of gold, he shoots as if he were blind. The skill of the archer is the same in all the cases; but (in the two latter cases) he is under the influence of solicitude, and looks on the external prize as most important. All who attach importance to what is external show stupidity in themselves.'

5. Thien Khâi-*k*ih[2] was having an interview with duke Wei of *K*âu[2], who said to him, 'I have heard that (your master) *K*û Hsin[2] has studied the subject of Life. What have you, good Sir, heard from him about it in your intercourse with him?' Thien Khâi-*k*ih replied, 'In my waiting on him in the courtyard with my broom, what should I have heard from my master?' Duke Wei said, 'Do not put the question off, Mr. Thien; I wish to hear what

---

[1] I think this is the meaning. 注 is defined by 射而賭物, 'to compete for anything by archery.'

[2] We have no information about who these personages and the others below were, and I have missed the story, if it be in Lieh-ȝze. The duke, it will be seen, had the appanage of *K*âu.

you have to say.' Khâi-*k*ih then replied, 'I have heard my master say that they who skilfully nourish their life are like shepherds, who whip up the sheep that they see lagging behind[1].' 'What did he mean?' asked the duke. The reply was, 'In Lû there was a Shan Pâo, who lived among the rocks, and drank only water. He would not share with the people in their toils and the benefits springing from them; and though he was now in his seventieth year, he had still the complexion of a child. Unfortunately he encountered a hungry tiger, which killed and ate him. There was also a *K*ang Î, who hung up a screen at his lofty door, and to whom all the people hurried (to pay their respects)[2]. In his fortieth year, he fell ill of a fever and died. (Of these two men), Pâo nourished his inner man, and a tiger ate his outer; while Î nourished his outer man, and disease attacked his inner. Both of them neglected whipping up their lagging sheep.'

*K*ung-nî said, 'A man should not retire and hide himself; he should not push forward and display himself; he should be like the decayed tree which stands in the centre of the ground. Where these three conditions are fulfilled, the name will reach its greatest height. When people fear the dangers of a path, if one man in ten be killed, then fathers and sons, elder brothers and younger, warn one another that they must not go out on a journey without a large number of retainers;—and is it not a mark of wisdom to do so? But there are dangers which

[1] Pay more attention to any part of their culture which they are neglecting.

[2] It served its purpose there, but had not been put in its place with any special object.

men incur on the mats of their beds, and in eating and drinking; and when no warning is given against them;—is it not a mark of error[1]?'

6. The officer of Prayer[2] in his dark and square-cut robes goes to the pig-pen, and thus counsels the pigs, 'Why should you shrink from dying? I will for three months feed you on grain. Then for ten days I will fast, and keep vigil for three days, after which I will put down the mats of white grass, and lay your shoulders and rumps on the carved stand;—will not this suit you?' If he had spoken from the standpoint of the pigs, he would have said, 'The better plan will be to feed us with our bran and chaff, and leave us in our pen.' When consulting for himself, he preferred to enjoy, while he lived, his carriage and cap of office, and after death to be borne to the grave on the ornamented carriage, with the canopy over his coffin. Consulting for the pigs, he did not think of these things, but for himself he would have chosen them. Why did he think so differently (for himself and) for the pigs[3]?

7. (Once), when duke Hwan[4] was hunting by a marsh, with Kwan *K*ung[5] driving the carriage, he saw a ghost. Laying his hand on that of Kwan

---

[1] This may seem to nourish the body, but in reality injures the life.

[2] Who had the charge also of the sacrifices.

[3] Lin Hsî-*k*ung says that the story shows the many troubles that arise from not renouncing the world. Ensnared by the world, men sacrifice for it their higher life, and are not so wise as pigs are for their life. The short paragraph bristles with difficulties.

[4] The first of the leading chieftains among the princes; B.C. 683–642.

[5] His chief minister.

Kung, he said to him, 'Do you see anything, Father Kung?' 'Your servant sees nothing,' was the reply. The duke then returned, talking incoherently and becoming ill, so that for several days he did not go out. Among the officers of Khî there was a Hwang-ȝze Kâo-âo[1], who said to the duke, 'Your Grace is injuring yourself; how could a ghost injure you? When a paroxysm of irritation is dispersed, and the breath does not return (to the body), what remains in the body is not sufficient for its wants. When it ascends and does not descend, the patient becomes accessible to gusts of anger. When it descends and does not ascend, he loses his memory of things. When it neither ascends nor descends, but remains about the heart in the centre of the body, it makes him ill.' The duke said, 'Yes, but are there ghostly sprites[2]?' The officer replied, 'There are. About mountain tarns there is the Lî; about furnaces, the Khieh; about the dust-heaps inside the door, the Lei-thing. In low-lying places in the north-east, the Pei-a and Wa-lung leap about, and in similar places in the north-west there dwells the Yî-yang. About rivers there is the Wang-hsiang; about mounds, the Hsin; about hills, the Khwei; about wilds, the Fang-hwang; about marshes, the Wei-tho.' 'Let me ask what is the Wei-tho like?' asked the duke. Hwang-ȝze said, 'It is the size of the

[1] An officer introduced here for the occasion, by surname Hwang, and designation Kâo-âo. The Ȝze simply=Mr.

[2] The commentators have a deal to say about the folklore of the various sprites mentioned. 'The whole shows that ghostly sprites are the fruit of a disordered mind.' It is a touch of nature that the prince recovers as soon as he knows that the ghost he had seen was of good presage.

nave of a chariot wheel, and the length of the shaft. It wears a purple robe and a red cap. It dislikes the rumbling noise of chariot wheels, and, when it hears it, it puts both its hands to its head and stands up. He who sees it is likely to become the leader of all the other princes.' Duke Hwan burst out laughing and said, 'This was what I saw.' On this he put his robes and cap to rights, and made Hwang-ȝze sit with him. Before the day was done, his illness was quite gone, he knew not how.

8. *K*î Hsing-ȝze was rearing a fighting-cock for the king[1]. Being asked after ten days if the bird were ready, he said, 'Not yet; he is still vain and quarrelsome, and relies on his own vigour.' Being asked the same after other ten days, he said, 'Not yet; he still responds to the crow and the appearance of another bird.' After ten days more, he replied, 'Not yet. He still looks angrily, and is full of spirit.' When a fourth ten days had passed, he replied to the question, 'Nearly so. Though another cock crows, it makes no change in him. To look at him, you would say he was a cock of wood. His quality is complete. No other cock will dare to meet him, but will run from him.'

9. Confucius was looking at the cataract near the gorge of Lü[2], which fell a height of 240 cubits, and

[1] According to the Lieh-ȝze version of this story (Bk. II, 17b), the king was king Hsüan, B.C. 827–782. The trainer's rule seems to have been that his bird should meet its antagonist, with all its vigour complete and undisturbed, and not wishing to fight.

[2] I think that there are two versions of this story in Lieh-ȝze. In Bk. VIII (4b, 5a), it appears that Confucius was on his way from Wei to Lû, when he stopped his carriage or cart at this spot to view the cataract, and the incident occurred, and he took the opportunity to give the lesson to his disciples.

the spray of which floated a distance of forty lî, (producing a turbulence) in which no tortoise, gavial, fish, or turtle could play. He saw, however, an old man swimming about in it, as if he had sustained some great calamity, and wished to end his life. Confucius made his disciples hasten along the stream to rescue the man; and by the time they had gone several hundred paces, he was walking along singing, with his hair dishevelled, and enjoying himself at the foot of the embankment. Confucius followed and asked him, saying, 'I thought you were a sprite; but, when I look closely at you, I see that you are a man. Let me ask if you have any particular way of treading the water.' The man said, 'No, I have no particular way. I began (to learn the art) at the very earliest time; as I grew up, it became my nature to practise it; and my success in it is now as sure as fate. I enter and go down with the water in the very centre of its whirl, and come up again with it when it whirls the other way. I follow the way of the water, and do nothing contrary to it of myself;—this is how I tread it.' Confucius said, 'What do you mean by saying that you began to learn the art at the very earliest time; that as you grew up, it became your nature to practise it, and that your success in it now is as sure as fate?' The man replied, 'I was born among these hills and lived contented among them;—that was why I say that I have trod this water from my earliest time. I grew up by it, and have been happy treading it;—that is why I said that to tread it had become natural to me. I know not how I do it, and yet I do it;—that is why I say that my success is as sure as fate.'

10. *Kh*ing, the Worker in Rottlera[1] wood, carved a bell-stand[2], and when it was completed, all who saw it were astonished as if it were the work of spirits. The marquis of Lû went to see it, and asked by what art he had succeeded in producing it. 'Your subject is but a mechanic,' was the reply; 'what art should I be possessed of? Nevertheless, there is one thing (which I will mention). When your servant had undertaken to make the bell-stand, I did not venture to waste any of my power, and felt it necessary to fast in order to compose my mind. After fasting for three days, I did not presume to think of any congratulation, reward, rank, or emolument (which I might obtain by the execution of my task); after fasting five days, I did not presume to think of the condemnation or commendation (which it would produce), or of the skill or want of skill (which it might display). At the end of the seven days, I had forgotten all about myself;—my four limbs and my whole person. By this time the thought of your Grace's court (for which I was to make the thing) had passed away; everything that could divert my mind from exclusive devotion to the exercise of my skill had disappeared. Then I went into the forest, and looked at the natural forms of the trees. When I saw one of a perfect form, then the figure of the bell-stand rose up to my view, and I applied my hand to the work. Had

[1] The 3ze or rottlera was and is a very famous tree, called 'the king of trees,' from its stately appearance and the excellence of its timber.

[2] The 'bell-stand' is celebrated in the Shih King, III, i, Ode 8. A complete peal consisted of twelve bells, suspended in two tiers one above the other.

I not met with such a tree, I must have abandoned the object; but my Heaven-given faculty and the Heaven-given qualities of the wood were concentrated on it. So it was that my spirit was thus engaged in the production of the bell-stand.'

11. Tung-yê *K*î[1] was introduced to duke *K*wang[2] to exhibit his driving. His horses went forwards and backwards with the straightness of a line, and wheeled to the right and the left with the exactness of a circle. The duke thought that the lines and circles could not be surpassed if they were woven with silken strings, and told him to make a hundred circuits on the same lines. On the road Yen Ho[3] met the equipage, and on entering (the palace), and seeing the duke, he said, '*K*î's horses will break down,' but the duke was silent, and gave him no reply. After a little the horses did come back, having broken down; and the duke then said, 'How did you know that it would be so?' Yen Ho said, 'The horses were exhausted, and he was still urging them on. It was this which made me say that they would break down.'

12. The artisan Shui[4] made things round (and square) more exactly than if he had used the circle

---

[1] *K*î would be the name of the charioteer, a gentleman of Lû, called Tung-yê, 'eastern country,' I suppose from the situation of his estate.

[2] Duke *K*wang would be the marquis Thung of Lû, B.C. 693–662.

[3] Yen Ho was probably the chief of the Yen family at the time. A scion of it, Yen Hui, afterwards became the favourite disciple of Confucius. He could hardly be the same Yen Ho who is mentioned in Bk. IV, par. 5. *K*î has had, and still has, his representatives in every country.

[4] Shui is mentioned in the Shû King, V, xxii, 19, as a famous maker of arrows. Some carry him back to the time of Shun.

and square. The operation of his fingers on (the forms of) things was like the transformations of them (in nature), and required no application of his mind; and so his Intelligence[1] was entire and encountered no resistance.

13. To be unthought of by the foot that wears it is the fitness of a shoe; to be unthought of by the waist is the fitness of a girdle. When one's wisdom does not think of the right or the wrong (of a question under discussion), that shows the suitability of the mind (for the question); when one is conscious of no inward change, or outward attraction, that shows the mastery of affairs. He who perceives at once the fitness, and never loses the sense of it, has the fitness that forgets all about what is fitting.

14. There was a Sun Hsiû[2] who went to the door of Ʒze-pien *Kh*ing-ʒze, and said to him in a strange perturbed way, 'When I lived in my village, no one took notice of me, but all said that I did not cultivate (my fields); in a time of trouble and attack, no one took notice of me, but all said that I had no courage. But that I did not cultivate my fields, was really because I never met with a good year; and that I did not do service for our ruler, was because I did not meet with the suitable opportunity to do so. I have been sent about my business by the villagers, and am driven away by the registrars of the district;—what is my crime? O Heaven! how is it that I have met with such a fate?'

---

[1] Literally, 'Tower of Intelligence,'—a Tâoistic name for the mind.

[2] A weakling, of whom we know only what we read here.

Pien-ȝze[1] said to him, 'Have you not heard how the perfect man deals with himself? He forgets that he has a liver and gall. He takes no thought of his ears and eyes. He seems lost and aimless beyond the dust and dirt of the world, and enjoys himself at ease in occupations untroubled by the affairs of business. He may be described as acting and yet not relying on what he does, as being superior and yet not using his superiority to exercise any control. But now you would make a display of your wisdom to astonish the ignorant; you would cultivate your person to make the inferiority of others more apparent; you seek to shine as if you were carrying the sun and moon in your hands. That you are complete in your bodily frame, and possess all its nine openings; that you have not met with any calamity in the middle of your course, such as deafness, blindness, or lameness, and can still take your place as a man among other men;—in all this you are fortunate. What leisure have you to murmur against Heaven? Go away, Sir.'

Sun-ȝze on this went out, and Pien-ȝze went inside. Having sitten down, after a little time he looked up to heaven, and sighed. His disciples asked him why he sighed, and he said to them, 'Hsiû came to me a little while ago, and I told him the characteristics of the perfect man. I am afraid he will be frightened, and get into a state of perplexity.' His disciples said, 'Not so. If what he said was right, and what you

---

[1] This must have been a man of more note. We find him here with a school of disciples in his house, and sought out for counsel by men like Sun Hsiû.

said was wrong, the wrong will certainly not be able to perplex the right. If what he said was wrong, and what you said was right, it was just because he was perplexed that he came to you. What was your fault in dealing with him as you did?' Pien-ȝze said, 'Not so. Formerly a bird came, and took up its seat in the suburbs of Lû[1]. The ruler of Lû was pleased with it, and provided an ox, a sheep, and a pig to feast it, causing also the *K*iû-shâo to be performed to delight it. But the bird began to be sad, looked dazed, and did not venture to eat or drink. This was what is called "Nourishing a bird, as you would nourish yourself." He who would nourish a bird as a bird should be nourished should let it perch in a deep forest, or let it float on a river or lake, or let it find its food naturally and undisturbed on the level dry ground. Now Hsiû (came to me), a man of slender intelligence, and slight information, and I told him of the characteristics of the perfect man, it was like using a carriage and horses to convey a mouse, or trying to delight a quail with the music of bells and drums;—could the creatures help being frightened?'

---

[1] Compare par. 5, Bk. XVIII.

BOOK XX.

PART II. SECTION XIII.

Shan Mû, or 'The Tree on the Mountain[1].'

1. *K*wang-ȝze was walking on a mountain, when he saw a great tree[2] with huge branches and luxuriant foliage. A wood-cutter was resting by its side, but he would not touch it, and, when asked the reason, said, that it was of no use for anything. *K*wang-ȝze then said to his disciples, 'This tree, because its wood is good for nothing, will succeed in living out its natural term of years.' Having left the mountain, the Master lodged in the house of an old friend, who was glad to see him, and ordered his waiting-lad to kill a goose and boil it. The lad said, 'One of our geese can cackle, and the other cannot;—which of them shall I kill?' The host said, 'Kill the one that cannot cackle.'

Next day, his disciples asked *K*wang-ȝze, saying, 'Yesterday the tree on the mountain (you said) would live out its years because of the uselessness of its wood, and now our host's goose has died because of its want of power (to cackle);—which of these conditions, Master, would you prefer to be in?' *K*wang-ȝze laughed and said, '(If I said that) I would prefer to be in a position between being fit to be useful and wanting that fitness, that would

---

[1] See vol. xxxix, p. 151.

[2] Compare the accounts of great trees in I, par. 6; IV, par. 1; et al.

seem to be the right position, but it would not be so, for it would not put me beyond being involved in trouble; whereas one who takes his seat on the Tâo and its Attributes, and there finds his ease and enjoyment, is not exposed to such a contingency. He is above the reach both of praise and of detraction; now he (mounts aloft) like a dragon, now he (keeps beneath) like a snake; he is transformed with the (changing) character of the time, and is not willing to addict himself to any one thing; now in a high position and now in a low, he is in harmony with all his surroundings; he enjoys himself at ease with the Author of all things [1]; he treats things as things, and is not a thing to them:—where is his liability to be involved in trouble? This was the method of Shăn Năng and Hwang-Tî. As to those who occupy themselves with the qualities of things, and with the teaching and practice of the human relations, it is not so with them. Union brings on separation; success, overthrow; sharp corners, the use of the file; honour, critical remarks; active exertion, failure; wisdom, scheming; inferiority, being despised:—where is the possibility of unchangeableness in any of these conditions? Remember this, my disciples. Let your abode be here,—in the Tâo and its Attributes [2].'

2. Î-liâo [3], an officer of Shih-nan [3], having an in-

[1] The Tâo; called 衆父父, in Bk. XII, par. 5.

[2] But after all it comes to be the same thing in point of fact with those who ground themselves in the Tâo, and with others.

[3] The Î-liâo here was a scion of the ruling House of *Khû*, and is mentioned fortunately in the Supplement to the Ȝo-*kh*wan, under the very year in which Confucius died (B.C. 479). His residence was in the south of the 'Market Place' of the city where he lived,

terview with the marquis of Lû[1], found him looking sad, and asked him why he was so. The marquis said, 'I have studied the ways of the former kings, and cultivated the inheritance left me by my predecessors. I reverence the spirits of the departed and honour the men of worth, doing this with personal devotion, and without the slightest intermission. Notwithstanding, I do not avoid meeting with calamity, and this it is which makes me sad.' The officer said, 'The arts by which you try to remove calamity are shallow. Think of the close-furred fox and of the elegantly-spotted leopard. They lodge in the forests on the hills, and lurk in their holes among the rocks;—keeping still. At night they go about, and during day remain in their lairs;—so cautious are they. Even if they are suffering from hunger, thirst, and other distresses, they still keep aloof from men, seeking their food about the *K*iang and the Ho;—so resolute are they. Still they are not able to escape the danger of the net or the trap; and what fault is it of theirs? It is their skins which occasion them the calamity.

'And is not the state of Lû your lordship's skin? I wish your lordship to rip your skin from your body, to cleanse your heart, to put away your desires, and to enjoy yourself where you will be

---

which is the meaning of the Shih-nan in the text. The description of his character is that no offer of gain could win him, and no threatening terrify him. We find him here at the court of Lû in friendly conference with the marquis, and trying to persuade him to adopt the ways of Tâoism, which he presents to him under the figure of an allegory, an utopia called 'the State of Established Virtue,' in the south of Yüeh.

[1] Probably known to us as 'duke Âi.'

without the presence of any one. In the southern state of Yüeh, there is a district called "the State of Established Virtue." The people are ignorant and simple; their object is to minimise the thought of self and make their desires few; they labour but do not lay up their gains; they give but do not seek for any return; they do not know what righteousness is required of them in any particular case, nor by what ceremonies their performances should be signalised; acting in a wild and eccentric way as if they were mad, they yet keep to the grand rules of conduct. Their birth is an occasion for joy; their death is followed by the rites of burial. I should wish your lordship to leave your state; to give up your ordinary ways, and to proceed to that country by the directest course.'

The ruler said, 'The way to it is distant and difficult; there are rivers and hills; and as I have neither boat nor carriage, how am I to go?' The officer from Shih-nan rejoined, 'If your lordship abjure your personal state, and give up your wish to remain here, that will serve you for a carriage.' The ruler rejoined, 'The way to it is solitary and distant, and there are no people on it;—whom shall I have as my companions? I have no provisions prepared, and how shall I get food?—how shall I be able to get (to the country)?' The officer said, 'Minimise your lordship's expenditure, and make your wants few, and though you have no provisions prepared, you will find you have enough. Wade through the rivers and float along on the sea, where however you look, you see not the shore, and, the farther you go, you do not see where your journey is to end;—those who escorted you to the shore will return, and after that you will feel yourself far away. Thus it is that he who owns men (as their ruler) is involved in troubles, and he who is owned by men (as their ruler) suffers from sadness; and hence Yâo would neither own men, nor be owned by them. I wish to remove your trouble, and take away your sadness, and it is only (to be done by inducing you) to enjoy yourself with the Tâo in the land of Great Vacuity.

'If a man is crossing a river in a boat, and another empty vessel comes into collision with it, even though he be a man of a choleric temper, he will not be angry with it. If there be a person, however, in that boat, he will bawl out to him to haul out of the way. If his shout be not heard, he will repeat it; and if the other do not then hear, he will call out a third time, following up the shout with abusive terms. Formerly he was not angry, but now he is; formerly (he thought) the boat was empty, but now there is a person in it. If a man can empty himself of himself, during his time in the world, who can harm him?'

3. Pei-kung Shê[1] was collecting taxes for duke Ling of Wei, to be employed in making (a peal of) bells. (In connexion with the work) he built an altar outside the gate of the suburban wall; and in three months the bells were completed, even to the suspending of the upper and lower (tiers). The king's son *Kh*ing-*k*î[2] saw them, and asked what

[1] Pei-kung, 'Northern Palace,' must have been the name of Shê's residence, and appears here as if it were his surname.

[2] A son, probably of king *K*ing of *K*âu (B.C. 544–529).—On the whole paragraph, see par. 10 of the preceding Book.

arts he had employed in the making of them. Shê replied, 'Besides my undivided attention to them, I did not venture to use any arts. I have heard the saying, "After all the carving and the chiselling, let the object be to return to simplicity." I was as a child who has no knowledge; I was extraordinarily slow and hesitating; they grew like the springing plants of themselves. In escorting those who went and meeting those who came, my object was neither to hinder the comers nor detain the goers. I suffered those who strongly opposed to take their way, and accepted those who did their best to come to terms. I allowed them all to do the utmost they could, and in this way morning and evening I collected the taxes. I did not have the slightest trouble, and how much more will this be the case with those who pursue the Great Way (on a grand scale)!'

4. Confucius was kept (by his enemies) in a state of siege between *Kh*ăn and 3hâi[1], and for seven days had no food cooked with fire to eat. The Thâi-kung *Z*ân[2] went to condole with him, and said, 'You had nearly met with your death.' 'Yes,' was the reply. 'Do you dislike death?' 'I do.' Then *Z*ăn continued, 'Let me try and describe a way by which (such a) death may be avoided.—In the eastern sea there are birds which go by the name of Î-îs[3]; they fly low and slowly as if they were deficient in power. They fly as if they were

[1] Compare Analects XI, ii.

[2] We might translate Thâi-kung by 'the grand-duke.' We know nothing about him. He tries to convert Confucius to Tâoism just as Î-liâo does the marquis of Lû in par. 2; and for a time at least, as *K*wang-3ze makes it appear, with more success.

[3] Were these Î-îs swallows? So some of the critics say.

leading and assisting one another, and they press on one another when they roost. No one ventures to take the lead in going forward, or to be the last in going backwards. In eating no one ventures to take the first mouthful, but prefers the fragments left by others. In this way (the breaks in) their line are not many[1], and men outside them cannot harm them, so that they escape injury.

'The straight tree is the first to be cut down; the well of sweet water is the first to be exhausted. Your aim is to embellish your wisdom so as to startle the ignorant, and to cultivate your person to show the unsightliness of others. A light shines around you as if you were carrying with you the sun and moon, and thus it is that you do not escape such calamity. Formerly I heard a highly accomplished man say, "Those who boast have no merit. The merit which is deemed complete will begin to decay. The fame which is deemed complete will begin to wane." Who can rid himself of (the ideas of) merit and fame, and return and put himself on the level of the masses of men? The practice of the Tâo flows abroad, but its master does not care to dwell where it can be seen; his attainments in it hold their course, but he does not wish to appear in its display. Always simple and commonplace, he may seem to be bereft of reason. He obliterates the traces of his action, gives up position and power, and aims not at merit and fame. Therefore he does not censure men, and men do not censure him. The perfect man does not seek to be heard of; how is it that you delight in doing so?'

---

[1] A clause of uncertain meaning.

Confucius said, 'Excellent;' and thereupon he took leave of his associates, forsook his disciples, retired to the neighbourhood of a great marsh, wore skins and hair cloth, and ate acorns and chestnuts. He went among animals without causing any confusion among their herds, and among birds without troubling their movements. Birds and beasts did not dislike him; how much less would men do so!

5. Confucius asked Ʒze-sang Hû[1], saying, 'I was twice driven from Lû; the tree was felled over me in Sung; I was obliged to disappear from Wei; I was reduced to extreme distress in Shang and *K*âu[2]; and I was kept in a state of siege between *Kh*ăn and Ʒhâi. I have encountered these various calamities; my intimate associates are removed from me more and more; my followers and friends are more and more dispersed;—why have all these things befallen me?' Ʒze-sang Hû replied, 'Have you not heard of the flight of Lin Hui of *K*iâ[3];—how he abandoned his round jade symbol of rank, worth a thousand pieces of silver, and hurried away with his infant son on his back? If it be asked, "Was it because of the market value of the child?" But that value was small (compared with the value of the jade token). If it be asked again, "Was it because of the troubles

---

[1] Supposed to have been a recluse.

[2] I do not know the particulars of this distress in Shang and *K*âu, or have forgotten them. A still more full recital of the sage's misfortunes occurs in Lieh-ʒze, VII, 8[a].

[3] The text here appears to be somewhat confused. Lin Hui is said to have been a man of the Yin dynasty, and of a state which was called *K*iâ, and for the verification of such a state I have searched in vain. The explanation of his conduct put here into his mouth is very good.

(of his office)?" But the child would occasion him much more trouble. Why was it then that, abandoning the jade token, worth a thousand pieces of silver, he hurried away with the child on his back? Lin Hui (himself) said, "The union between me and the token rested on the ground of gain; that between me and the child was of Heaven's appointment." Where the bond of union is its profitableness, when the pressure of poverty, calamity, distress, and injury come, the parties abandon one another; when it is of Heaven's appointment, they hold in the same circumstances to one another. Now between abandoning one another, and holding to one another, the difference is great. Moreover, the intercourse of superior men is tasteless as water, while that of mean men is sweet as new wine. But the tastelessness of the superior men leads on to affection, and the sweetness of the mean men to aversion. The union which originates without any cause will end in separation without any cause.'

Confucius said, 'I have reverently received your instructions.' And hereupon, with a slow step and an assumed air of ease, he returned to his own house. There he made an end of studying and put away his books. His disciples came no more to make their bow to him (and be taught), but their affection for him increased the more.

Another day Sang Hû said further to him, 'When Shun was about to die, he charged[1] Yü, saying, 'Be

[1] The 眞泠 of the text here are allowed on all hands to be spurious, and 其命 have been substituted for them. What follows, however, from Shun to Yü, is far from being clear, in itself, or in its connexion.

upon your guard. (The attraction of) the person is not like that of sympathy; the (power of) affection is not like the leading (of example). Where there is sympathy, there will not be separation; where there is (the leading of) example, there will be no toil. Where there is neither separation nor toil, you will not have to seek the decoration of forms to make the person attractive, and where there is no such need of those forms, there will certainly be none for external things.'

6. *K*wang-ʒze in a patched dress of coarse cloth, and having his shoes tied together with strings, was passing by the king of Wei, who said to him, 'How great, Master, is your distress?' *K*wang-ʒze replied, 'It is poverty, not distress! While a scholar possesses the Tâo and its Attributes, he cannot be going about in distress. Tattered clothes and shoes tied on the feet are the sign of poverty, and not of distress. This is what we call not meeting with the right time. Has your majesty not seen the climbing monkey? When he is among the plane trees, rottleras, oaks, and camphor trees, he grasps and twists their branches (into a screen), where he reigns quite at his ease, so that not even Î[1] or Phăng Măng[1] could spy him out. When, however, he finds himself among the prickly mulberry and date trees, and other thorns, he goes cautiously, casts sidelong glances, and takes every trembling movement with apprehension;—it is not that his sinews and bones

[1] Î;—see Book V, par. 2. Phăng Măng was a contemporary of Î, learned archery from him, and then slew him, that he might himself be the foremost archer in the kingdom;—see Mencius IV, ii, 24.

are straitened, and have lost their suppleness, but the situation is unsuitable for him, and he cannot display his agility. And now when I dwell under a benighted ruler, and seditious ministers, how is it possible for me not to be in distress? My case might afford an illustration of the cutting out the heart of Pî-kan[1]!'

7. When Confucius was reduced to great distress between *Kh*ăn and *Kh*âi, and for seven days he had no cooked food to eat, he laid hold of a decayed tree with his left hand, and with his right hand tapped it with a decayed branch, singing all the while the ode of Piâo-shih[2]. He had his instrument, but the notes were not marked on it. There was a noise, but no blended melody. The sound of the wood and the voice of the man came together like the noise of the plough through the ground, yet suitably to the feelings of the disciples around. Yen Hui, who was standing upright, with his hands crossed on his breast, rolled his eyes round to observe him. *K*ung-nî, fearing that Hui would go to excess in manifesting how he honoured himself, or be plunged in sorrow through his love for him, said to him, 'Hui, not to receive (as evils) the inflictions of Heaven is easy; not to receive (as benefits) the favours of men is difficult. There is no beginning which was not an end. The Human and the Heavenly may be one

[1] 'A spurious paragraph, no doubt.' Lin Hsî-*k*ung thus concludes what he has to say on this paragraph; but it is not without its interest and lessons.

[2] I do not know who this was, nor what his ode or air was. Lû Teh-ming read the character 猋, and says that Piâo-shih was one of the old royal Tîs who did nothing. In all my texts it is wrongly printed with three 火.

and the same. Who, for instance, is it that is now singing[1]?' Hui said, 'I venture to ask how not to receive (as evils) the inflictions of Heaven is easy.' *K*ung-nî said, 'Hunger, thirst, cold, and heat, and having one's progress entirely blocked up;—these are the doings of Heaven and Earth, necessary incidents in the revolutions of things. They are occurrences of which we say that we will pass on (composedly) along with them. The minister of another does not dare to refuse his commands; and if he who is discharging the duty of a minister feels it necessary to act thus, how much more should we wait with ease on the commands of Heaven[2]!' 'What do you mean by saying that not to receive (as benefits) the favours of men is difficult?' *K*ung-nî said, 'As soon as one is employed in office, he gets forward in all directions; rank and emolument come to him together, and without end. But these advantages do not come from one's self;—it is my appointed lot to have such external good. The superior man is not a robber; the man of worth is no filcher;—if I prefer such things, what am I[3]? Hence it is said, "There is no bird wiser than the swallow." Where its eye lights on a place that is not suitable for it, it does not give it a second glance. Though it may drop the food from its

[1] This question arose out of the previous statement that man and Heaven might be one,—acting with the same spontaneity.

[2] Confucius recognises here, as he often does, a power beyond his own, 'his appointed lot,' what we call destiny, to which the Tâo requires submission. This comes very near to our idea of God.

[3] Human gifts had such an attraction, that they tended to take from man his heavenly spontaneity; and were to be eschewed, or received only with great caution.

mouth, it abandons it, and hurries off. It is afraid of men, and yet it stealthily takes up its dwelling by his; finding its protection in the altars of the Land and Grain [1].

'What do you mean by saying that there is no beginning which was not an end?' Kung-nî said, 'The change—rise and dissolution—of all things (continually) goes on, but we do not know who it is that maintains and continues the process. How do we know when any one begins? How do we know when he will end? We have simply to wait for it, and nothing more [2].'

'And what do you mean by saying that the Human and the Heavenly are one and the same?' Kung-nî said, 'Given man, and you have Heaven; given Heaven, and you still have Heaven (and nothing more). That man can not have Heaven is owing to the limitation of his nature [3]. The sagely man quietly passes away with his body, and there is an end of it.'

8. As Kwang Kâu was rambling in the park of Tiâo-ling [4] he saw a strange bird which came from the south. Its wings were seven cubits in width, and

---

[1] What is said here about the swallow is quite obscure. Hsî-kung says that all the old attempts to explain it are ridiculous, and then propounds an ingenious one of his own; but I will leave the passage with my reader to deal with it as he best can.

[2] Compare with this how in Book XVIII we find Kwang-3ze singing by the dead body of his wife.

[3] That man is man and not Heaven is simply from the limitation of his nature,—his 'appointed lot.'

[4] Tiâo-ling might be translated 'Eagle Mount.' Where it was I do not know; perhaps the name originated with Kwang-3ze, and thus has become semi-historical.

its eyes were large, an inch in circuit. It touched the forehead of *K*âu as it passed him, and lighted in a grove of chestnut trees. 'What bird is this?' said he, 'with such great wings not to go on! and with such large eyes not to see me!' He lifted up his skirts, and hurried with his cross-bow, waiting for (an opportunity to shoot) it. (Meanwhile) he saw a cicada, which had just alighted in a beautiful shady spot, and forgot its (care for its) body. (Just then), a preying mantis raised its feelers, and pounced on the cicada, in its eagerness for its prey, (also) forgetting (its care for) its body; while the strange bird took advantage of its opportunity to secure them both, in view of that gain forgetting its true (instinct of preservation)[1]. *K*wang *K*âu with an emotion of pity, said, 'Ah! so it is that things bring evil on one another, each of these creatures invited its own calamity.' (With this) he put away his cross-bow, and was hurrying away back, when the forester pursued him with terms of reproach.

When he returned and went into his house, he did not appear in his courtyard[2] for three months[2]. (When he came out), Lan 3ü[3] (his disciple) asked him, saying, 'Master, why have you for this some time avoided the courtyard so much?' *K*wang-3ze replied, 'I was guarding my person, and forgot myself; I was looking at turbid water, till I

[1] *K*wang-3ze might now have shot the bird, but we like him the better for letting it alone.

[2] So then, masters of schools, like *K*wang-3ze, received and taught their disciples in the courtyard of their house;—in China as elsewhere. For three 'months,' it is conjectured, we should read three 'days.'

[3] The disciple Lan 3ü appears here, but not, so far as I know, elsewhere.

mistook the clear pool. And moreover I have heard the Master say[1], "Going where certain customs prevail, you should follow those customs." I was walking about in the park of Tiâo-ling, and forgot myself. A strange bird brushed past my forehead, and went flying about in the grove of chestnuts, where it forgot the true (art of preserving itself). The forester of the chestnut grove thought that I was a fitting object for his reproach. These are the reasons why I have avoided the courtyard.'

9. Yang-ȝze, having gone to Sung, passed the night in a lodging-house, the master of which had two concubines;—one beautiful, the other ugly[2]. The ugly one was honoured, however, and the beautiful one contemned. Yang-ȝze asked the reason, and a little boy of the house replied, 'The beauty knows her beauty, and we do not recognise it. The ugly one knows her ugliness, and we do not recognise it.' Yang-ȝze said, 'Remember it, my disciples. Act virtuously, and put away the practice of priding yourselves on your virtue. If you do this, where can you go to that you will not be loved[3]?'

---

[1] Who was this 'Master?'

[2] The story here is found in Lieh-ȝze II, 15 a, b. The Yang-ȝze is there Yang *K*û, against whom Mencius so often directed his arguments.

[3] See the greater part of this paragraph in Prémare's 'Notitia Linguae Sinicae,' p. 200, with his remarks on the style.

BOOK XXI.

PART II. SECTION XIV.

Thien Ʒze-fang[1].

1. Thien Ʒze-fang, sitting in attendance on the marquis Wăn of Wei[2], often quoted (with approbation) the words of *Kh*î Kung[3]. The marquis said, 'Is *Kh*î Kung your preceptor?' Ʒze-fang replied, 'No. He only belongs to the same neighbourhood. In speaking about the Tâo, his views are often correct, and therefore I quote them as I do.' The marquis went on, 'Then have you no preceptor?' 'I have.' 'And who is he?' 'He is Tung-kwo Shun-ʒze[4].' 'And why, my Master, have I never heard you quote his words?' Ʒze-fang replied, 'He is a man who satisfies the true (ideal of humanity)[5]; a man in appearance, but (having the mind of) Heaven. Void of any thought of himself, he accommodates himself to others, and nourishes the true ideal that belongs to him. With all his purity, he is forbearing to others. Where they are without the Tâo, he rectifies his demeanour, so that they understand it, and in consequence their own ideas melt

---

[1] See vol. xxxix, pp. 151, 152. [2] B.C. 424–387.

[3] Some well-known worthy of Wei.

[4] A greater worthy still. He must have lived near the outside suburban wall of the capital, and his residence became a sort of surname.

[5] The Human and the Heavenly were blended in his personality.

away and disappear. How should one like me be fit to quote his words?'

When Ȝze-fang went out, the marquis Wăn continued in a state of dumb amazement all the day. He then called Lung Lî-*kh*ăn, and said to him, 'How far removed from us is the superior man of complete virtue! Formerly I thought the words of the sages and wise men, and the practice of benevolence and righteousness, to be the utmost we could reach to. Since I have heard about the preceptor of Ȝze-fang, my body is all unstrung, and I do not wish to move, and my mouth is closed up, and I do not wish to speak;—what I have learned has been only a counterfeit of the truth[1]. Yes, (the possession of Wei) has been an entanglement to me.'

2. Wăn-po Hsüeh-ȝze[2], on his way to *Kh*î, stayed some time in Lû, where some persons of the state begged to have an interview with him. He refused them, saying, 'I have heard that the superior men of these Middle States[3] understand the (subjects of) ceremony and righteousness, but are deplorably ignorant of the minds of men. I do not wish to see them.' He went on to *Kh*î; and on his way back (to the south), he again stayed in Lû, when the same persons begged as before for an interview. He then said, 'Formerly they asked to see me, and now again they seek an interview. They will afford me

[1] So the Khang-hsî dictionary defines the phrase;—'a wooden image made of earth,' says Lû Shû-*k*ih.

[2] A Tâoist of note from some region in the south, perhaps from *Kh*û, having his own share of the Tâoistic contempt for knowledge and culture.

[3] Probably Lû and the northern states grouped closely round the royal domain.

some opportunity of bringing out my sentiments.' He went out accordingly and saw the visitors, and came in again with a sigh. Next day the same thing occurred, and his servant said to him, 'How is it that whenever you see those visitors, you are sure to come in again sighing?' 'I told you before,' was the reply, 'that the people of these Middle States understand (the subjects of) ceremony and righteousness, but are deplorably ignorant of the minds of men. Those men who have just seen me, as they came in and went out would describe, one a circle and another a square, and in their easy carriage would be like, one a dragon and another a tiger. They remonstrated with me as sons (with their fathers), and laid down the way for me as fathers (for their sons). It was this which made me sigh.'

*K*ung-nî saw the man, but did not speak a word to him. 3ze-lû said, 'You have wished, Sir, to see this Wăn-po Hsüeh-ȝze for a long time; what is the reason that when you have seen him, you have not spoken a word?' *K*ung-nî replied, 'As soon as my eyes lighted on that man, the Tâo in him was apparent. The situation did not admit of a word being spoken.'

3. Yen Yüan asked *K*ung-nî, saying, 'Master, when you pace quietly along, I also pace along; when you go more quickly, I also do the same; when you gallop, I also gallop; but when you race along and spurn the dust, then I can only stand and look, and keep behind you[1].' The Master said, 'Hui, what do you mean?' The reply was, 'In saying that "when you, Master, pace quietly along, I also pace

[1] They are both supposed to be on horseback.

along," I mean[1] that when you speak, I also speak. By saying, "When you go more quickly, I also do the same," I mean[1] that when you reason, I also reason. By saying, "When you gallop, I also gallop," I mean[1] that when you speak of the Way, I also speak of the Way; but by saying, "When you race along and spurn the dust, then I can only stare, and keep behind you," I am thinking how though you do not speak, yet all men believe you; though you are no partisan, yet all parties approve your catholicity; and though you sound no instrument, yet people all move on harmoniously before you, while (all the while) I do not know how all this comes about; and this is all which my words are intended to express[2].'

*K*ung-nî said, 'But you must try and search the matter out. Of all causes for sorrow there is none so great as the death of the mind;—the death of man's (body) is only next to it. The sun comes forth in the east, and sets in the extreme west;—all things have their position determined by these two points. All that have eyes and feet wait for this (sun), and then proceed to do what they have to do. When this comes forth, they appear in their places; when it sets, they disappear. It is so with all things. They have that for which they wait, and (on its arrival) they die; they have that for which they wait, and then (again) they live. When once I receive my frame thus completed, I remain unchanged, awaiting the consummation of my course.

[1] In these three cases the 也 of the text should be 者.

[2] So Hui is made to represent the master as a mental Thaumaturgist, and Confucius is made to try to explain the whole thing to him;—but not to my mind successfully. Still a distinction is maintained between the mind and the body.

I move as acted on by things, day and night without cessation, and I do not know when I will come to an end. Clearly I am here a completed frame, and even one who (fancies that he) knows what is appointed cannot determine it beforehand. I am in this way daily passing on, but all day long I am communicating my views to you; and now, as we are shoulder to shoulder you fail (to understand me);—is it not matter for lamentation? You are able in a measure to set forth what I more clearly set forth; but that is passed away, and you look for it, as if it were still existing, just as if you were looking for a horse in the now empty place where it was formerly exhibited for sale. You have very much forgotten my service to you, and I have very much forgotten wherein I served you. But nevertheless why should you account this such an evil? What you forget is but my old self; that which cannot be forgotten remains with me.'

4. Confucius went to see Lâo Tan, and arrived just as he had completed the bathing of his head, and was letting his dishevelled hair get dry. There he was, motionless, and as if there were not another man in the world[1]. Confucius waited quietly; and, when in a little time he was introduced, he said, 'Were my eyes dazed? Is it really you? Just now, your body, Sir, was like the stump of a rotten tree. You looked as if you had no thought of anything, as if you had left the society of men, and were standing in the solitude (of yourself).' Lâo Tan replied, 'I was enjoying myself in thinking about the commencement

[1] He was in the Tâoistic trance, like Nan-kwo Ȝze-*kh*î, at the beginning of the second Book.

of things[1].' 'What do you mean?' 'My mind is so cramped, that I hardly know it; my tongue is so tied that I cannot tell it; but I will try to describe it to you as nearly as I can. When the state of Yin was perfect, all was cold and severe; when the state of Yang was perfect, all was turbulent and agitated. The coldness and severity came forth from Heaven; the turbulence and agitation issued from Earth. The two states communicating together, a harmony ensued and things were produced. Some one regulated and controlled this, but no one has seen his form. Decay and growth; fulness and emptiness; darkness and light; the changes of the sun and the transformations of the moon:—these are brought about from day to day; but no one sees the process of production. Life has its origin from which it springs, and death has its place from which it returns. Beginning and ending go on in mutual contrariety without any determinable commencement, and no one knows how either comes to an end. If we disallow all this, who originates and presides over all these phenomena?'

Confucius said, 'I beg to ask about your enjoyment in these thoughts.' Lâo Tan replied, 'The

[1] This 'commencement of things' was not the equivalent of 'our creation out of nothing,' for Lâo Tan immediately supposes the existence of the primary ether in its twofold state, as Yin and Yang; and also of Heaven and Earth, as a twofold Power working, under some regulation and control, yet invisible; that is, under the Tâo. In the same way the process of beginning and ending, growth and decay, life and death go on, no one knows how, or how long. And the contemplation of all this is the cause of unceasing delight to the Perfect man, the possessor of the Tâo. Death is a small matter, merely as a change of feature; and Confucius acknowledges his immeasurable inferiority to Lâo-ȝze.

comprehension of this is the most admirable and the most enjoyable (of all acquisitions). The getting of the most admirable and the exercise of the thoughts in what is the most enjoyable, constitutes what we call the Perfect man.' Confucius said, 'I should like to hear the method of attaining to it.' The reply was, 'Grass-eating animals do not dislike to change their pastures; creatures born in the water do not dislike to change their waters. They make a small change, but do not lose what is the great and regular requirement (of their nature); joy, anger, sadness, and delight do not enter into their breasts (in connexion with such events). Now the space under the sky is occupied by all things in their unity. When they possess that unity and equally share it, then the four limbs and hundred members of their body are but so much dust and dirt, while death and life, their ending and beginning, are but as the succession of day and night, which cannot disturb their enjoyment; and how much less will they be troubled by gains and losses, by calamity and happiness! Those who renounce the paraphernalia of rank do it as if they were casting away so much mud;—they know that they are themselves more honourable than those paraphernalia. The honour belonging to one's self is not lost by any change (of condition). Moreover, a myriad transformations may take place before the end of them is reached. What is there in all this sufficient to trouble the mind? Those who have attained to the Tâo understand the subject.'

Confucius said, 'O Master, your virtue is equal to that of Heaven and Earth, and still I must borrow (some of your) perfect words (to aid me) in the cultivation of my mind. Who among the superior men of antiquity could give such expression to them?' Lâo Tan replied, 'Not so. Look at the spring, the water of which rises and overflows;—it does nothing, but it naturally acts so. So with the perfect man and his virtue;—he does not cultivate it, and nothing evades its influence. He is like heaven which is high of itself, like earth which is solid of itself, like the sun and moon which shine of themselves;—what need is there to cultivate it?'

Confucius went out and reported the conversation to Yen Hui, saying, 'In the (knowledge of the) Tâo am I any better than an animalcule in vinegar? But for the Master's lifting the veil from me, I should not have known the grand perfection of Heaven and Earth.'

5. At an interview of *K*wang-ȝze with duke Âi[1] of Lû, the duke said, 'There are many of the Learned class in Lû; but few of them can be compared with you, Sir.' *K*wang-ȝze replied, 'There are few Learned men in Lû.' 'Everywhere in Lû,' rejoined the duke, 'you see men wearing the dress of the Learned[2];—how can you say that they are few?' 'I have heard,' said *K*wang-ȝze, 'that those of them who wear round caps know the times of heaven; that those who wear square shoes know the contour of the ground; and that those who saunter about with semicircular stones at their

[1] Duke Âi of Lû died in B.C. 468, a century and more before the birth of *K*wang-ȝze. On that, as well as on other grounds, the paragraph cannot be genuine.

[2] Compare the thirty-eighth Book of the Lî *K*î, where Confucius denies that there was any dress peculiar to the scholar.

girdle-pendents settle matters in dispute as they come before them. But superior men who are possessed of such knowledge will not be found wearing the dress, and it does not follow that those who wear the dress possess the knowledge. If your Grace think otherwise, why not issue a notification through the state, that it shall be a capital offence to wear the dress without possessing the knowledge.' On this the duke issued such a notification, and in five days, throughout all Lû, there was no one who dared to wear the dress of the Learned. There was only one old man who came and stood in it at the duke's gate. The duke instantly called him in, and questioned him about the affairs of the state, when he talked about a thousand points and ten thousand divergences from them. *K*wang-ȝze said, 'When the state of Lû can thus produce but one man of the Learned class, can he be said to be many?'

6. The ideas of rank and emolument did not enter the mind of Pâi-lî Hsî[1], and so he became a cattle-feeder, and his cattle were all in fine condition. This made duke Mû of *Kh*in forget the meanness of his position, and put the government (of his state) into his hands. Neither life nor death entered into the mind of (Shun), the Lord of Yü, and therefore he was able to influence others[2].

7. The ruler Yüan[3] of Sung wishing to have a map

[1] Pâi-lî Hsî, a remarkable character of the seventh century B.C., who rose to be chief minister to Mû, the earl (or duke) of *Kh*in, the last of the five Leading Princes of the kingdom. Mû died in B.C. 621. Mencius has much to say of Pâi-lî Hsî.

[2] Shun's parents wished to kill him; but that did not trouble his mind; his filial piety even affected them.

[3] His first year as duke of Sung was B.C. 530. The point of the story is not clear.

drawn, the masters of the pencil all came (to undertake the task). Having received his instructions and made their bows, they stood, licking their pencils and preparing their ink. Half their number, however, remained outside. There was one who came late, with an air of indifference, and did not hurry forward. When he had received his instructions and made his bow, he did not keep standing, but proceeded to his shed. The duke sent a man to see him, and there he was, with his upper garment off, sitting cross-legged, and nearly naked. The ruler said, 'He is the man; he is a true draughtsman.'

8. King Wăn was (once) looking about him at 3ang[1], when he saw an old man fishing[2]. But his fishing was no fishing. It was not the fishing of one whose business is fishing. He was always fishing (as if he had no object in the occupation). The king wished to raise him to office, and put the government into his hands, but was afraid that such a step would give dissatisfaction to his great ministers, his uncles, and cousins. He then wished to dismiss the man altogether from his mind, but he could not bear the thought that his people should be without (such a) Heaven (as their Protector). On this, (next) morning, he called together his great officers, and said to them, 'Last night, I dreamt that I saw a good man, with a dark complexion and a

[1] Where 3ang was cannot be told.

[2] The old fisherman here was, no doubt, the first marquis of *K*h̆î, after the establishment of the dynasty of *K*âu, known by various names, as Lü Shang, Thâi-kung Wang, and *K*iang 3ze-yâ. He did much for the new rule, but his connexion with kings Wăn and Wû is a mass of fables. The fishing as if he were not fishing betokened in him the aimlessness of the Tâo.

beard, riding on a piebald horse, one half of whose hoofs were red, who commanded me, saying, "Lodge your government in the hands of the old man of Ȝang; and perhaps the evils of your people will be cured."' The great officers said eagerly, 'It was the king, your father.' King Wăn said, 'Let us then submit the proposal to the tortoise-shell.' They replied, 'It is the order of your father. Let not your majesty think of any other. Why divine about it?' (The king) then met the old man of Ȝang, and committed the government to him.

The statutes and laws were not changed by him; not a one-sided order (of his own) was issued; but when the king made a survey of the kingdom after three years, he found that the officers had destroyed the plantations (which harboured banditti), and dispersed their occupiers, that the superintendents of the official departments did not plume themselves on their successes, and that no unusual grain measures were allowed within the different states[1]. When the officers had destroyed the dangerous plantations and dispersed their occupants, the highest value was set on the common interests; when the chiefs of departments did not plume themselves on their successes, the highest value was set on the common business; when unusual grain measures did not enter the different states, the different princes had no jealousies. On this king Wăn made the old man his Grand Preceptor, and asked him, with his own face to the north, whether his government might be extended to all the kingdom. The old

[1] That is, that all combinations formed to resist and warp the course of justice had been put an end to.

man looked perplexed and gave no reply, but with aimless look took his leave. In the morning he had issued his orders, and at night he had gone his way; nor was he heard of again all his life. Yen Yüan questioned Confucius, saying, 'Was even king Wăn unequal to determine his course? What had he to do with resorting to a dream?' Kung-nî replied, 'Be silent and do not say a word! King Wăn was complete in everything. What have you to do with criticising him? He only had recourse (to the dream) to meet a moment's difficulty.'

9. Lieh Yü-khâu was exhibiting his archery[1] to Po-hwăn Wû-zăn[2]. Having drawn the bow to its full extent, with a cup of water placed on his elbow, he let fly. As the arrow was discharged, another was put in its place; and as that was sent off, a third was ready on the string. All the while he stood like a statue. Po-hwăn Wû-zăn said, 'That is the shooting of an archer, but not of one who shoots without thinking about his shooting. Let me go up with you to the top of a high mountain, treading with you among the tottering rocks, till we arrive at the brink of a precipice, 800 cubits deep, and (I will then see) if you can shoot.' On this they went up a high mountain, making their way among the tottering rocks, till they came to the brink of a precipice 800 cubits deep. Then Wû-zăn turned round and walked backwards, till his feet were two-

[1] This must be the meaning of the 爲, 'for.' The whole story is found in Lieh-ȝze, II, p. 5. From Lieh's Book VIII, p. 2, we learn that Lieh-ȝze's teacher in archery was Yin Hsî, the warden of the pass famous in the history of Lâo-ȝze.

[2] Mentioned in Book V, par. 2.

thirds of their length outside the edge, and beckoned Yü-khâu to come forward. He, however, had fallen prostrate on the ground, with the sweat pouring down to his heels. Then the other said, 'The Perfect man looks up to the azure sky above, or dives down to the yellow springs beneath, or soars away to the eight ends of the universe, without any change coming over his spirit or his breath. But now the trepidation of your mind appears in your dazed eyes; your inward feeling of peril is extreme!'

10. *K*ien Wû asked Sun-shû Âo[1], saying, 'You, Sir, were thrice chief minister, and did not feel elated; you were thrice dismissed from that position, without manifesting any sorrow. At first I was in doubt about you, (but I am not now, since) I see how regularly and quietly the breath comes through your nostrils. How is it that you exercise your mind?' Sun-shû Âo replied, 'In what do I surpass other men? When the position came to me, I thought it should not be rejected; when it was taken away, I thought it could not be retained. I considered that the getting or losing it did not make me what I was, and was no occasion for any manifestation of sorrow;—that was all. In what did I surpass other men? And moreover, I did not know whether the honour of it belonged to the dignity, or to myself. If it belonged to the dignity, it was nothing to me; if it belonged to me, it had nothing

[1] Sun-shû Âo;—see Mencius VI, ii, 15. He was, no doubt, a good and able man, chief minister to king *K*wang of *Kh*û. The legends or edifying stories about him are many; but *K*wang-ȝze, I think, is the author of his being thrice raised and thrice dismissed from office.

to do with the dignity. While occupied with these uncertainties, and looking round in all directions, what leisure had I to take knowledge of whether men honoured me or thought me mean?'

*K*ung-nî heard of all this, and said, 'The True men of old could not be fully described by the wisest, nor be led into excess by the most beautiful, nor be forced by the most violent robber. Neither Fû-hsî nor Hwang-Tî could compel them to be their friends. Death and life are indeed great considerations, but they could make no change in their (true) self; and how much less could rank and emolument do so? Being such, their spirits might pass over the Thâi mountain and find it no obstacle to them[1]; they might enter the greatest gulphs, and not be wet by them; they might occupy the lowest and smallest positions without being distressed by them. Theirs was the fulness of heaven and earth; the more that they gave to others, the more they had.'

The king of *Kh*û and the ruler of Fan[2] were sitting together. After a little while, the attendants of the king said, 'Fan has been destroyed three times.' The ruler of Fan rejoined, 'The destruction of Fan has not been sufficient to destroy what we had that was most deserving to be preserved.' Now,

[1] It is difficult to see why this should be predicated of the 'spirits' of the True men.

[2] Fan was a small state, held at one time by descendants of the famous duke of *K*âu;—see the Ȝo *Kh*wan, I, vii, 6; V, xxiv, 2. But we do not know what had been the relations between the powerful *Kh*û and the feeble Fan, which gave rise to and could explain the remarks made at the entertainment, more honourable to Fan than to *Kh*û.

if the destruction of Fan had not been sufficient to destroy that which it had most deserving to be preserved, the preservation of *Kh*û had not been sufficient to preserve that in it most deserving to be preserved. Looking at the matter from this point of view, Fan had not begun to be destroyed, and *Kh*û had not begun to be preserved.

BOOK XXII.

PART II. SECTION XV.

*K*ih Pei Yû, or 'Knowledge Rambling in the North[1].'

1. Knowledge[2] had rambled northwards to the region of the Dark Water[3], where he ascended the height of Imperceptible Slope[3], when it happened that he met with Dumb Inaction[2]. Knowledge addressed him, saying, 'I wish to ask you some questions:—By what process of thought and anxious consideration do we get to know the Tâo? Where should we dwell and what should we do to find our rest in the Tâo? From what point should we start and what path should we pursue to make the Tâo our own?' He asked these three questions, but Dumb Inaction[2] gave him no reply. Not only did he not answer, but he did not know how to answer.

Knowledge[2], disappointed by the fruitlessness of his questions, returned to the south of the Bright

---

[1] See vol. xxxix, p. 152.

[2] All these names are metaphorical, having more or less to do with the qualities of the Tâo, and are used as the names of personages, devoted to the pursuit of it. It is difficult to translate the name *Kh*wang *Kh*ü (狂屈). An old reading is 詘, which Medhurst explains by 'Bent or Crooked Discourse.' 'Blurter,' though not an elegant English term, seems to express the idea our author would convey by it. Hwang-Tî is different from the other names, but we cannot regard him as here a real personage.

[3] These names of places are also metaphorical and Tâoistic.

Water[1], and ascended the height of the End of Doubt[1], where he saw Heedless Blurter, to whom he put the same questions, and who replied, 'Ah! I know, and will tell you.' But while he was about to speak, he forgot what he wanted to say.

Knowledge, (again) receiving no answer to his questions, returned to the palace of the Tî[2], where he saw Hwang-Tî[3], and put the questions to him. Hwang-Tî said, 'To exercise no thought and no anxious consideration is the first step towards knowing the Tâo; to dwell nowhere and do nothing is the first step towards resting in the Tâo; to start from nowhere and pursue no path is the first step towards making the Tâo your own.'

Knowledge then asked Hwang-Tî, saying, 'I and you know this; those two did not know it; which of us is right?' The reply was, 'Dumb Inaction[3] is truly right; Heedless Blurter has an appearance of being so; I and you are not near being so. (As it is said), "Those who know (the Tâo) do not speak of it; those who speak of it do not know it[4];" and "Hence the sage conveys his instructions without the use of speech[4]." The Tâo cannot be made ours by constraint; its characteristics will not come to us (at our call). Benevolence may be practised; Righteousness may be partially attended to; by Ceremonies men impose on one another. Hence it

[1] See note 3, on preceding page.

[2] Tî might seem to be used here for 'God,' but its juxtaposition with Hwang-Tî is against our translating it so.

[3] See note 2, on preceding page.

[4] See the Tâo Teh *K*ing, chaps. 56 and 2. *K*wang-ȝze is quoting, no doubt, these two passages, as he vaguely intimates I think by the 夫, with which the sentence commences.

is said, "When the Tâo was lost, its Characteristics appeared. When its Characteristics were lost, Benevolence appeared. When Benevolence was lost, Righteousness appeared. When Righteousness was lost, Ceremonies appeared. Ceremonies are but (the unsubstantial) flowers of the Tâo, and the commencement of disorder[1]." Hence (also it is further said), "He who practises the Tâo, daily diminishes his doing. He diminishes it and again diminishes it, till he arrives at doing nothing. Having arrived at this non-inaction, there is nothing that he does not do[1]." Here now there is something, a regularly fashioned utensil;—if you wanted to make it return to the original condition of its materials, would it not be difficult to make it do so? Could any but the Great Man accomplish this easily[2]?

'Life is the follower of death, and death is the predecessor of life; but who knows the Arranger (of this connexion between them)[3]? The life is due to the collecting of the breath. When that is collected, there is life; when it is dispersed, there is death. Since death and life thus attend on each other, why should I account (either of) them an evil?

'Therefore all things go through one and the same experience. (Life) is accounted beautiful because it is spirit-like and wonderful, and death is accounted ugly because of its foetor and putridity. But the foetid and putrid is transformed again into the spirit-like and wonderful, and the spirit-like and wonderful is transformed again into the foetid and

---

[1] See the Tâo Teh *K*ing, chaps. 38 and 48.

[2] This sentence is metaphorical of the Tâo, whose spell is broken by the intrusion of Knowledge.

[3] This 'Arranger' is the Tâo.

putrid. Hence it is said, "All under the sky there is one breath of life, and therefore the sages prized that unity[1].""

Knowledge[2] said to Hwang-Tî[2], 'I asked Dumb Inaction[2], and he did not answer me. Not only did he not answer me, but he did not know how to answer me. I asked Heedless Blurter, and while he wanted to tell me, he yet did not do so. Not only did he not tell me, but while he wanted to tell me, he forgot all about my questions. Now I have asked you, and you knew (all about them);—why (do you say that) you are not near doing so?' Hwang-Tî replied, 'Dumb Inaction[2] was truly right, because he did not know the thing. Heedless Blurter[2] was nearly right, because he forgot it. I and you are not nearly right, because we know it.' Heedless Blurter[2] heard of (all this), and considered that Hwang-Tî[2] knew how to express himself (on the subject).

2. (The operations of) Heaven and Earth proceed in the most admirable way, but they say nothing about them; the four seasons observe the clearest laws, but they do not discuss them; all things have their complete and distinctive constitutions, but they say nothing about them[3].

The sages trace out the admirable operations of Heaven and Earth, and reach to and understand the distinctive constitutions of all things; and thus it is that the Perfect Man (is said to) do nothing and the Greatest Sage to originate nothing, such language showing that they look to Heaven and Earth as

[1] I have not been able to trace this quotation to its source.
[2] See note 2, p. 57. [3] Compare Analects XVII, xix, 3.

their model[1]. Even they, with their spirit-like and most exquisite intelligence, as well as all the tribes that undergo their transformations, the dead and the living, the square and the round, do not understand their root and origin, but nevertheless they all from the oldest time by it preserve their being.

Vast as is the space included within the six cardinal points, it all (and all that it contains) lies within (this twofold root of Heaven and Earth); small as is an autumn hair, it is indebted to this for the completion of its form. All things beneath the sky, now rising, now descending, ever continue the same through this. The Yin and Yang, and the four seasons revolve and move by it, each in its proper order. Now it seems to be lost in obscurity, but it continues; now it seems to glide away, and have no form, but it is still spirit-like. All things are nourished by it, without their knowing it. This is what is called the Root and Origin; by it we may obtain a view of what we mean by Heaven[2].

3. Nieh *Kh*üeh[3] asked about the Tâo from Phei-î[3], who replied, 'If you keep your body as it should be, and look only at the one thing, the Harmony of Heaven will come to you. Call in your knowledge, and make your measures uniform, and the spiritual (belonging to you) will come and lodge with you; the Attributes (of the Tâo) will be your beauty, and the Tâo (itself) will be your dwelling-place. You will have the simple look of a new-born calf, and

[1] Compare the Tâo Teh *K*ing, ch. 25.

[2] The binomial 'Heaven and Earth' here gives place to the one term 'Heaven,' which is often a synonym of Tâo.

[3] See his character in Book XII, par. 5, where Phei-î also is mentioned.

will not seek to know the cause (of your being what you are).' Phei-î had not finished these words when the other dozed off into a sleep.

Phei-î was greatly pleased, and walked away, singing as he went,

'Like stump of rotten tree his frame,
Like lime when slaked his mind became[1].
Real is his wisdom, solid, true,
Nor cares what's hidden to pursue.
O dim and dark his aimless mind!
No one from him can counsel find.
What sort of man is he?'

4. Shun asked (his attendant) *Kh*ăng[2], saying, 'Can I get the Tâo and hold it as mine?' The reply was, 'Your body is not your own to hold;—how then can you get and hold the Tâo?' Shun resumed, 'If my body be not mine to possess and hold, who holds it?' *Kh*ăng said, 'It is the bodily form entrusted to you by Heaven and Earth. Life is not yours to hold. It is the blended harmony (of the Yin and Yang), entrusted to you by Heaven and Earth. Your nature, constituted as it is, is not yours to hold. It is entrusted to you by Heaven and Earth to act in accordance with it. Your grandsons and sons are not yours to hold. They are the exuviae[3] entrusted to you by Heaven and Earth. Therefore when we walk, we should not know where we are going; when we stop and rest, we should not know what to occupy ourselves with;

[1] See the account of Nan-kwo Ȝze-*kh*î in Book II, par. 1.
[2] Not the name of a man, but an office.
[3] The term in the text denotes the cast-off skin or shell of insects, snakes, and crabs. See the account of death and life in par. 1.

when we eat, we should not know the taste of our food;—all is done by the strong Yang influence of Heaven and Earth[1]. How then can you get (the Tâo), and hold it as your own?'

5. Confucius asked Lâo Tan, saying, 'Being at leisure to-day, I venture to ask you about the Perfect Tâo.' Lâo Tan replied, 'You must, as by fasting and vigil, clear and purge your mind, wash your spirit white as snow, and sternly repress your knowledge. The subject of the Tâo is deep, and difficult to describe;—I will give you an outline of its simplest attributes.

'The Luminous was produced from the Obscure; the Multiform from the Unembodied; the Spiritual from the Tâo; and the bodily from the seminal essence. After this all things produced one another from their bodily organisations. Thus it is that those which have nine apertures are born from the womb, and those with eight from eggs[2]. But their coming leaves no trace, and their going no monument; they enter by no door; they dwell in no apartment[3]:—they are in a vast arena reaching in all directions. They who search for and find (the Tâo) in this are strong in their limbs, sincere and far-reaching in their thinking, acute in their hearing, and clear in their seeing. They exercise their minds without being toiled; they respond to everything aright without regard to place or circumstance. Without this heaven would not be high, nor earth

[1] It is an abstruse point why only the Yang is mentioned here, and described as 'strong.'

[2] It is not easy to see the pertinence of this illustration.

[3] Hû Wăn-ying says, 'With this one word our author sweeps away the teaching of Purgatorial Sufferings.'

broad; the sun and moon would not move, and nothing would flourish:—such is the operation of the Tâo.

'Moreover, the most extensive knowledge does not necessarily know it; reasoning will not make men wise in it;—the sages have decided against both these methods. However you try to add to it, it admits of no increase; however you try to take from it, it admits of no diminution;—this is what the sages maintain about it. How deep it is, like the sea! How grand it is, beginning again when it has come to an end! If it carried along and sustained all things, without being overburdened or weary, that would be like the way of the superior man, merely an external operation; when all things go to it, and find their dependence in it;—this is the true character of the Tâo.

'Here is a man (born) in one of the middle states[1]. He feels himself independent both of the Yin and Yang[2], and dwells between heaven and earth; only for the present a mere man, but he will return to his original source. Looking at him in his origin, when his life begins, we have (but) a gelatinous substance in which the breath is collecting. Whether his life be long or his death early, how short is the space between them! It is but the name for a moment of time, insufficient to play the part of a good Yâo or a bad *K*ieh in.

'The fruits of trees and creeping plants have their distinctive characters, and though the relation-

---

[1] The commentators suppose that by 'the man' here there is intended 'a sage;' and they would seem to be correct.

[2] Compare the second sentence in the Tâo Teh *K*ing, ch. 42.

ships of men, according to which they are classified, are troublesome, the sage, when he meets with them, does not set himself in opposition to them, and when he has passed through them, he does not seek to retain them; he responds to them in their regular harmony according to his virtue; and even when he accidentally comes across any of them, he does so according to the Tâo. It was thus that the Tîs flourished, thus that the kings arose.

'Men's life between heaven and earth is like a white[1] colt's passing a crevice, and suddenly disappearing. As with a plunge and an effort they all come forth; easily and quietly they all enter again. By a transformation they live, and by another transformation they die. Living things are made sad (by death), and mankind grieve for it; but it is (only) the removal of the bow from its sheath, and the emptying the natural satchel of its contents. There may be some confusion amidst the yielding to the change; but the intellectual and animal souls are taking their leave, and the body will follow them:—This is the Great Returning home.

'That the bodily frame came from incorporeity, and will return to the same, is what all men in common know, and what those who are on their way to (know) it need not strive for. This is what the multitudes of men discuss together. Those whose (knowledge) is complete do not discuss it;—such discussion shows that their (knowledge) is not complete. Even the most clear-sighted do not meet

[1] Why is it the colt here is 'white?' Is it to heighten the impression made by his speedy disappearing? or is it merely the adoption of the phrase from the Shih, II, iv, 2?

(with the Tâo);—it is better to be silent than to reason about it. The Tâo cannot be heard with the ears;—it is better to shut the ears than to try and hear it. This is what is called the Great Attainment.'

6. Tung-kwo Ȝze[1] asked *K*wang-ȝze, saying, 'Where is what you call the Tâo to be found?' *K*wang-ȝze replied, 'Everywhere.' The other said, 'Specify an instance of it. That will be more satisfactory.' 'It is here in this ant.' 'Give a lower instance.' 'It is in this panic grass.' 'Give me a still lower instance.' 'It is in this earthenware tile.' 'Surely that is the lowest instance?' 'It is in that excrement[2].' To this Tung-kwo Ȝze gave no reply. *K*wang-ȝze said, 'Your questions, my master, do not touch the fundamental point (of the Tâo). They remind me of the questions addressed by the superintendents of the market to the inspector about examining the value of a pig by treading on it, and testing its weight as the foot descends lower and lower on the body[3]. You should not specify any particular thing. There is not a single thing without (the Tâo). So it is with the Perfect Tâo. And if we call it the Great (Tâo), it is just the same. There are the three terms,—"Complete," "All-embracing," "the Whole." These names are differ-

[1] Perhaps the Tung-kwo Shun-ȝze of Bk. XXI, par. 1.

[2] A contemptuous reply, provoked by Tung-kwo's repeated interrogation as to where the Tâo was to be found, the only question being as to what it was.

[3] We do not know the practices from which our author draws his illustrations here sufficiently to make out his meaning clearly. The signification of the characters 正 and 獲 may be gathered indeed from the Î Lî, Books 7–9; but that is all.

ent, but the reality (sought in them) is the same; referring to the One thing[1].

'Suppose we were to try to roam about in the palace of No-where;—when met there, we might discuss (about the subject) without ever coming to an end. Or suppose we were to be together in (the region of) Non-action;—should we say that (the Tâo was) Simplicity and Stillness? or Indifference and Purity? or Harmony and Ease? My will would be aimless. If it went nowhere, I should not know where it had got to; if it went and came again, I should not know where it had stopped; if it went on going and coming, I should not know when the process would end. In vague uncertainty should I be in the vastest waste. Though I entered it with the greatest knowledge, I should not know how inexhaustible it was. That which makes things what they are has not the limit which belongs to things, and when we speak of things being limited, we mean that they are so in themselves. (The Tâo) is the limit of the unlimited, and the boundlessness of the unbounded.

'We speak of fulness and emptiness; of withering and decay. It produces fulness and emptiness, but is neither fulness nor emptiness; it produces withering and decay, but is neither withering nor decay. It produces the root and branches, but is neither root nor branch; it produces accumulation and dispersion, but is itself neither accumulated nor dispersed.'

7. A-ho Kan[2] and Shăn Năng studied together

[1] The meaning of this other illustration is also very obscure to me; and much of what follows to the end of the paragraph.

[2] We can hardly be said to know anything more of the first and third of these men than what is mentioned here.

under Lăo-lung *K*î. Shăn Năng[1] was leaning forward on his stool, having shut the door and gone to sleep in the day time. At midday A-ho Kan pushed open the door and entered, saying, 'Lâo-lung is dead.' Shăn Năng leant forward on his stool, laid hold of his staff and rose. Then he laid the staff aside with a clash, laughed and said, 'That Heaven knew how cramped and mean, how arrogant and assuming I was, and therefore he has cast me off, and is dead. Now that there is no Master to correct my heedless words, it is simply for me to die!' Yen Kang, (who had come in) to condole, heard these words, and said, 'It is to him who embodies the Tâo that the superior men everywhere cling. Now you who do not understand so much as the tip of an autumn hair of it, not even the ten-thousandth part of the Tâo, still know how to keep hidden your heedless words about it and die;—how much more might he who embodied the Tâo do so! We look for it, and there is no form; we hearken for it, and there is no sound. When men try to discuss it, we call them dark indeed. When they discuss the Tâo, they misrepresent it.'

Hereupon Grand Purity[2] asked Infinitude[2], saying, 'Do you know the Tâo?' 'I do not know it,' was the reply. He then asked Do-nothing[2], who replied, 'I know it.' 'Is your knowledge of it de-

[1] Shăn Năng is well known, as coming in the chronological list between Fû-hsî and Hwang-Tî; and we are surprised that a higher place is not given to him among the Tâoist patriarchs than our author assigns to him here.

[2] These names, like those in the first paragraph of the Book, are metaphorical, intended, no doubt, to set forth attributes of the Tâo, and to suggest to the reader what it is or what it is not.

termined by various points?' 'It is.' 'What are they?' Do-nothing[1] said, 'I know that the Tâo may be considered noble, and may be considered mean, that it may be bound and compressed, and that it may be dispersed and diffused. These are the marks by which I know it.' Grand Purity took the words of those two, and asked No-beginning[1], saying, 'Such were their replies; which was right? and which was wrong? Infinitude's saying that he did not know it? or Do-nothing's saying that he knew it?' No-beginning said, 'The "I do not know it" was profound, and the "I know it" was shallow. The former had reference to its internal nature; the latter to its external conditions. Grand Purity looked up and sighed, saying, 'Is "not to know it" then to know it? And is "to know it" not to know it? But who knows that he who does not know it (really) knows it?' No-beginning replied, 'The Tâo cannot be heard; what can be heard is not It. The Tâo cannot be seen; what can be seen is not It. The Tâo cannot be expressed in words; what can be expressed in words is not It. Do we know the Formless which gives form to form? In the same way the Tâo does not admit of being named.'

No-beginning (further) said, 'If one ask about the Tâo and another answer him, neither of them knows it. Even the former who asks has never learned anything about the Tâo. He asks what does not admit of being asked, and the latter answers where answer is impossible. When one asks what does not admit of being asked, his questioning is in (dire)

[1] See note 2 on last page.

extremity. When one answers where answer is impossible, he has no internal knowledge of the subject. When people without such internal knowledge wait to be questioned by others in dire extremity, they show that externally they see nothing of space and time, and internally know nothing of the Grand Commencement[1]. Therefore they cannot cross over the Khwăn-lun[2], nor roam in the Grand Void.'

8. Starlight[3] asked Non-entity[3], saying, 'Master, do you exist? or do you not exist?' He got no answer to his question, however, and looked stedfastly to the appearance of the other, which was that of a deep void. All day long he looked to it, but could see nothing; he listened for it, but could hear nothing; he clutched at it, but got hold of nothing[4]. Starlight then said, 'Perfect! Who can attain to this? I can (conceive the ideas of) existence and non-existence, but I cannot (conceive the ideas of) non-existing non-existence, and still there be a non-existing existence. How is it possible to reach to this?'

9. The forger of swords for the Minister of War had reached the age of eighty, and had not lost a hair's-breadth of his ability[5]. The Minister said to

[1] The first beginning of all things or of anything.

[2] The Khwăn-lun may be considered the Sacred Mountain of Tâoism.

[3] The characters Kwang Yâo denote the points of light all over the sky, 'dusted with stars.' I can think of no better translation for them, as personified here, than 'starlight.' 'Non-entity' is a personification of the Tâo; as no existing thing, but the idea of the order that pervades and regulates throughout the universe.

[4] A quotation from the Tâo Teh *K*ing, ch. 14.

[5] Compare the case of the butcher in Bk. III, and other similar passages.

him, 'You are indeed skilful, Sir. Have you any method that makes you so?' The man said, 'Your servant has (always) kept to his work. When I was twenty, I was fond of forging swords. I looked at nothing else. I paid no attention to anything but swords. By my constant practice of it, I came to be able to do the work without any thought of what I was doing. By length of time one acquires ability at any art; and how much more one who is ever at work on it! What is there which does not depend on this, and succeed by it?'

10. *Z*ăn *Kh*iû[1] asked *K*ung-nî, saying, 'Can it be known how it was before heaven and earth?' The reply was, 'It can. It was the same of old as now.' *Z*ăn *Kh*iû asked no more and withdrew. Next day, however, he had another interview, and said, 'Yesterday I asked whether it could be known how it was before heaven and earth, and you, Master, said, "It can. As it is now, so it was of old." Yesterday, I seemed to understand you clearly, but to-day it is dark to me. I venture to ask you for an explanation of this.' *K*ung-nî said, 'Yesterday you seemed to understand me clearly, because your own spiritual nature had anticipated my reply. To-day it seems dark to you, for you are in an unspiritual mood, and are trying to discover the meaning. (In this matter) there is no old time and no present; no beginning and no ending. Could it be that there were grandchildren and children before there were (other) grandchildren and children[2]?'

---

[1] One of the disciples of Confucius;—Analects VI, 3.

[2] Hû Wăn-ying says, 'Before there can be grandsons and sons there must be grandfathers and fathers to transmit them, so before

*Z*ăn *Kh*iû had not made any reply, when *K*ung-nî went on, 'Let us have done. There can be no answering (on your part). We cannot with life give life to death; we cannot with death give death to life. Do death and life wait (for each other)? There is that which contains them both in its one comprehension [1]. Was that which was produced before Heaven and Earth a thing? That which made things and gave to each its character was not itself a thing. Things came forth and could not be before things, as if there had (previously) been things;—as if there had been things (producing one another) without end. The love of the sages for others, and never coming to an end, is an idea taken from this [2].'

11. Yen Yüan asked *K*ung-nî, saying, 'Master, I have heard you say, "There should be no demonstration of welcoming; there should be no movement to meet;"—I venture to ask in what way this affection of the mind may be shown.' The reply was, 'The ancients, amid (all) external changes, did not change internally; now-a-days men change internally, but take no note of external changes. When one only notes the changes of things, himself continuing one and the same, he does not change. How should there be (a difference between) his changing and not changing? How should he put himself in contact with (and come under the influence of) those external changes? He is sure, however,

there were (the present) heaven and earth, there must have been another heaven and earth.' But I am not sure that he has in this remark exactly caught our author's meaning.

[1] Meaning the Tâo. [2] An obscure remark.

to keep his pcints of contact with them from being many. The park of Shih-wei[1], the garden of Hwang-Tî, the palace of the Lord of Yü, and the houses of Thang and Wû;—(these all were places in which this was done). But the superior men (so called, of later days), such as the masters of the Literati and of Mohism, were bold to attack each other with their controversies; and how much more so are the men of the present day! Sages in dealing with others do not wound them; and they who do not wound others cannot be wounded by them. Only he whom others do not injure is able to welcome and meet men.

'Forests and marshes make me joyful and glad; but before the joy is ended, sadness comes and succeeds to it. When sadness and joy come, I cannot prevent their approach; when they go, I cannot retain them. How sad it is that men should only be as lodging-houses for things, (and the emotions which they excite)! They know what they meet, but they do not know what they do not meet; they use what power they have, but they cannot be strong where they are powerless. Such ignorance and powerlessness is what men cannot avoid. That they should try to avoid what they cannot avoid, is not this also sad? Perfect speech is to put speech away; perfect action is to put action away; to digest all knowledge that is known is a thing to be despised.'

---

[1] This personage has occurred before in Bk. VI, par. 7,—at the head of the most ancient sovereigns, who were in possession of the Tâo. His 'park' as a place for moral and intellectual inquiry is here mentioned;—so early was there a certain quickening of the mental faculties in China.

BOOK XXIII.

PART III. SECTION I.

Kăng-sang *Kh*û[1].

1. Among the disciples[2] of Lâo Tan there was a Kăng-sang *Kh*û, who had got a greater knowledge than the others of his doctrines, and took up his residence with it in the north at the hill of Wei-lêi[3]. His servants who were pretentious and knowing he sent away, and his concubines who were officious and kindly he kept at a distance; living (only) with those who were boorish and rude, and employing (only) the bustling and ill-mannered[4]. After three years there was great prosperity[5] in Wei-lêi, and the people said to one another, 'When Mr. Kăng-sang first came here, he alarmed us, and we thought him strange; our estimate of him after a short acquaintance was that he could not do us much good; but now that we have known him for years, we find him a more than ordinary benefit. Must he not be near being a sage? Why should you not

[1] See vol. xxxix, p. 153.

[2] The term in the text commonly denotes 'servants.' It would seem here simply to mean 'disciples.'

[3] Assigned variously. Probably the mount Yü in the 'Tribute of Yü,'—a hill in the present department of Tăng-*k*âu, Shan-tung.

[4] The same phraseology occurs in Bk. XI, par. 5; and also in the Shih, II, vi, 1, q. v.

[5] That is, abundant harvests. The 壤 of the common text should, probably, be 穰.

unite in blessing him as the representative of our departed (whom we worship), and raise an altar to him as we do to the spirit of the grain[1]?' Kăng-sang heard of it, kept his face indeed to the south[2], but was dissatisfied.

His disciples thought it strange in him, but he said to them, 'Why, my disciples, should you think this strange in me? When the airs of spring come forth, all vegetation grows; and, when the autumn arrives, all the previous fruits of the earth are matured. Do spring and autumn have these effects without any adequate cause? The processes of the Great Tâo have been in operation. I have heard that the Perfect man dwells idly in his apartment within its surrounding walls[3], and the people get wild and crazy, not knowing how they should repair to him. Now these small people of Wei-lêi in their opinionative way want to present their offerings to me, and place me among such men of ability and virtue. But am I a man to be set up as such a model? It is on this account that I am dissatisfied when I think of the words of Lâo Tan[4].'

2. His disciples said, 'Not so. In ditches eight cubits wide, or even twice as much, big fishes cannot turn their bodies about, but minnows and eels find them sufficient for them[5]; on hillocks six or

---

[1] I find it difficult to tell what these people wanted to make of *Kh*û, further than what he says himself immediately to his disciples. I cannot think that they wished to make him their ruler.

[2] This is the proper position for the sovereign in his court, and for the sage as the teacher of the world. *Kh*û accepts it in the latter capacity, but with dissatisfaction.

[3] Compare the Lî *K*î, Bk. XXXVIII, par. 10, et al.

[4] As if he were one with the Tâo.

[5] I do not see the appropriateness here of the 制 in the text.

seven cubits high, large beasts cannot conceal themselves, but foxes of evil omen find it a good place for them. And moreover, honour should be paid to the wise, offices given to the able, and preference shown to the good and the beneficial. From of old Yâo and Shun acted thus;—how much more may the people of Wei-lêi do so! O Master, let them have their way!'

Kăng-sang replied, 'Come nearer, my little children. If a beast that could hold a carriage in its mouth leave its hill by itself, it will not escape the danger that awaits it from the net; or if a fish that could swallow a boat be left dry by the flowing away of the water, then (even) the ants are able to trouble it. Thus it is that birds and beasts seek to be as high as possible, and fishes and turtles seek to lie as deep as possible. In the same way men who wish to preserve their bodies and lives keep their persons concealed, and they do so in the deepest retirement possible. And moreover, what was there in those sovereigns to entitle them to your laudatory mention? Their sophistical reasonings (resembled) the reckless breaking down of walls and enclosures and planting the wild rubus and wormwood in their place; or making the hair thin before they combed it; or counting the grains of rice before they cooked them[1]. They would do such things with careful discrimination; but what was there in them to benefit the world? If you raise the men of talent to office, you will create disorder; making the people strive with one

[1] All these condemnatory descriptions of Yâo and Shun are eminently Tâoistic, but so metaphorical that it is not easy to appreciate them.

another for promotion; if you employ men for their wisdom, the people will rob one another (of their reputation)[1]. These various things are insufficient to make the people good and honest. They are very eager for gain;—a son will kill his father, and a minister his ruler (for it). In broad daylight men will rob, and at midday break through walls. I tell you that the root of the greatest disorder was planted in the times of Yâo and Shun. The branches of it will remain for a thousand ages; and after a thousand ages men will be found eating one another[2].'

3. (On this) Nan-yung *Kh*û[3] abruptly sat right up and said, 'What method can an old man like me adopt to become (the Perfect man) that you have described?' Kăng-sang Ȝze said, 'Maintain your body complete; hold your life in close embrace; and do not let your thoughts keep working anxiously:—do this for three years, and you may become the man of whom I have spoken.' The other rejoined, 'Eyes are all of the same form, I do not know any difference between them:—yet the blind have no power of vision. Ears are all of the same form; I do not know any difference between them:—yet the deaf have no power of hearing. Minds are all of the same nature, I do not know any difference between them;—yet the mad cannot make the minds of other men their own. (My) personality is indeed like (yours), but things seem to separate

[1] Compare the Tâo Teh *K*ing, ch. 3.

[2] *Kh*û is in all this too violent.

[3] A disciple of Kăng-sang *Kh*û;—'a sincere seeker of the Tâo, very much to be pitied,' says Lin Hsî-*k*ung.

between us[1]. I wish to find in myself what there is in you, but I am not able to do so[1]. You have now said to me, "Maintain your body complete; hold your life in close embrace; and do not let your thoughts keep working anxiously." With all my efforts to learn your Way, (your words) reach only my ears.' Kăng-sang replied, 'I can say nothing more to you,' and then he added, 'Small flies cannot transform the bean caterpillar[2]; Yüeh[3] fowls cannot hatch the eggs of geese, but Lû fowls[3] can. It is not that the nature of these fowls is different; the ability in the one case and inability in the other arise from their different capacities as large and small. My ability is small and not sufficient to transform you. Why should you not go south and see Lâo-ʒze?'

4. Nan-yung *Kh*û hereupon took with him some rations, and after seven days and seven nights arrived at the abode of Lâo-ʒze, who said to him, 'Are you come from *Kh*û's?' 'I am,' was the reply. 'And why, Sir, have you come with such a multitude of attendants[4]?' Nan-yung was frightened, and turned his head round to look behind him. Lâo-ʒze said, 'Do you not understand my meaning?' The other held his head down and was ashamed, and then he lifted it up, and sighed, saying, 'I forgot at the moment what I should reply to your

---

[1] The 辟 in the former of these sentences is difficult. I take it in the sense of 譬, and read it phî.

[2] Compare the Shih, II, v, Ode 2, 3.

[3] I believe the fowls of Shan-tung are still larger than those of *K*ih-*k*iang or Fû-*k*ien.

[4] A good instance of Lâo's metaphorical style.

question, and in consequence I have lost what I wished to ask you.' 'What do you mean?' 'If I have not wisdom, men say that I am stupid[1], while if I have it, it occasions distress to myself. If I have not benevolence, then (I am charged) with doing hurt to others, while if I have it, I distress myself. If I have not righteousness, I (am charged with) injuring others, while if I have it, I distress myself. How can I escape from these dilemmas? These are the three perplexities that trouble me; and I wish at the suggestion of *Kh*û to ask you about them.' Lâo-ȝze replied, 'A little time ago, when I saw you and looked right into your eyes[2], I understood you, and now your words confirm the judgment which I formed. You look frightened and amazed. You have lost your parents, and are trying with a pole to find them at the (bottom of) the sea. You have gone astray; you are at your wit's end. You wish to recover your proper nature, and you know not what step to take first to find it. You are to be pitied!'

5. Nan-yung *Kh*û asked to be allowed to enter (the establishment), and have an apartment assigned to him[3]. (There) he sought to realise the qualities which he loved, and put away those which he hated. For ten days he afflicted himself, and then waited again on Lâo-ȝze, who said to him, 'You must purify yourself thoroughly! But from your symptoms of

---

[1] In the text 朱愚. The 朱 must be an erroneous addition. or probably it is a mistake for the speaker's name 趎.

[2] Literally, 'between the eye-brows and eye-lashes.'

[3] Thus we are as it were in the school of Lâo-ȝze, and can see how he deals with his pupils.

distress, and signs of impurity about you, I see there still seem to cling to you things that you dislike. When the fettering influences from without become numerous, and you try to seize them (you will find it a difficult task); the better plan is to bar your inner man against their entrance. And when the similar influences within get intertwined, it is a difficult task to grasp (and hold them in check); the better plan is to bar the outer door against their exit. Even a master of the Tâo and its characteristics will not be able to control these two influences together, and how much less can one who is only a student of the Tâo do so!' Nan-yung *Kh*û said, 'A certain villager got an illness, and when his neighbours asked about it, he was able to describe the malady, though it was one from which he had not suffered before. When I ask you about the Grand Tâo, it seems to me like drinking medicine which (only serves to) increase my illness. I should like to hear from you about the regular method of guarding the life;—that will be sufficient for me.' Lâo-ȝze replied, '(You ask me about) the regular method of guarding the life;—can you hold the One thing fast in your embrace? Can you keep from losing it? Can you know the lucky and the unlucky without having recourse to the tortoise-shell or the divining stalks? Can you rest (where you ought to rest)? Can you stop (when you have got enough)? Can you give over thinking of other men, and seek what you want in yourself (alone)? Can you flee (from the allurements of desire)? Can you maintain an entire simplicity? Can you become a little child? The child will cry all the day, without its throat becoming hoarse;—so perfect is the harmony (of its physical constitution). It will keep its fingers closed all the day without relaxing their grasp;—such is the concentration of its powers. It will keep its eyes fixed all day, without their moving;—so is it unaffected by what is external to it. It walks it knows not whither; it rests where it is placed, it knows not why; it is calmly indifferent to things, and follows their current. This is the regular method of guarding the life[1].'

6. Nan-yung *Kh*û said, 'And are these all the characteristics of the Perfect man?' Lâo-ȝze replied, 'No. These are what we call the breaking up of the ice, and the dissolving of the cold. The Perfect man, along with other men, gets his food from the earth, and derives his joy from his Heaven (-conferred nature). But he does not like them allow himself to be troubled by the consideration of advantage or injury coming from men and things; he does not like them do strange things, or form plans, or enter on undertakings; he flees from the allurements of desire, and pursues his way with an entire simplicity. Such is the way by which he guards his life.' 'And is this what constitutes his perfection?' 'Not quite. I asked you whether you could become a little child. The little child moves unconscious of what it is doing, and walks unconscious of whither it is going. Its body is like the branch of a rotten tree, and its mind is like slaked lime[2]. Being such, misery does not come to it, nor happiness. It has

[1] In this long reply there are many evident recognitions of passages in the Tâo Teh *K*ing;—compare chapters 9, 10, 55, 58.

[2] See the description of Ȝze-*kh*î's Tâoistic trance at the beginning of the second Book.

neither misery nor happiness;—how can it suffer from the calamities incident to men[1]?'

7. [2] He whose mind[3] is thus grandly fixed emits a Heavenly light. In him who emits this heavenly light men see the (True) man. When a man has cultivated himself (up to this point), thenceforth he remains constant in himself. When he is thus constant in himself, (what is merely) the human element will leave him[4], but Heaven will help him. Those whom their human element has left we call the people of Heaven[4]. Those whom Heaven helps we call the Sons of Heaven. Those who would by learning attain to this[5] seek for what they cannot

[1] Nan-yung *Kh*û disappears here. His first master, Kăng-sang *Kh*û, disappeared in paragraph 4. The different way in which his name is written by Sze-mâ *Kh*ien is mentioned in the brief introductory note on p. 153. It should have been further stated there that in the Fourth Book of Lieh-ʒze (IV, 2b–3b) some account of him is given with his name as written by *Kh*ien. A great officer of *Kh*ăn is introduced as boasting of him that he was a sage, and, through his mastery of the principles of Lâo Tan, could hear with his eyes and see with his ears. Hereupon Khăng-ʒhang is brought to the court of the marquis of Lû to whom he says that the report of him which he had heard was false, adding that he could dispense with the use of his senses altogether, but could not alter their several functions. This being reported to Confucius, he simply laughs at it, but makes no remark.

[2] I suppose that from this to the end of the Book we have the sentiments of *K*wang-ʒze himself. Whether we consider them his, or the teachings of Lâo-ʒze to his visitor, they are among the depths of Tâoism, which I will not attempt to elucidate in the notes here.

[3] The character which I have translated 'mind' here is 宇, meaning 'the side walls of a house,' and metaphorically used for 'the breast,' as the house of the mind. Hû explains it by 心胸.

[4] He is emancipated from the human as contrary to the heavenly.

[5] The Tâo.

learn. Those who would by effort attain to this, attempt what effort can never effect. Those who aim by reasoning to reach it reason where reasoning has no place. To know to stop where they cannot arrive by means of knowledge is the highest attainment. Those who cannot do this will be destroyed on the lathe of Heaven.

8. Where things are all adjusted to maintain the body; where a provision against unforeseen dangers is kept up to maintain the life of the mind; where an inward reverence is cherished to be exhibited (in all intercourse) with others;—where this is done, and yet all evils arrive, they are from Heaven, and not from the men themselves. They will not be sufficient to confound the established (virtue of the character), or be admitted into the Tower of Intelligence. That Tower has its Guardian, who acts unconsciously, and whose care will not be effective, if there be any conscious purpose in it[1]. If one who has not this entire sincerity in himself make any outward demonstration, every such demonstration will be incorrect. The thing will enter into him, and not let go its hold. Then with every fresh demonstration there will be still greater failure. If he do what is not good in the light of open day, men will have the opportunity of punishing him; if he do it in darkness and secrecy, spirits[2] will inflict the punishment. Let a man understand this—his relation both to men and spirits, and then he will do what is good in the solitude of himself.

[1] This Guardian of the Mind or Tower of Intelligence is the Tâo.

[2] One of the rare introductions of spiritual agency in the early Tâoism.

He whose rule of life is in himself does not act for the sake of a name. He whose rule is outside himself has his will set on extensive acquisition. He who does not act for the sake of a name emits a light even in his ordinary conduct; he whose will is set on extensive acquisition is but a trafficker. Men see how he stands on tiptoe, while he thinks that he is overtopping others. Things enter (and take possession of) him who (tries to) make himself exhaustively (acquainted with them), while when one is indifferent to them, they do not find any lodgment in his person. And how can other men find such lodgment? But when one denies lodgment to men, there are none who feel attachment to him. In this condition he is cut off from other men. There is no weapon more deadly than the will[1];—even Mû-yê[2] was inferior to it. There is no robber greater than the Yin and Yang, from whom nothing can escape of all between heaven and earth. But it is not the Yin and Yang that play the robber;—it is the mind that causes them to do so.

9. The Tâo is to be found in the subdivisions (of its subject); (it is to be found) in that when complete, and when broken up. What I dislike in considering it as subdivided, is that the division leads to the multiplication of it;—and what I dislike in that multiplication is that it leads to the (thought of) effort to secure it. Therefore when (a man)

[1] That is, the will, man's own human element, in opposition to the Heavenly element of the Tâo.

[2] One of the two famous swords made for Ho-lü, the king of Wû. See the account of their making in the seventy-fourth chapter of the 'History of the Various States;' very marvellous, but evidently, and acknowledged to be, fabulous.

comes forth (and is born), if he did not return (to his previous non-existence), we should have (only) seen his ghost; when he comes forth and gets this (return), he dies (as we say). He is extinguished, and yet has a real existence:—(this is another way of saying that in life we have) only man's ghost. By taking the material as an emblem of the immaterial do we arrive at a settlement of the case of man. He comes forth, but from no root; he re-enters, but by no aperture. He has a real existence, but it has nothing to do with place; he has continuance, but it has nothing to do with beginning or end. He has a real existence, but it has nothing to do with place, such is his relation to space; he has continuance, but it has nothing to do with beginning or end, such is his relation to time; he has life; he has death; he comes forth; he enters; but we do not see his form;—all this is what is called the door of Heaven. The door of Heaven is Non-Existence. All things come from non-existence. The (first) existences could not bring themselves into existence; they must have come from non-existence. And non-existence is just the same as non-existing. Herein is the secret of the sages.

10. Among the ancients there were those whose knowledge reached the extreme point. And what was that point? There were some who thought that in the beginning there was nothing. This was the extreme point, the completest reach of their knowledge, to which nothing could be added. Again, there were those who supposed that (in the beginning) there were existences, proceeding to consider life to be a (gradual) perishing, and death a returning (to the original state). And there they stopped,

making, (however), a distinction between life and death. Once again there were those who said, 'In the beginning there was nothing; by and by there was life; and then in a little time life was succeeded by death. We hold that non-existence was the head, life the body, and death the os coccygis. But of those who acknowledge that existence and non-existence, death and life, are all under the One Keeper, we are the friends.' Though those who maintained these three views were different, they were so as the different branches of the same ruling Family (of *Kh*û)[1],—the *K*âos and the *K*ings, bearing the surname of the lord whom they honoured as the author of their branch, and the *K*iâs named from their appanage;—(all one, yet seeming) not to be one.

The possession of life is like the soot that collects under a boiler. When that is differently distributed, the life is spoken of as different. But to say that life is different in different lives, and better in one than in another, is an improper mode of speech. And yet there may be something here which we do not know. (As for instance), at the lâ sacrifice the paunch and the divided hoofs may be set forth on separate dishes, but they should not be considered as parts of different victims; (and again), when one is inspecting a house, he goes over it all, even the adytum for the shrines of the temple, and visits also the most private apartments; doing this, and setting a different estimate on the different parts.

Let me try and speak of this method of appor-

[1] Both Lâo and *K*wang belonged to *Kh*û, and this illustration was natural to them.

tioning one's approval:—life is the fundamental consideration in it; knowledge is the instructor. From this they multiply their approvals and disapprovals, determining what is merely nominal and what is real. They go on to conclude that to themselves must the appeal be made in everything, and to try to make others adopt them as their model; prepared even to die to make good their views on every point. In this way they consider being employed in office as a mark of wisdom, and not being so employed as a mark of stupidity, success as entitling to fame, and the want of it as disgraceful. The men of the present day who follow this differentiating method are like the cicada and the little dove[1];—there is no difference between them.

11. When one treads on the foot of another in the market-place, he apologises on the ground of the bustle. If an elder tread on his younger brother, he proceeds to comfort him; if a parent tread on a child, he says and does nothing. Hence it is said, 'The greatest politeness is to show no special respect to others; the greatest righteousness is to take no account of things; the greatest wisdom is to lay no plans; the greatest benevolence is to make no demonstration of affection; the greatest good faith is to give no pledge of sincerity.'

Repress the impulses of the will; unravel the errors of the mind; put away the entanglements to virtue; and clear away all that obstructs the free course of the Tâo. Honours and riches, distinctions and austerity, fame and profit; these six things produce the impulses of the will. Personal appearance

---

[1] See in Bk. I, par. 2.

and deportment, the desire of beauty and subtle reasonings, excitement of the breath and cherished thoughts; these six things produce errors of the mind. Hatred and longings, joy and anger, grief and delight; these six things are the entanglements to virtue. Refusals and approachments, receiving and giving, knowledge and ability; these six things obstruct the course of the Tâo. When these four conditions, with the six causes of each, do not agitate the breast, the mind is correct. Being correct, it is still; being still, it is pellucid; being pellucid, it is free from pre-occupation; being free from pre-occupation, it is in the state of inaction, in which it accomplishes everything.

The Tâo is the object of reverence to all the virtues. Life is what gives opportunity for the display of the virtues. The nature is the substantive character of the life. The movement of the nature is called action. When action becomes hypocritical, we say that it has lost (its proper attribute).

The wise communicate with what is external to them and are always laying plans. This is what with all their wisdom they are not aware of;—they look at things askance. When the action (of the nature) is from external constraint, we have what is called virtue; when it is all one's own, we have what is called government. These two names seem to be opposite to each other, but in reality they are in mutual accord.

12. Î[1] was skilful in hitting the minutest mark, but stupid in wishing men to go on praising him without end. The sage is skilful Heavenwards, but stupid

[1] See on V, par. 2.

manwards. It is only the complete man who can be both skilful Heavenwards and good manwards.

Only an insect can play the insect, only an insect show the insect nature. Even the complete man hates the attempt to exemplify the nature of Heaven. He hates the manner in which men do so, and how much more would he hate the doing so by himself before men!

When a bird came in the way of Î, he was sure to obtain it;—such was his mastery with his bow. If all the world were to be made a cage, birds would have nowhere to escape to. Thus it was that Thang caged Î Yin by making him his cook[1], and that duke Mû of *Kh*in caged Pâi-lî Hsî by giving the skins of five rams for him[2]. But if you try to cage men by anything but what they like, you will never succeed.

A man, one of whose feet has been cut off, discards ornamental (clothes);—his outward appearance will not admit of admiration. A criminal under sentence of death will ascend to any height without fear;—he has ceased to think of life or death.

When one persists in not reciprocating the gifts (of friendship), he forgets all others. Having forgotten all others, he may be considered as a Heaven-like man. Therefore when respect is shown to a man, and it awakens in him no joy, and when contempt awakens no anger, it is only one who shares in the Heaven-like harmony that can be thus. When he would display anger and yet is not angry, the anger comes out in that repression of it. When he would put forth action, and yet does not do so,

[1] See Mencius V, i, 7.

[2] Mencius V, i, 9.

the action is in that not-acting. Desiring to be quiescent, he must pacify all his emotions ; desiring to be spirit-like, he must act in conformity with his mind. When action is required of him, he wishes that it may be right; and it then is under an inevitable constraint. Those who act according to that inevitable constraint pursue the way of the sage.

BOOK XXIV.

PART III. SECTION II.

Hsü Wû-kwei[1].

1. Hsü Wû-kwei having obtained through Nü Shang[2] an introduction to the marquis Wû of Wei[3], the marquis, speaking to him with kindly sympathy[4], said, 'You are ill, Sir; you have suffered from your hard and laborious toils[4] in the forests, and still you have been willing to come and see poor me[5].' Hsü Wû-kwei replied, 'It is I who have to comfort your lordship; what occasion have you to comfort me? If your lordship go on to fill up the measure of your sensual desires, and to prolong your likes and dislikes, then the condition of your mental nature will be diseased, and if you discourage and repress those desires, and deny your likings and dislikings, that will be an affliction to your ears and eyes

---

[1] See vol. xxxix, pp. 153, 154.

[2] A favourite and minister of the marquis Wû.

[3] This was the second marquis of Wei, one of the three principalities into which the great state of Ȝin had been broken up, and which he ruled as the marquis *K*î for sixteen years, B.C. 386–371. His son usurped the title of king, and was the 'king Hui of Liang,' whom Mencius had interviews with. Wû, or 'martial,' was *K*î's honorary, posthumous epithet.

[4] The character (勞) which I thus translate, has two tones, the second and fourth. Here and elsewhere in this paragraph and the next, it is with one exception in the fourth tone, meaning 'to comfort or reward for toils endured.' The one exception is its next occurrence,—'hard and laborious toils.'

[5] The appropriate and humble designation of himself by the ruler of a state.

(deprived of their accustomed pleasures);—it is for me to comfort your lordship, what occasion have you to comfort me?' The marquis looked contemptuous, and made no reply.

After a little time, Hsü Wû-kwei said, 'Let me tell your lordship something:—I look at dogs and judge of them by their appearance[1]. One of the lowest quality seizes his food, satiates himself, and stops;—he has the attributes of a fox. One of a medium quality seems to be looking at the sun. One of the highest quality seems to have forgotten the one thing,—himself. But I judge still better of horses than I do of dogs. When I do so, I find that one goes straightforward, as if following a line; that another turns off, so as to describe a hook; that a third describes a square as if following the measure so called; and that a fourth describes a circle as exactly as a compass would make it. These are all horses of a state; but they are not equal to a horse of the kingdom. His qualities are complete. Now he looks anxious; now to be losing the way; now to be forgetting himself. Such a horse prances along, or rushes on, spurning the dust and not knowing where he is.' The marquis was greatly pleased and laughed.

When Hsü Wû-kwei came out, Nü Shang said to him, 'How was it, Sir, that you by your counsels produced such an effect on our ruler? In my counsellings of him, now indirectly, taking my subjects from the Books of Poetry, History, Rites, and Music; now directly, from the Metal Tablets[2], and the six Bow-cases[2], all calculated for the service (of the

---

[1] Literally, 'I physiognomise dogs.'

[2] The names of two Books, or Collections of Tablets, the former

state), and to be of great benefit;—in these counsellings, repeated times without number, I have never seen the ruler show his teeth in a smile:—by what counsels have you made him so pleased to-day?' Hsü Wû-kwei replied, 'I only told him how I judged of dogs and horses by looking at their appearance.' 'So?' said Nü Shang, and the other rejoined, 'Have you not heard of the wanderer[1] from Yüeh? when he had been gone from the state several days, he was glad when he saw any one whom he had seen in it; when he had been gone a month, he was glad when he saw any one whom he had known in it; and when he had been gone a round year, he was glad when he saw any one who looked like a native of it. The longer he was gone, the more longingly did he think of the people;—was it not so? The men who withdraw to empty valleys, where the hellebore bushes stop up the little paths made by the weasels, as they push their way or stand amid the waste, are glad when they seem to hear the sounds of human footsteps; and how much more would they be so, if it were their brothers and relatives talking and laughing by their side! How long it is since the words of a True[2] man were heard as he talked and laughed by our ruler's side!'

2. At (another) interview of Hsü Wû-kwei with the marquis Wû, the latter said, 'You, Sir, have been dwelling in the forests for a long time, living

---

containing Registers of the Population, the latter treating of military subjects.

[1] Kwo Hsiang makes this 'a banished criminal.' This is not necessary.

[2] Wû-kwei then had a high opinion of his own attainments in Tâoism, and a low opinion of Nü Shang and the other courtiers.

on acorns and chestnuts, and satiating yourself with onions and chives, without thinking of poor me. Now (that you are here), is it because you are old? or because you wish to try again the taste of wine and meat? or because (you wish that) I may enjoy the happiness derived from the spirits of the altars of the Land and Grain?' Hsü Wû-kwei replied, 'I was born in a poor and mean condition, and have never presumed to drink of your lordship's wine, or eat of your meat. My object in coming was to comfort your lordship under your troubles.' 'What? comfort me under my troubles?' 'Yes, to comfort both your lordship's spirit and body.' The marquis said, 'What do you mean?' His visitor replied, 'Heaven and Earth have one and the same purpose in the production (of all men). However high one man be exalted, he should not think that he is favourably dealt with; and however low may be the position of another, he should not think that he is unfavourably dealt with. You are indeed the one and only lord of the 10,000 chariots (of your state), but you use your dignity to embitter (the lives of) all the people, and to pamper your ears, eyes, nose, and mouth. But your spirit does not acquiesce in this. The spirit (of man) loves to be in harmony with others and hates selfish indulgence[1]. This selfish indulgence is a disease, and therefore I would comfort you under it. How is it that your lordship more than others brings this disease on yourself?' The marquis said, 'I have wished to see you, Sir, for a long time. I want to love my people, and by the exercise of righteous-

[1] Wû-kwei had a high idea of the constitution of human nature.

ness to make an end of war;—will that be sufficient?' Hsü Wû-kwei replied, 'By no means. To love the people is the first step to injure them[1]. By the exercise of righteousness to make an end of war is the root from which war is produced[1]. If your lordship try to accomplish your object in this way, you are not likely to succeed. All attempts to accomplish what we think good (with an ulterior end) is a bad contrivance. Although your lordship practise benevolence and righteousness (as you propose), it will be no better than hypocrisy. You may indeed assume the (outward) form, but successful accomplishment will lead to (inward) contention, and the change thence arising will produce outward fighting. Your lordship also must not mass files of soldiers in the passages of your galleries and towers, nor have footmen and horsemen in the apartments about your altars[2]. Do not let thoughts contrary to your success lie hidden in your mind; do not think of conquering men by artifice, or by (skilful) plans, or by fighting. If I kill the officers and people of another state, and annex its territory, to satisfy my selfish desires, while in my spirit I do not know whether the fighting be good, where is the victory that I gain? Your lordship's best plan is to abandon (your purpose). If you will cultivate in your breast the sincere purpose (to love the people), and so respond to the feeling of Heaven and Earth, and not (further) vex yourself, then your people will already have escaped death;—what

[1] Tâoistic teaching, but questionable.

[2] We need more information about the customs of the feudal princes fully to understand the language of this sentence.

occasion will your lordship have to make an end of war?'

3. Hwang-Tî was going to see Tâ-kwei[1] at the hill of *K*ü-ȝhze. Fang Ming was acting as charioteer, and *Kh*ang Yü was occupying the third place in the carriage. *K*ang *Z*o and Hsî Phăng went before the horses; and Khwăn Hwun and Kû *Kh*î followed the carriage. When they arrived at the wild of Hsiang-*kh*ăng, the seven sages were all perplexed, and could find no place at which to ask the way. Just then they met with a boy tending some horses, and asked the way of him. 'Do you know,' they said, 'the hill of *K*ü-ȝhze?' and he replied that he did. He also said that he knew where Tâ-kwei was living. 'A strange boy is this!' said Hwang-Tî. 'He not only knows the hill of *K*ü-ȝhze, but he also knows where Tâ-kwei is living. Let me ask him about the government of mankind.' The boy said, 'The administration of the kingdom is like this (which I am doing);—what difficulty should there be in it? When I was young, I enjoyed myself roaming over all within the six confines of the world of space, and then I began to suffer from indistinct sight. A wise elder taught me, saying, "Ride in the chariot of the

[1] Tâ (or Thâi)-kwei (or wei) appears here as the name of a person. It cannot be the name of a hill, as it is said by some to be. The whole paragraph is parabolic or allegorical; and Tâ-kwei is probably a personification of the Great Tâo itself, though no meaning of the character kwei can be adduced to justify this interpretation. The horseherd boy is further supposed to be a personification of the 'Great Simplicity,' which is characteristic of the Tâo, the spontaneity of it, unvexed by the wisdom of man. The lesson of the paragraph is that taught in the eleventh Book, and many other places.

sun, and roam in the wild of Hsiang-*Kh*ăng." Now the trouble in my eyes is a little better, and I am again enjoying myself roaming outside the six confines of the world of space. As to the government of the kingdom, it is like this (which I am doing);—what difficulty should there be in it?' Hwang-Tî said, 'The administration of the world is indeed not your business, my son; nevertheless, I beg to ask you about it.' The little lad declined to answer, but on Hwang-Tî putting the question again, he said, 'In what does the governor of the kingdom differ from him who has the tending of horses, and who has only to put away whatever in him would injure the horses?'

Hwang-Tî bowed to him twice with his head to the ground, called him his 'Heavenly Master[1],' and withdrew.

4. If officers of wisdom do not see the changes which their anxious thinking has suggested, they have no joy; if debaters are not able to set forth their views in orderly style, they have no joy; if critical examiners find no subjects on which to exercise their powers of vituperation, they have no joy:—they are all hampered by external restrictions.

Those who try to attract the attention of their age (wish to) rise at court; those who try to win the regard of the people[2] count holding office a glory; those who possess muscular strength boast of doing what is difficult; those who are bold and daring exert themselves in times of calamity; those who are able

[1] This is the title borne to the present day by the chief or pope of Tâoism, the representative of *K*ang Tâo-ling of our first century.

[2] Taking the initial *k*ung in the third tone. If we take it in the first tone, the meaning is different.

swordmen and spearmen delight in fighting; those whose powers are decayed seek to rest in the name (they have gained); those who are skilled in the laws seek to enlarge the scope of government; those who are proficient in ceremonies and music pay careful attention to their deportment; and those who profess benevolence and righteousness value opportunities (for displaying them).

The husbandmen who do not keep their fields well weeded are not equal to their business, nor are traders who do not thrive in the markets. When the common people have their appropriate employment morning and evening, they stimulate one another to diligence; the mechanics who are masters of their implements feel strong for their work. If their wealth does not increase, the greedy are distressed; if their power and influence is not growing, the ambitious are sad.

Such creatures of circumstance and things delight in changes, and if they meet with a time when they can show what they can do, they cannot keep themselves from taking advantage of it. They all pursue their own way like (the seasons of) the year, and do not change as things do. They give the reins to their bodies and natures, and allow themselves to sink beneath (the pressure of) things, and all their lifetime do not come back (to their proper selves):—is it not sad[1]?

5. *K*wang-ȝze said, 'An archer, without taking aim beforehand, yet may hit the mark. If we say that he is a good archer, and that all the world may

[1] All the parties in this paragraph disallow the great principle of Tâoism, which does everything by doing nothing.

be Îs[1], is this allowable?' Hui-ȝze replied, 'It is.' *K*wang-ȝze continued, 'All men do not agree in counting the same thing to be right, but every one maintains his own view to be right; (if we say) that all men may be Yâos, is this allowable?' Hui-ȝze (again) replied, 'It is;' and *K*wang-ȝze went on, 'Very well; there are the literati, the followers of Mo (Tî), of Yang (*K*û), and of Ping[2];—making four (different schools). Including yourself, Master, there are five. Which of your views is really right? Or will you take the position of Lû *K*ü[3]? One of his disciples said to him, "Master, I have got hold of your method. I can in winter heat the furnace under my tripod, and in summer can produce ice." Lû *K*ü said, "That is only with the Yang element to call out the same, and with the Yin to call out the yin;—that is not my method. I will show you what my method is." On this he tuned two citherns, placing one of them in the hall, and the other in one of the inner apartments. Striking the note Kung[4] in the one, the same note vibrated in the other, and so it was with the note *K*io[4]; the two instruments being tuned in the same way. But if he had differently tuned them on other strings different

[1] The famous archer of the Hsiâ dynasty, in the twenty-second century B.C.

[2] The name of Kung-sun Lung, the Lung Li-*kh*ăn of Bk. XXI, par. 1.

[3] Only mentioned here. The statement of his disciple and his remark on it are equally obscure, though the latter is partially illustrated from the twenty-third, twenty-fourth, and other hexagrams of the Yih *K*ing.

[4] The sounds of the first and third notes of the Chinese musical scale, corresponding to our A and E. I know too little of music myself to pronounce further on Lû *K*ü's illustration.

from the normal arrangement of the five notes, the five-and-twenty strings would all have vibrated, without any difference of their notes, the note to which he had tuned them ruling and guiding all the others. Is your maintaining your view to be right just like this?'

Hui-ȝze replied, 'Here now are the literati, and the followers of Mo, Yang, and Ping. Suppose that they have come to dispute with me. They put forth their conflicting statements; they try vociferously to put me down; but none of them have ever proved me wrong:—what do you say to this?' *K*wang-ȝze said, 'There was a man of *Kh*î who cast away his son in Sung to be a gate-keeper there, and thinking nothing of the mutilation he would incur; the same man, to secure one of his sacrificial vessels or bells, would have it strapped and secured, while to find his son who was lost, he would not go out of the territory of his own state:—so forgetful was he of the relative importance of things. If a man of *Kh*û, going to another state as a lame gate-keeper, at midnight, at a time when no one was nigh, were to fight with his boatman, he would not be able to reach the shore, and he would have done what he could to provoke the boatman's animosity[1].'

6. As *K*wang-ȝze was accompanying a funeral, when passing by the grave of Hui-ȝze[2], he looked

[1] The illustrations in this last member of the paragraph are also obscure. Lin Hsî-*k*ung says that all the old explanations of them are defective; his own explanation has failed to make itself clear to me.

[2] The expression in the last sentence of the paragraph, 'the Master,' makes it certain that this was the grave of *K*wang-ȝze's friend with whom he had had so many conversations and arguments.

round, and said to his attendants, 'On the top of the nose of that man of Ying[1] there is a (little) bit of mud like a fly's wing.' He sent for the artisan Shih to cut it away. Shih whirled his axe so as to produce a wind, which immediately carried off the mud entirely, leaving the nose uninjured, and the (statue of) the man of Ying[1] standing undisturbed. The ruler Yüan of Sung[2] heard of the feat, called the artisan Shih, and said to him, 'Try and do the same thing on me.' The artisan said, 'Your servant has been able to trim things in that way, but the material on which I have worked has been dead for a long time.' *K*wang-ȝze said, 'Since the death of the Master, I have had no material to work upon. I have had no one with whom to talk.'

7. Kwan *K*ung being ill, duke Hwan went to ask for him, and said, 'Your illness, father *K*ung, is very severe; should you not speak out your mind to me? Should this prove the great illness, to whom will it be best for me to entrust my State?' Kwan *K*ung said, 'To whom does your grace wish to entrust it?' 'To Pâo Shû-yâ[3],' was the reply. 'He will not do. He is an admirable officer, pure and incorruptible, but with others who are not like himself he will not associate. And when he once hears

[1] Ying was the capital of *Kh*û. I have seen in China about the graves of wealthy and distinguished men many life-sized statues of men somehow connected with them.

[2] Yüan is called the 'ruler' of Sung. That duchy was by this time a mere dependency of *Kh*î. The sacrifices of its old ruling House were finally extinguished by *Kh*î in B. C. 206.

[3] Pâo Shû-yâ had been the life-long friend of the dying premier, and to him in the first place had been owing the elevation of Hwan to the marquisate.

of another man's faults, he never forgets them. If you employ him to administer the state, above, he will take the leading of your Grace, and, below, he will come into collision with the people;—in no long time you will be holding him as an offender.' The duke said, 'Who, then, is the man?' The reply was, 'If I must speak, there is Hsî Phăng[1];—he will do. He is a man who forgets his own high position, and against whom those below him will not revolt. He is ashamed that he is not equal to Hwang-Tî, and pities those who are not equal to himself. Him who imparts of his virtue to others we call a sage; him who imparts of his wealth to others we call a man of worth. He who by his worth would preside over others, never succeeds in winning them; he who with his worth condescends to others, never but succeeds in winning them. Hsî Phăng has not been (much) heard of in the state; he has not been (much) distinguished in his own clan. But as I must speak, he is the man for you.'

8. The king of Wû, floating about on the *K*iang, (landed and) ascended the Hill of monkeys, which all, when they saw him, scampered off in terror, and hid themselves among the thick hazels. There was one, however, which, in an unconcerned way, swung about on the branches, displaying its cleverness to the king, who thereon discharged an arrow at it. With a nimble motion it caught the swift arrow, and the king ordered his attendants to hurry forward and shoot it; and thus the monkey was seized and killed. The king then, looking round, said to his friend Yen

---

[1] For a long time a great officer of *Kh*î, but he died in the same year as Kwan *K*ung himself.

Pû-î[1], 'This monkey made a display of its artfulness, and trusted in its agility, to show me its arrogance;—this it was which brought it to this fate. Take warning from it. Ah! do not by your looks give yourself haughty airs!' Yen Pû-î[1], when he returned home, put himself under the teaching of Tung Wû[1], to root up[2] his pride. He put away what he delighted in and abjured distinction. In three years the people of the kingdom spoke of him with admiration.

9. Nan-po 3ze-*kh*î[3] was seated, leaning forward on his stool, and sighing gently as he looked up to heaven. (Just then) Yen *Kh*ăng-3ze[3] came in, and said, when he saw him, 'Master, you surpass all others. Is it right to make your body thus like a mass of withered bones, and your mind like so much slaked lime?' The other said, 'I formerly lived in a grotto on a hill. At that time Thien Ho[4] once came to see me, and all the multitudes of *Kh*î congratulated him thrice (on his having found the proper man). I must first have shown myself, and so it was that he knew me; I must first have been selling (what I had), and so it was that he came to buy. If I had not shown what I possessed, how should he have known it; if I had not been selling (myself), how should he have come to buy me? I pity

---

[1] We know these names only from their occurrence here. Tung Wû must have been a professor of Tâoism.

[2] The text here is 助, 'to help;' but it is explained as = 鋤, 'a hoe.' The Khang-hsî dictionary does not give this meaning of the character, but we find it in that of Yen Yüan.

[3] See the first paragraph of Bk. II.

[4] 田禾 must be the 田和 of Sze-mâ *Kh*ien, who became marquis of *Kh*î in B.C. 389.

the men who lose themselves[1]; I also pity the men who pity others (for not being known); and I also pity the men who pity the men who pity those that pity others. But since then the time is long gone by; (and so I am in the state in which you have found me)[2].

10. *K*ung-nî, having gone to *Kh*û, the king ordered wine to be presented to him. Sun Shû-âo[3] stood, holding the goblet in his hand. Î-liâo of Shih-nan[3], having received (a cup), poured its contents out as a sacrificial libation, and said, 'The men of old, on such an occasion as this, made some speech.' *K*ung-nî said, 'I have heard of speech without words; but I have never spoken it; I will do so now. Î-liâo of Shih-nan kept (quietly) handling his little spheres,

[1] In seeking for worldly honours.

[2] That is, I have abjured all desire for worldly honour, and desire attainment in the Tâo alone.

[3] See Mencius VI, ii, 15. Sun Shû-âo was chief minister to king *Kh*wang who died in B.C. 591, and died, probably, before Confucius was born, and Î-liâo (p. 28, n. 3) appears in public life only after the death of the sage. The three men could not have appeared together at any time. This account of their doing so was devised by our author as a peg on which to hang his own lessons in the rest of the paragraph. The two historical events referred to I have found it difficult to discover. They are instances of doing nothing, and yet thereby accomplishing what is very great. The action of Î-liâo in 'quietly handling his balls' recalls my seeing the same thing done by a gentleman at *Kh*ü-fâu, the city of Confucius, in 1873. Being left there with a companion, and not knowing how to get to the Grand Canal, many gentlemen came to advise with us how we should proceed. Among them was one who, while tendering his advice, kept rolling about two brass balls in one palm with the fingers of the other hand. When I asked the meaning of his action, I was told, 'To show how he is at his ease and master of the situation.' I mention the circumstance because I have nowhere found the phrase in the text adequately explained.

and the difficulties between the two Houses were resolved; Sun Shû-âo slept undisturbed on his couch, with his (dancer's) feather in his hand, and the men of Ying enrolled themselves for the war. I wish I had a beak three cubits long[1].'

In the case of those two (ministers) we have what is called 'The Way that cannot be trodden[2];' in (the case of *K*ung-nî) we have what is called 'the Argument without words[2].' Therefore when all attributes are comprehended in the unity of the Tâo, and speech stops at the point to which knowledge does not reach, the conduct is complete. But where there is (not)[3] the unity of the Tâo, the attributes cannot (always) be the same, and that which is beyond the reach of knowledge cannot be exhibited by any reasoning. There may be as many names as those employed by the Literati and the Mohists, but (the result is) evil. Thus when the sea does not reject the streams that flow into it in their eastward course, we have the perfection of greatness. The sage embraces in his regard both Heaven and Earth; his beneficent influence extends to all under the sky; and we do not know from whom it comes. Therefore though when living one may have no rank, and when dead no honorary epithet; though the reality (of what he is) may not be acknowledged and his name not established; we have in him what is called 'The Great Man.'

A dog is not reckoned good because it barks well; and a man is not reckoned wise because he speaks

[1] This strange wish concludes the speech of Confucius. What follows is from *K*wang-ȝze.

[2] Compare the opening chapters of the Tâo Teh *K*ing.

[3] The Tâo is greater than any and all of its attributes.

skilfully;—how much less can he be deemed Great! If one thinks he is Great, he is not fit to be accounted Great;—how much less is he so from the practice of the attributes (of the Tâo)[1]! Now none are so grandly complete as Heaven and Earth; but do they seek for anything to make them so grandly complete? He who knows this grand completion does not seek for it; he loses nothing and abandons nothing; he does not change himself from regard to (external) things; he turns in on himself, and finds there an inexhaustible store; he follows antiquity and does not feel about (for its lessons);—such is the perfect sincerity of the Great Man.

11. Ȝze-*kh*î[2] had eight sons. Having arranged them before him, he called *K*iû-fang Yăn[3], and said to him, 'Look at the physiognomy of my sons for me;—which will be the fortunate one?' Yăn said, 'Khwăn is the fortunate one.' Ȝze-*kh*î looked startled, and joyfully said, 'In what way?' Yăn replied, 'Khwăn will share the meals of the ruler of a state to the end of his life.' The father looked uneasy, burst into tears, and said, 'What has my son done that he should come to such a fate?' Yăn replied, 'When one shares the meals of the ruler of a state, blessings reach to all within the three branches of his kindred[4], and how much more to his father and mother! But you, Master, weep when you hear this;—you oppose (the idea of) such happiness. It is the good fortune of your son, and

[1] See note 3 on previous page.

[2] This can hardly be any other but Nan-kwo Ȝze-*kh*î.

[3] A famous physiognomist; some say, of horses. Hwâi-nan Ȝze calls him *K*iû-fang Kâo (皐).

[4] See Mayers's Manual, p. 303.

you count it his misfortune.' Ȝze-*kh*î said, 'O Yăn, what sufficient ground have you for knowing that this will be Khwăn's good fortune? (The fortune) that is summed up in wine and flesh affects only the nose and the mouth, but you are not able to know how it will come about. I have never been a shepherd, and yet a ewe lambed in the south-west corner of my house. I have never been fond of hunting, and yet a quail hatched her young in the south-east corner. If these were not prodigies, what can be accounted such? Where I wish to occupy my mind with my son is in (the wide sphere of) heaven and earth; I wish to seek his enjoyment and mine in (the idea of) Heaven, and our support from the Earth. I do not mix myself up with him in the affairs (of the world); nor in forming plans (for his advantage); nor in the practice of what is strange. I pursue with him the perfect virtue of Heaven and Earth, and do not allow ourselves to be troubled by outward things. I seek to be with him in a state of undisturbed indifference, and not to practise what affairs might indicate as likely to be advantageous. And now there is to come to us this vulgar recompense. Whenever there is a strange realisation, there must have been strange conduct. Danger threatens;—not through any sin of me or of my son, but as brought about, I apprehend, by Heaven. It is this which makes me weep!'

Not long after this, Ȝze-*kh*î sent off Khwăn to go to Yen[1], when he was made prisoner by some robbers on the way. It would have been difficult to sell him if he were whole and entire, and they thought

[1] The state so called.

their easiest plan was to cut off (one of his) feet first. They did so, and sold him in *Kh*î, where he became Inspector of roads for a Mr. *Kh*ü[1]. Nevertheless he had flesh to eat till he died.

12. Nieh *Kh*üeh met Hsü Yû (on the way), and said to him, 'Where, Sir, are you going to?' 'I am fleeing from Yâo,' was the reply. 'What do you mean?' 'Yâo has become so bent on his benevolence that I am afraid the world will laugh at him, and that in future ages men will be found eating one another[2]. Now the people are collected together without difficulty. Love them, and they respond with affection; benefit them, and they come to you; praise them, and they are stimulated (to please you); make them to experience what they dislike, and they disperse. When the loving and benefiting proceed from benevolence and righteousness, those who forget the benevolence and righteousness, and those who make a profit of them, are the many. In this way the practice of benevolence and righteousness comes to be without sincerity and is like a borrowing of the instruments with which men catch birds[3]. In all this the one man's seeking to benefit the world by his decisions and enactments (of such a nature) is as if he were to cut through (the nature of all) by one operation;—Yâo knows how wise and superior men can benefit the world, but he does not

[1] One expert supposes the text here to mean 'duke *Kh*ü;' but there was no such duke of *Kh*î. The best explanation seems to be that *Kh*ü was a rich gentleman, inspector of the roads of *Kh*î, or of the streets of its capital, who bought Khwăn to take his duties for him.

[2] Compare in Bk. XXIII, par. 2.

[3] A scheming for one's own advantage.

also know how they injure it. It is only those who stand outside such men that know this[1].'

There are the pliable and weak; the easy and hasty; the grasping and crooked. Those who are called the pliable and weak learn the words of some one master, to which they freely yield their assent, being secretly pleased with themselves, and thinking that their knowledge is sufficient, while they do not know that they have not yet begun (to understand) a single thing. It is this which makes them so pliable and weak. The easy and hasty are like lice on a pig. The lice select a place where the bristles are more wide apart, and look on it as a great palace or a large park. The slits between the toes, the overlappings of its skin, about its nipples and its thighs,—all these seem to them safe apartments and advantageous places;—they do not know that the butcher one morning, swinging about his arms, will spread the grass, and kindle the fire, so that they and the pig will be roasted together. So do they appear and disappear with the place where they harboured:—this is why they are called the easy and hasty.

Of the grasping and crooked we have an example in Shun. Mutton has no craving for ants, but ants have a craving for mutton, for it is rank. There was a rankness about the conduct of Shun, and the people were pleased with him. Hence when he thrice changed his residence, every one of them became a capital city[2]. When he came to the wild

[1] I suppose that the words of Hsü Yû stop with this sentence, and that from this to the end of the paragraph we have the sentiments of Kwang-ʒze himself. The style is his,—graphic but sometimes coarse.

[2] See note on Mencius V, i, 2, 3.

of Tăng[1], he had 100,000 families about him. Yâo having heard of the virtue and ability of Shun, appointed him to a new and uncultivated territory, saying, 'I look forward to the benefit of his coming here.' When Shun was appointed to this new territory, his years were advanced, and his intelligence was decayed;—and yet he could not find a place of rest or a home. This is an example of being grasping and wayward.

Therefore (in opposition to such) the spirit-like man dislikes the flocking of the multitudes to him. When the multitudes come, they do not agree; and when they do not agree, no benefit results from their coming. Hence there are none whom he brings very near to himself, and none whom he keeps at a great distance. He keeps his virtue in close embrace, and warmly nourishes (the spirit of) harmony, so as to be in accordance with all men. This is called the True man[2]. Even the knowledge of the ant he puts away; his plans are simply those of the fishes[3]; even the notions of the sheep he discards. His seeing is simply that of the eye; his hearing that of the ear; his mind is governed by its general exercises. Being such, his course is straight and level as if marked out by a line, and its every change is in accordance (with the circumstances of the case).

13. The True men of old waited for the issues of events as the arrangements of Heaven, and did not by their human efforts try to take the place of Heaven. The True men of old (now) looked on

[1] Situation unknown.

[2] The spirit-like man and the true man are the same.

[3] Fishes forget everything in the water.

success as life and on failure as death; and (now) on success as death and on failure as life. The operation of medicines will illustrate this:—there are monk's-bane, the *k*ieh-kăng, the tribulus fruit, and china-root; each of these has the time and case for which it is supremely suitable; and all such plants and their suitabilities cannot be mentioned particularly. Kâu-*k*ien[1] took his station on (the hill of) Kwâi-*kh*î with 3,000 men with their buff-coats and shields:—(his minister) *K*ung knew how the ruined (Yüeh) might still be preserved, but the same man did not know the sad fate in store for himself[1]. Hence it is said, 'The eye of the owl has its proper fitness; the leg of the crane has its proper limit, and to cut off any of it would distress (the bird).' Hence (also) it is (further) said, 'When the wind passes over it, the volume of the river is diminished, and so it is when the sun passes over it. But let the wind and sun keep a watch together on the river, and it will not begin to feel that they are doing it any injury:—it relies on its springs and flows on.' Thus, water does its part to the ground with undeviating exactness; and so does the shadow to the substance; and one thing to another. Therefore there is danger from the power of vision in the eyes, of hearing in the ears, and of the inordinate thinking of the mind; yea, there is danger from the exercise of every power of which man's constitution is the depository.

---

[1] See the account of the struggle between Kâu-*k*ien of Yüeh and Fû-*kh*âi of Wû in the eightieth and some following chapters of the 'History of the various States of the Eastern *K*âu (Lieh Kwo *K*ih).' We have sympathy with Kâu-*k*ien, till his ingratitude to his two great ministers, one of whom was Wăn *K*ung (the *K*ung of the text), shows the baseness of his character.

When the danger has come to a head, it cannot be averted, and the calamity is perpetuated, and goes on increasing. The return from this (to a state of security) is the result of (great) effort, and success can be attained only after a long time; and yet men consider (their power of self-determination) as their precious possession:—is it not sad? It is in this way that we have the ruin of states and the slaughtering of the people without end; while no one knows how to ask how it comes about.

14. Therefore, the feet of man on the earth tread but on a small space, but going on to where he has not trod before, he traverses a great distance easily; so his knowledge is but small, but going on to what he does not already know, he comes to know what is meant by Heaven[1]. He knows it as The Great Unity; The Great Mystery; The Great Illuminator; The Great Framer; The Great Boundlessness; The Great Truth; The Great Determiner. This makes his knowledge complete. As The Great Unity, he comprehends it; as The Great Mystery, he unfolds it; as the Great Illuminator, he contemplates it; as the Great Framer, it is to him the Cause of all; as the Great Boundlessness, all is to him its embodiment; as The Great Truth, he examines it; as The Great Determiner, he holds it fast.

Thus Heaven is to him all; accordance with it is the brightest intelligence. Obscurity has in this its pivot; in this is the beginning. Such being the

[1] This paragraph grandly sets forth the culmination of all inquiries into the Tâo as leading to the knowledge of Heaven; and the means by which it may be attained to.

case, the explanation of it is as if it were no explanation; the knowledge of it is as if it were no knowledge. (At first) he does not know it, but afterwards he comes to know it. In his inquiries, he must not set to himself any limits, and yet he cannot be without a limit. Now ascending, now descending, then slipping from the grasp, (the Tâo) is yet a reality, unchanged now as in antiquity, and always without defect:—may it not be called what is capable of the greatest display and expansion? Why should we not inquire into it? Why should we be perplexed about it? With what does not perplex let us explain what perplexes, till we cease to be perplexed. So may we arrive at a great freedom from all perplexity!

BOOK XXV.

Part III. Section III.

Ȝeh-yang[1].

1. Ȝeh-yang having travelled to *Kh*û, Î *K*ieh[2] spoke of him to the king, and then, before the king had granted him an interview, (left him, and) returned home. Ȝeh-yang went to see Wang Kwo[3], and said to him, 'Master, why do you not mention me to the king?' Wang Kwo replied, 'I am not so good a person to do that as Kung-yüeh Hsiû[4].' 'What sort of man is he?' asked the other, and the reply was, 'In winter he spears turtles in the *K*iang, and in summer he rests in shady places on the mountain. When passers-by ask him (what he is doing there), he says, "This is my abode." Since Î *K*ieh was not able to induce the king to see you, how much less should I, who am not equal to him, be able to do so! Î *K*ieh's character is this:—he has no (real) virtue, but he has knowledge. If you do not freely yield yourself to him, but employ him to carry on his spirit-like influence (with you), you will certainly get upset and benighted in the region of riches and honours. His help will not be of a virtuous character, but will go to make your virtue

---

[1] See vol. xxxix, pp. 154, 155.

[2] A native of *Kh*û, and, probably, a parasite of the court.

[3] An officer of *Kh*û, 'a worthy man.'

[4] A recluse of *Kh*û, but not keeping quite aloof from the court.

less;—it will be like heaping on clothes in spring as a protection against cold, or bringing back the cold winds of winter as a protection against heat (in summer). Now the king of *Kh*û is of a domineering presence and stern. He has no forgiveness for offenders, but is merciless as a tiger. It is only a man of subtle speech, or one of correct virtue, who can bend him from his purpose [1].

'But the sagely man [2], when he is left in obscurity, causes the members of his family to forget their poverty; and, when he gets forward to a position of influence, causes kings and dukes to forget their rank and emoluments, and transforms them to be humble. With the inferior creatures, he shares their pleasures, and they enjoy themselves the more; with other men, he rejoices in the fellowship of the Tâo, and preserves it in himself. Therefore though he may not speak, he gives them to drink of the harmony (of his spirit). Standing in association with them, he transforms them till they become in their feeling towards him as sons with a father. His wish is to return to the solitude of his own mind, and this is the effect of his occasional intercourse with them. So far-reaching is his influence on the minds of men; and therefore I said to you, "Wait for Kung-yüeh Hsiû."'

2. The sage comprehends the connexions between himself and others, and how they all go to constitute him of one body with them, and he does not know how it is so;—he naturally does so. In fulfilling his constitution, as acted on and acting, he

[1] Much of the description of Î *K*ieh is difficult to construe.

[2] Kung-yüeh Hsiû.

(simply) follows the direction of Heaven; and it is in consequence of this that men style him (a sage). If he were troubled about (the insufficiency of) his knowledge, what he did would always be but small, and sometimes would be arrested altogether;—how would he in this case be (the sage)? When (the sage) is born with all his excellence, it is other men who see it for him. If they did not tell him, he would not know that he was more excellent than others. And when he knows it, he is as if he did not know it; when he hears it, he is as if he did not hear it. His source of joy in it has no end, and men's admiration of him has no end;—all this takes place naturally[1]. The love of the sage for others receives its name from them. If they did not tell him of it, he would not know that he loved them; and when he knows it, he is as if he knew it not; when he hears it, he is as if he heard it not. His love of others never has an end, and their rest in him has also no end:—all this takes place naturally[1].

3. When one sees at a distance his old country and old city, he feels a joyous satisfaction[2]. Though it be full of mounds and an overgrowth of trees and grass, and when he enters it he finds but a tenth part remaining, still he feels that satisfaction. How much more when he sees what he saw, and hears what he heard before! All this is to him like a tower eighty cubits high exhibited in the sight of all men.

---

[1] That is, 'he does so in the spontaneity of his nature.' The 性 requires the employment of the term 'nature' here, not according to any abstract usage of the term, but meaning the natural constitution. Compare the 性之 in Mencius VII, i, 30.

[2] So does he rejoice in attaining to the knowledge of his nature.

(The sovereign) *Z*ăn-hsiang[1] was possessed of that central principle round which all things revolve[2], and by it he could follow them to their completion. His accompanying them had neither ending nor beginning, and was independent of impulse or time. Daily he witnessed their changes, and himself underwent no change; and why should he not have rested in this? If we (try to) adopt Heaven as our Master, we incapacitate ourselves from doing so. Such endeavour brings us under the power of things. If one acts in this way, what is to be said of him? The sage never thinks of Heaven nor of men. He does not think of taking the initiative, nor of anything external to himself. He moves along with his age, and does not vary or fail. Amid all the completeness of his doings, he is never exhausted. For those who wish to be in accord with him, what other course is there to pursue?

When Thang got one to hold for him the reins of government, namely, Măn-yin Tăng-hăng[3], he employed him as his teacher. He followed his master, but did not allow himself to be hampered by him, and so he succeeded in following things to their completion. The master had the name; but that name was a superfluous addition to his laws, and the twofold character of his government was made apparent[4]. *K*ung-nî's 'Task your thoughts to the utmost' was his expression of the duties of a

[1] A sage sovereign prior to the three Hwang or August ones.

[2] See the same phraseology in Book II, par. 3.

[3] I have followed Lin Hsî-*k*ung in taking these four characters as the name of one man.

[4] There was a human element in it instead of the Heavenly only: but some critics think the text here is erroneous or defective.

master. Yung-khăng said, 'Take the days away and there will be no year; without what is internal there will be nothing external[1].'

4. (King) Yung[2] of Wei made a treaty with the marquis Thien Mâu[3] (of *Kh*î), which the latter violated. The king was enraged, and intended to send a man to assassinate him. When the Minister of War[4] heard of it, he was ashamed, and said (to the king), 'You are a ruler of 10,000 chariots, and by means of a common man would avenge yourself on your enemy. I beg you to give me, Yen, the command of 200,000 soldiers to attack him for you. I will take captive his people and officers, halter (and lead off) his oxen and horses, kindling a fire within him that shall burn to his backbone. I will then storm his capital; and when he shall run away in terror, I will flog his back and break his spine.' *K*î-ȝze[5] heard of this advice, and was ashamed of it, and said (to the king), 'We have been raising the wall (of our capital) to a height of eighty cubits, and the work has been completed. If we now get it thrown down, it will be a painful toil to the convict builders. It is now seven years

[1] Said to have been employed by Hwang-Tî to make the calendar.

[2] B.C. 370–317.

[3] I do not find the name Mâu as belonging to any of the Thien rulers of *Kh*î. The name of the successor of Thien Ho, who has been before us, was 午, Wû, for which 牟, Mâu, may be a mistake; or 'the marquis Mâu' may be a creation of our author.

[4] Literally, 'the Rhinoceros' Head,' the title of 'the Minister of War' in Wei, who was at this time a Kung-sun Yen. See the memoir of him in Sze-mâ *Kh*ien, Book IX of his Biographies.

[5] I do not know that anything more can be said of *K*î and Hwâ than that they were officers of Wei.

since our troops were called out, and this is the foundation of the royal sway. Yen would introduce disorder;—he should not be listened to.' Hwâ-ȝze[1] heard of this advice, and, greatly disapproving of it, said (to the king), 'He who shows his skill in saying "Attack *Kh*î" would produce disorder; and he who shows his skill in saying "Do not attack it" would also produce disorder. And one who should (merely) say, "The counsellors to attack *Kh*î and not to attack it would both produce disorder," would himself also lead to the same result.' The king said, 'Yes, but what am I to do?' The reply was, 'You have only to seek for (the rule of) the Tâo (on the subject).'

Hui-ȝze, having heard of this counsel, introduced to the king Tâi Ȝin-zăn[2], who said, 'There is the creature called a snail; does your majesty know it?' 'I do.' 'On the left horn of the snail there is a kingdom which is called Provocation, and on the right horn another which is called Stupidity. These two kingdoms are continually striving about their territories and fighting. The corpses that lie on the ground amount to several myriads. The army of one may be defeated and put to flight, but in fifteen days it will return.' The king said, 'Pooh! that is empty talk!' The other rejoined, 'Your servant begs to show your majesty its real significance. When your majesty thinks of space—east, west, north, and south, above and beneath—can you set any limit to it?' 'It is illimitable,' said the king; and his visitor went on, 'Your majesty knows

---

[1] See note 5 on preceding page.

[2] Evidently a man of considerable reach of thought.

how to let your mind thus travel through the illimitable, and yet (as compared with this) does it not seem insignificant whether the kingdoms that communicate one with another exist or not?' The king replies, 'It does so;' and Tâi Ȝin-zăn said, finally, 'Among those kingdoms, stretching one after another, there is this Wei; in Wei there is this (city of) Liang[1]; and in Liang there is your majesty. Can you make any distinction between yourself, and (the king of that kingdom of) Stupidity?' To this the king answered, 'There is no distinction,' and his visitor went out, while the king remained disconcerted and seemed to have lost himself.

When the visitor was gone, Hui-ȝze came in and saw the king, who said, 'That stranger is a Great man. An (ordinary) sage is not equal to him.' Hui-ȝze replied, 'If you blow into a flute, there come out its pleasant notes; if you blow into a sword-hilt, there is nothing but a wheezing sound. Yâo and Shun are the subjects of men's praises, but if you speak of them before Tâi Ȝin-zăn, there will be but the wheezing sound.'

5. Confucius, having gone to *Kh*û, was lodging in the house of a seller of Congee at Ant-hill. On the roof of a neighbouring house there appeared the husband and his wife, with their servants, male and female[2]. Ȝze-lû said, 'What are those people doing,

[1] Liang, the capital, came to be used also as the name of the state;—as in Mencius.

[2] 'They were on the roof, repairing it,' say some. 'They had got on the roof, to get out of the way of Confucius,' say others. The sequel shows that this second interpretation is correct; but we do not see how the taking to the roof facilitated their departure from the house.

collected there as we see them?' *K*ung-nî replied, 'The man is a disciple of the sages. He is burying himself among the people, and hiding among the fields. Reputation has become little in his eyes, but there is no bound to his cherished aims. Though he may speak with his mouth, he never tells what is in his mind. Moreover, he is at variance with the age, and his mind disdains to associate with it;—he is one who may be said to lie hid at the bottom of the water on the dry land. Is he not a sort of Î Liâo of Shih-nan?' Ȝze-lû asked leave to go and call him, but Confucius said, 'Stop. He knows that I understand him well. He knows that I am come to *Kh*û, and thinks that I am sure to try and get the king to invite him (to court). He also thinks that I am a man swift to speak. Being such a man, he would feel ashamed to listen to the words of one of voluble and flattering tongue, and how much more to come himself and see his person! And why should we think that he will remain here?' Ȝze-lû, however, went to see how it was, but found the house empty.

6. The Border-warden of *Kh*ang-wû[1], in questioning Ȝze-lâo[2], said, 'Let not a ruler in the exercise of his government be (like the farmer) who leaves the clods unbroken, nor, in regulating his people, (like one) who recklessly plucks up the shoots. Formerly, in ploughing my corn-fields, I left the clods unbroken, and my recompense was in the rough unsatisfactory crops; and in weeding, I destroyed and tore up (many good plants), and my recompense was in the scantiness of my harvests. In subse-

[1] Probably the same as the *Kh*ang-wû Ȝze in Book II, par. 9.

[2] See Analects IX, vi, 4.

quent years I changed my methods, ploughing deeply and carefully covering up the seed; and my harvests were rich and abundant, so that all the year I had more than I could eat.' When *K*wang-ʒze heard of his remarks, he said, 'Now-a-days, most men, in attending to their bodies and regulating their minds, correspond to the description of the Border-warden. They hide from themselves their Heaven(-given being); they leave (all care of) their (proper) nature; they extinguish their (proper) feelings; and they leave their spirit to die:—abandoning themselves to what is the general practice. Thus dealing with their nature like the farmer who is negligent of the clods in his soil, the illegitimate results of their likings and dislikings become their nature. The bushy sedges, reeds, and rushes, which seem at first to spring up to support our bodies, gradually eradicate our nature, and it becomes like a mass of running sores, ever liable to flow out, with scabs and ulcers, discharging in flowing matter from the internal heat. So indeed it is!'

7. Po *K*ü[1] was studying with Lâo Tan, and asked his leave to go and travel everywhere. Lâo Tan said, 'Nay;—elsewhere it is just as here.' He repeated his request, and then Lâo Tan said, 'Where would you go first?' 'I would begin with *Kh*î,' replied the disciple. 'Having got there, I would go to look at the criminals (who had been executed). With my arms I would raise (one of) them up and set him on his feet, and, taking off my court robes, I would cover him with them, appealing at

[1] We can only say of Po *K*ü that he was a disciple of Lâo-ʒze.

the same time to Heaven and bewailing his lot, while I said [1], "My son, my son, you have been one of the first to suffer from the great calamities that afflict the world [2].''' (Lâo Tan) said [1], '(It is said), "Do not rob. Do not kill." (But) in the setting up of (the ideas of) glory and disgrace, we see the cause of those evils; in the accumulation of property and wealth, we see the causes of strife and contention. If now you set up the things against which men fret; if you accumulate what produces strife and contention among them; if you put their persons in such a state of distress, that they have no rest or ease, although you may wish that they should not come to the end of those (criminals), can your wish be realised?

'The superior men (and rulers) of old considered that the success (of their government) was to be found in (the state of) the people, and its failure to be sought in themselves; that the right might be with the people, and the wrong in themselves. Thus it was that if but a single person lost his life, they retired and blamed themselves. Now, however, it is not so. (Rulers) conceal what they want done, and hold those who do not know it to be stupid; they require what is very difficult, and condemn those who do not dare to undertake it; they impose heavy burdens, and punish those who are unequal to them; they require men to go far, and put them to death when they cannot accomplish the distance. When the people know that the utmost of their

---

[1] There are two 曰 here, and the difficulty in translating is to determine the subject of each.

[2] The 離 of the text here is taken as = 罹.

strength will be insufficient, they follow it up with deceit. When (the rulers) daily exhibit much hypocrisy, how can the officers and people not be hypocritical? Insufficiency of strength produces hypocrisy; insufficiency of knowledge produces deception; insufficiency of means produces robbery. But in this case against whom ought the robbery and theft to be charged?'

8. When *K*ü Po-yü was in his sixtieth year, his views became changed in the course of it[1]. He had never before done anything but consider the views which he held to be right, but now he came to condemn them as wrong; he did not know that what he now called right was not what for fifty-nine years he had been calling wrong. All things have the life (which we know), but we do not see its root; they have their goings forth, but we do not know the door by which they depart. Men all honour that which lies within the sphere of their knowledge, but they do not know their dependence on what lies without that sphere which would be their (true) knowledge:—may we not call their case one of great perplexity? Ah! Ah! there is no escaping from this dilemma. So it is! So it is!

9. *K*ung-nî asked the Grand Historiographer[2] Tâ Thâo, (along with) Po *Kh*ang-*kh*ien and *Kh*ih-wei, saying, 'Duke Ling of Wei was so addicted to

[1] Confucius thought highly of this *K*ü Po-yü, and they were friends (Analects, XIV, 26; XV, 6). It would seem from this paragraph that, in his sixtieth year, he adopted the principles of Tâoism. Whether he really did so we cannot tell. See also Book IV, par. 5.

[2] We must translate here in the singular, for in the historiographer's department there were only two officers with the title of 'Grand;' Po *Kh*ang-*kh*ien and *Kh*ih-wei would be inferior members of it.

drink, and abandoned to sensuality, that he did not attend to the government of his state. Occupied in his pursuit of hunting with his nets and bows, he kept aloof from the meetings of the princes. In what was it that he showed his title to the epithet of Ling[1]?' Tâ Thâo said, 'It was on account of those very things.' Po *Kh*ang-*kh*ien said, 'Duke Ling had three mistresses with whom he used to bathe in the same tub. (Once, however), when Shih-ȝhiû came to him with presents from the imperial court, he made his servants support the messenger in bearing the gifts[2]. So dissolute was he in the former case, and when he saw a man of worth, thus reverent was he to him. It was on this account that he was styled "Duke Ling."' *Kh*ih-wei said, 'When duke Ling died, and they divined about burying him in the old tomb of his House, the answer was unfavourable; when they divined about burying him on Shâ-*kh*iû, the answer was favourable. Accordingly they dug there to the depth of several fathoms, and found a stone coffin. Having washed and inspected it, they discovered an inscription, which said,

"This grave will not be available for your
posterity;
Duke Ling will appropriate it for himself."

[1] Ling (靈), as a posthumous epithet, has various meanings, none of them very bad, and some of them very good. Confucius ought to have been able to solve his question himself better than any of the historiographers, but he propounded his doubt to them for reasons which he, no doubt, had.

[2] We are not to suppose that the royal messenger found him in the tub with his three wives or mistresses. The two incidents mentioned illustrate two different phases of his character, as some of the critics, and even the text itself, clearly indicate.

Thus that epithet of Ling had long been settled for the duke[1]. But how should those two be able to know this?'

10. Shâo *K*ih[2] asked Thâi-kung Thiâo[2], saying, 'What do we mean by "The Talk of the Hamlets and Villages?"' The reply was, 'Hamlets and Villages are formed by the union—say of ten surnames and a hundred names, and are considered to be (the source of) manners and customs. The differences between them are united to form their common character, and what is common to them is separately apportioned to form the differences. If you point to the various parts which make up the body of a horse, you do not have the horse; but when the horse is before you, and all its various parts stand forth (as forming the animal), you speak of "the horse." So it is that the mounds and hills are made to be the elevations that they are by accumulations of earth which individually are but low. (So also rivers like) the *K*iang and the Ho obtain their greatness by the union of (other smaller) waters with them. And (in the same way) the Great man exhibits the common sentiment of humanity by the union in himself of all its individualities. Hence when ideas come to him from without, though he

[1] This explanation is, of course, absurd.

[2] These two names are both metaphorical, the former meaning 'Small Knowledge,' and the latter, 'The Grand Public and Just Harmonizer.' Small Knowledge would look for the Tâo in the ordinary talk of ordinary men. The other teaches him that it is to be found in 'the Great man,' blending in himself what is 'just' in the sentiments and practice of all men. And so it is to be found in all the phenomena of nature, but it has itself no name, and does nothing.

has his own decided view, he does not hold it with bigotry; and when he gives out his own decisions, which are correct, the views of others do not oppose them. The four seasons have their different elemental characters, but they are not the partial gifts of Heaven, and so the year completes its course. The five official departments have their different duties, but the ruler does not partially employ any one of them, and so the kingdom is governed. (The gifts of) peace and war (are different), but the Great man does not employ the one to the prejudice of the other, and so the character (of his administration) is perfect. All things have their different constitutions and modes of actions, but the Tâo (which directs them) is free from all partiality, and therefore it has no name. Having no name, it therefore does nothing. Doing nothing, there is nothing which it does not do.

'Each season has its ending and beginning; each age has its changes and transformations; misery and happiness regularly alternate. Here our views are thwarted, and yet the result may afterwards have our approval; there we insist on our own views, and looking at things differently from others, try to correct them, while we are in error ourselves. The case may be compared to that of a great marsh, in which all its various vegetation finds a place, or we may look at it as a great hill, where trees and rocks are found on the same terrace. Such may be a description of what is intended by "The Talk of the Hamlets and Villages."'

Shâo *K*ih said, 'Well, is it sufficient to call it (an expression of) the Tâo?' Thâi-kung Thiâo said, 'It is not so. If we reckon up the number of things, they are not 10,000 merely. When we speak of them as "the Myriad Things," we simply use that large number by way of accommodation to denominate them. In this way Heaven and Earth are the greatest of all things that have form; the Yin and Yang are the greatest of all elemental forces. But the Tâo is common to them. Because of their greatness to use the Tâo or (Course) as a title and call it "the Great Tâo" is allowable. But what comparison can be drawn between it and "the Talk of the Hamlets and Villages?" To argue from this that it is a sufficient expression of the Tâo, is like calling a dog and a horse by the same name, while the difference between them is so great.'

11. Shâo *K*ih said, 'Within the limits of the four cardinal points, and the six boundaries of space, how was it that there commenced the production of all things?' Thâi-kung Thiâo replied, 'The Yin and Yang reflected light on each other, covered each other, and regulated each the other; the four seasons gave place to one another, produced one another, and brought one another to an end. Likings and dislikings, the avoidings of this and movements towards that, then arose (in the things thus produced), in their definite distinctness; and from this came the separation and union of the male and female. Then were seen now security and now insecurity, in mutual change; misery and happiness produced each other; gentleness and urgency pressed on each other; the movements of collection and dispersion were established:—these names and processes can be examined, and, however minute, can be recorded. The rules determining the order in which they follow one another, their mutual influence

now acting directly and now revolving, how, when they are exhausted, they revive, and how they end and begin again; these are the properties belonging to things. Words can describe them and knowledge can reach to them; but with this ends all that can be said of things. Men who study the Tâo do not follow on when these operations end, nor try to search out how they began:—with this all discussion of them stops.'

Shâo *K*ih said, '*K*î *K*ăn [1] holds that (the Tâo) forbids all action, and *K*ieh-ȝze [1] holds that it may perhaps allow of influence. Which of the two is correct in his statements, and which is one-sided in his ruling?' Thâi-kung Thiâo replied, 'Cocks crow and dogs bark;—this is what all men know. But men with the greatest wisdom cannot describe in words whence it is that they are formed (with such different voices), nor can they find out by thinking what they wish to do. We may refine on this small point; till it is so minute that there is no point to operate on, or it may become so great that there is no embracing it. "Some one caused it;" "No one did it;" but we are thus debating about things; and the end is that we shall find we are in error. "Some one caused it;"—then there was a real Being. "No one did it;"—then there was mere vacancy. To have a name and a real existence,—that is the condition of a thing. Not to have a name, and not

[1] Two masters of schools of Tâoism. Who the former was I do not know; but Sze-mâ *Kh*ien in the seventy-fourth Book of his Records mentions several Tâoist masters, and among them *K*ieh-ȝze, a native of *Kh*î, 'a student of the arts of the Tâo and its Characteristics, as taught by Hwang-Tî and Lâo-ȝze, and who also published his views on the subject.'

to have real being;—that is vacancy and no thing. We may speak and we may think about it, but the more we speak, the wider shall we be of the mark. Birth, before it comes, cannot be prevented; death, when it has happened, cannot be traced farther. Death and life are not far apart; but why they have taken place cannot be seen. That some one has caused them, or that there has been no action in the case are but speculations of doubt. When I look for their origin, it goes back into infinity; when I look for their end, it proceeds without termination. Infinite, unceasing, there is no room for words about (the Tâo). To regard it as in the category of things is the origin of the language that it is caused or that it is the result of doing nothing; but it would end as it began with things. The Tâo cannot have a (real) existence; if it has, it cannot be made to appear as if it had not. The name Tâo is a metaphor, used for the purpose of description[1]. To say that it causes or does nothing is but to speak of one phase of things, and has nothing to do with the Great Subject. If words were sufficient for the purpose, in a day's time we might exhaust it; since they are not sufficient, we may speak all day, and only exhaust (the subject of) things. The Tâo is the extreme to which things conduct us. Neither speech nor silence is sufficient to convey the notion of it. Neither by speech nor by silence can our thoughts about it have their highest expression.

[1] A very important statement with regard to the meaning of the name Tâo.

BOOK XXVI.

Part III. Section IV.

Wâi Wû, or 'What comes from Without[1].'

1. What comes from without cannot be determined beforehand. So it was that Lung-făng[2] was killed; Pi-kan immolated; and the count of *K*î (made to feign himself) mad, (while) O-lâi died[3], and *K*ieh and *K*âu both perished. Rulers all wish their ministers to be faithful, but that faithfulness may not secure their confidence; hence Wû Yün became a wanderer along the *K*iang[4], and *Kh*ang Hung died in Shû, where (the people) preserved his blood for three years, when it became changed into green jade[5]. Parents all wish their sons to be filial, but that filial duty may not secure their love; hence

[1] See vol. xxxix, p. 155.

[2] The name of Kwan Lung-făng, a great officer of *K*ieh, the tyrant of Hsiâ;—see Bk. IV, par. 1, et al.

[3] A scion of the line of *Kh*in whose fortunes culminated in Shih Hwang-Tî. O-lâi assisted the tyrant of Shang, and was put to death by king Wû of *K*âu.

[4] The famous Wû 3ze-hsü, the hero of Revenge, who made his escape along the *K*iang, in about B. C. 512, to Wû, after the murder of his father and elder brother by the king of *Kh*û.

[5] See Bk. X, par. 2. In the 3o-*k*wan, under the third year of duke Âi, it is related that the people of *K*âu killed *Kh*ang Hung; but nothing is said of this being done in Shû, or of his blood turning to green jade! This we owe to the *Kh*un *Kh*iû of Lü.

Hsiâo-*k*î[1] had to endure his sorrow, and 3ăng Shăn his grief[2].

When wood is rubbed against wood, it begins to burn; when metal is subjected to fire, it (melts and) flows. When the Yin and Yang act awry, heaven and earth are greatly perturbed; and on this comes the crash of thunder, and from the rain comes fire, which consumes great locust trees[3]. (The case of men) is still worse. They are troubled between two pitfalls[4], from which they cannot escape. Chrysalis-like, they can accomplish nothing. Their minds are as if hung up between heaven and earth. Now comforted, now pitied, they are plunged in difficulties. The ideas of profit and of injury rub against each other, and produce in them a very great fire. The harmony (of the mind) is consumed in the mass of men. Their moonlike intelligence cannot overcome the (inward) fire. They thereupon fall away more and more, and the Course (which they should pursue) is altogether lost.

2. The family of *K*wang *K*âu being poor, he went to ask the loan of some rice from the Marquis Superintendent of the Ho[5], who said, 'Yes, I shall be

[1] Said to have been the eldest son of king Wû Ting or Kâo 3ung of the Yin dynasty. I do not know the events in his experience to which our author must be referring.

[2] The well-known disciple of Confucius, famous for his filial piety.

[3] The lightning accompanying a thunderstorm.

[4] The ideas of profit and injury immediately mentioned.

[5] In another version of this story, in Liû Hsiang's Shwo Yüan, XI, art. 13, the party applied to is 'duke Wăn of Wei;' but this does not necessarily conflict with the text. The genuineness of the paragraph is denied by Lin Hsî-*k*ung and others; but I seem to see the hand of *K*wang-3ze in it.

getting the (tax-) money from the people (soon), and I will then lend you three hundred ounces of silver;—will that do?' *K*wang *K*âu flushed with anger, and said, 'On the road yesterday, as I was coming here, I heard some one calling out. On looking round, I saw a goby in the carriage rut, and said to it, "Goby fish, what has brought you here?" The goby said, "I am Minister of Waves in the Eastern Sea. Have you, Sir, a gallon or a pint of water to keep me alive?" I replied, "Yes, I am going south to see the kings of Wû and Yüeh, and I will then lead a stream from the Western *K*iang to meet you;—will that do?" The goby flushed with anger, and said, "I have lost my proper element, and I can here do nothing for myself; but if I could get a gallon or a pint of water, I should keep alive. Than do what you propose, you had better soon look for me in a stall of dry fish."'

3. A son of the duke of *Z*ăn[1], having provided himself with a great hook, a powerful black line, and fifty steers to be used as bait, squatted down on (mount) Kwâi *Kh*î, and threw the line into the Eastern Sea. Morning after morning he angled thus, and for a whole year caught nothing. At the end of that time, a great fish swallowed the bait, and dived down, dragging the great hook with him. Then it rose to the surface in a flurry, and flapped with its fins, till the white waves rose like hills, and the waters were lashed into fury. The noise was like that of imps and spirits, and spread terror

[1] I suppose this was merely a district of *Kh*û, and the duke of it merely the officer in charge of it;—according to the practice of the rulers of *Kh*û, after they usurped the title of King.

for a thousand lî. The prince having got such a fish, cut it in slices and dried them. From the *K*eh river[1] to the east, and from Ȝhang-wû[2] to the north, there was not one who did not eat his full from that fish; and in subsequent generations, story-tellers of small abilities have all repeated the story to one another with astonishment. (But) if the prince had taken his rod, with a fine line, and gone to pools and ditches, and watched for minnows and gobies, it would have been difficult for him to get a large fish. Those who dress up their small tales to obtain favour with the magistrates are far from being men of great understanding; and therefore one who has not heard the story of this scion of *Z*ăn is not fit to take any part in the government of the world;—far is he from being so[3].

4. Some literati, students of the Odes and Ceremonies, were breaking open a mound over a grave[4]. The superior among them spoke down to the others, 'Day is breaking in the east; how is the thing going on?' The younger men replied, 'We have not yet opened his jacket and skirt, but there is a pearl in the mouth. As it is said in the Ode,

"The bright, green grain
Is growing on the sides of the mound.

---

[1] The 制河 of the text = the 浙江, still giving its name to the province so called.

[2] Where Shun was buried.

[3] This last sentence is difficult to construe, and to understand.—The genuineness of this paragraph is also questioned, and the style is inferior to that of the preceding.

[4] I can conceive of *K*wang-ȝze telling this story of some literati who had been acting as resurrectionists, as a joke against their class; but not of his writing it to form a part of his work.

While living, he gave nothing away;
Why, when dead, should he hold a pearl in his mouth[1]?"'

Thereupon they took hold of the whiskers and pulled at the beard, while the superior introduced a piece of fine steel into the chin, and gradually separated the jaws, so as not to injure the pearl in the mouth.

5. A disciple of Lâo Lâi-ȝze[2], while he was out gathering firewood, met with *K*ung-nî. On his return, he told (his master), saying, 'There is a man there, the upper part of whose body is long and the lower part short. He is slightly hump-backed, and his ears are far back. When you look at him, he seems occupied with the cares of all within the four seas; I do not know whose son he is.' Lâo Lâi-ȝze said, 'It is *Kh*iû; call him here;' and when *K*ung-nî came, he said to him, '*Kh*iû, put away your personal conceit, and airs of wisdom, and show yourself to be indeed a superior man.' *K*ung-nî bowed and was retiring, when he abruptly changed his manner, and asked, 'Will the object I am pursuing be thereby advanced?' Lâo Lâi-ȝze replied, 'You cannot bear the sufferings of this one age, and are stubbornly regardless of the

---

[1] This verse is not found, so far as I know, anywhere else.

[2] Lâo Lâi-ȝze appears here as a contemporary of Confucius, and the master of a Tâoistic school, and this also is the view of him which we receive from the accounts in Sze-mâ *Kh*ien and Hwang-fû Mi. Sze-mâ says he published a work in fifteen sections on the usefulness of Tâoism. Some have imagined that he was the same as Lâo-ȝze himself, but there does not appear any ground for that opinion. He is one of the twenty-four examples of Filial Piety so celebrated among the Chinese; but I suspect that the accounts of him as such are fabrications. He certainly lectures Confucius here in a manner worthy of Lâo Tan.

evils of a myriad ages:—is it that you purposely make yourself thus unhappy? or is it that you have not the ability to comprehend the case? Your obstinate purpose to make men rejoice in a participation of your joy is your life-long shame, the procedure of a mediocre man. You would lead men by your fame; you would bind them to you by your secret art. Than be praising Yâo and condemning *K*ieh, you had better forget them both, and shut up your tendency to praise. If you reflect on it, it does nothing but injury; your action in it is entirely wrong. The sage is full of anxiety and indecision in undertaking anything, and so he is always successful. But what shall I say of your conduct? To the end it is all affectation.'

6. The ruler Yüan of Sung [1] (once) dreamt at midnight that a man with dishevelled hair peeped in on him at a side door and said, 'I was coming from the abyss of Ȝâi-lû, commissioned by the Clear *K*iang to go to the place of the Earl of the Ho; but the fisherman Yü Ȝü has caught me.' When the ruler Yüan awoke, he caused a diviner to divine the meaning (of the dream), and was told, 'This is a marvellous tortoise.' The ruler asked if among the fishermen there was one called Yü Ȝü, and being told by his attendants that there was, he gave orders that he should be summoned to court. Accordingly the man next day appeared at court, and the ruler said, 'What have you caught (lately) in fishing?' The reply was, 'I have caught in my net a white tortoise, sieve-like, and five cubits round.' 'Present the prodigy here,' said the ruler; and, when it came, once and

[1] Compare in Bk. XXI, par. 7.

again he wished to kill it, once and again he wished to keep it alive. Doubting in his mind (what to do), he had recourse to divination, and obtained the answer, 'To kill the tortoise for use in divining will be fortunate.' Accordingly they cut the creature open, and perforated its shell in seventy-two places, and there was not a single divining slip which failed[1].

*K*ung-nî said, 'The spirit-like tortoise could show itself in a dream to the ruler Yüan, and yet it could not avoid the net of Yü Ȝü. Its wisdom could respond on seventy-two perforations without failing in a single divination, and yet it could not avoid the agony of having its bowels all scooped out. We see from this that wisdom is not without its perils, and spirit-like intelligence does not reach to everything. A man may have the greatest wisdom, but there are a myriad men scheming against him. Fishes do not fear the net, though they fear the pelican. Put away your small wisdom, and your great wisdom will be bright; discard your skilfulness, and you will become naturally skilful. A child when it is born needs no great master, and yet it becomes able to speak, living (as it does) among those who are able to speak.'

7. Hui-ȝze said to *K*wang-ȝze, 'You speak, Sir, of what is of no use.' The reply was, 'When a man knows what is not useful, you can then begin to speak to him of what is useful. The earth for instance is certainly spacious and great; but what a

[1] The story of this wonderful tortoise is found at much greater length, and with variations, in Sze-mâ *Kh*ien's Records, Bk. LXVIII, q. v. The moral of it is given in the concluding remarks from Confucius.

man uses of it is only sufficient ground for his feet. If, however, a rent were made by the side of his feet, down to the yellow springs, could the man still make use of it?' Hui-ȝze said, 'He could not use it,' and *K*wang-ȝze rejoined, 'Then the usefulness of what is of no use is clear [1].'

8. *K*wang-ȝze said, 'If a man have the power to enjoy himself (in any pursuit), can he be kept from doing so? If he have not the power, can he so enjoy himself? There are those whose aim is bent on concealing themselves, and those who are determined that their doings shall leave no trace. Alas! they both shirk the obligations of perfect knowledge and great virtue. The (latter) fall, and cannot recover themselves; the (former) rush on like fire, and do not consider (what they are doing). Though men may stand to each other in the relation of ruler and minister, that is but for a time. In a changed age, the one of them would not be able to look down on the other. Hence it is said, "The Perfect man leaves no traces of his conduct."

'To honour antiquity and despise the present time is the characteristic of learners [2]; but even the disciples of *Kh*ih-wei [3] have to look at the present age; and who can avoid being carried along by its course? It is only the Perfect man who is able to enjoy himself in the world, and not be deflected from the right,

---

[1] See Bk. I, par. 6, and XXIV, par. 14. The conversations between our author and Hui-ȝze often turned on this subject.

[2] Does our author mean by 'learners' the literati, the disciples of Confucius?

[3] *Kh*ih-wei,—see Bk. VI, par. 7. Perhaps 'the disciples of *Kh*ih-wei' are those who in our author's time called themselves such, but were not.

to accommodate himself to others and not lose himself. He does not learn their lessons; he only takes their ideas into consideration, and does not discard them as different from his own.

9. 'It is the penetrating eye that gives clear vision, the acute ear that gives quick hearing, the discriminating nose that gives discernment of odours, the practised mouth that gives the enjoyment of flavours, the active mind that acquires knowledge, and the far-reaching knowledge that constitutes virtue. In no case does the connexion with what is without like to be obstructed; obstruction produces stoppage; stoppage, continuing without intermission, arrests all progress; and with this all injurious effects spring up.

'The knowledge of all creatures depends on their breathing[1]. But if their breath be not abundant, it is not the fault of Heaven, which tries to penetrate them with it, day and night without ceasing; but men notwithstanding shut their pores against it. The womb encloses a large and empty space; the heart has its spontaneous and enjoyable movements. If their apartment be not roomy, wife and mother-in-law will be bickering; if the heart have not its spontaneous and enjoyable movements, the six faculties of perception[2] will be in mutual collision. That

[1] There seems to underlie this statement the Tâoist dogma about the regulation of the 'breath,' as conducive to long life and mental cultivation.

[2] Probably what in Buddhist literature are called 'the Six Entrances (六入),' what Mayers denominates 'The Six Organs of Admittance, or Bodily Sensations,' the Shadâyatana, the eye, ear, nose, mouth, body, and mind,—one of the twelve Nidânas in the Buddhist system.

the great forests, the heights and hills, are pleasant to men, is because their spirits cannot overcome (those distracting influences). Virtue overflows into (the love of) fame; (the love of) fame overflows into violence; schemes originate in the urgency (of circumstances); (the show of) wisdom comes from rivalry; the fuel (of strife) is produced from the obstinate maintenance (of one's own views); the business of offices should be apportioned in accordance with the approval of all. In spring, when the rain and the sunshine come seasonably, vegetation grows luxuriantly, and sickles and hoes begin to be prepared. More than half of what had fallen down becomes straight, and we do not know how.

10. 'Stillness and silence are helpful to those who are ill; rubbing the corners of the eyes is helpful to the aged; rest serves to calm agitation; but they are the toiled and troubled who have recourse to these things. Those who are at ease, and have not had such experiences, do not care to ask about them. The spirit-like man has had no experience of how it is that the sagely man keeps the world in awe, and so he does not inquire about it; the sagely man has had no experience of how it is that the man of ability and virtue keeps his age in awe, and so he does not inquire about it; the man of ability and virtue has had no experience of how it is that the superior man keeps his state in awe, and so he does not inquire about it. The superior man has had no experience of how it is that the small man keeps himself in agreement with his times that he should inquire about it.'

11. The keeper of the Yen Gate[1], on the death of

[1] The name of one of the gates in the wall of the capital of Sung.

his father, showed so much skill in emaciating his person[1] that he received the rank of 'Pattern for Officers.' Half the people of his neighbourhood (in consequence) carried their emaciation to such a point that they died. When Yâo wished to resign the throne to Hsü Yû, the latter ran away. When Thang offered his to Wû Kwang[2], Wû Kwang became angry. When *K*î Thâ[3] heard it, he led his disciples, and withdrew to the river Kho, where the feudal princes came and condoled with him, and after three years, Shăn Thû-tî[4] threw himself into the water. Fishing-stakes[5] are employed to catch fish; but when the fish are got, the men forget the stakes. Snares are employed to catch hares, but when the hares are got, men forget the snares. Words are employed to convey ideas; but when the ideas are apprehended, men forget the words. Fain would I talk with such a man who has forgot the words!

---

[1] The abstinences and privations in mourning were so many that there was a danger of their seriously injuring the health;—which was forbidden.

[2] See Bk. VI, par. 3; but in the note there, Wû Kwang is said to have been of the time of Hwang-Tî; which is probably an error.

[3] See IV, par. 3; but I do not know who *K*î Thâ was, nor can I explain what is said of him here.

[4] See again IV, par. 3.

[5] According to some, 'baskets.' This illustration is quoted in the Inscription on the Nestorian Monument, II, 7.

BOOK XXVII.

PART III. SECTION V.

Yü Yen, or 'Metaphorical Language[1].'

1. Of my sentences nine in ten are metaphorical; of my illustrations seven in ten are from valued writers. The rest of my words are like the water that daily fills the cup, tempered and harmonised by the Heavenly element in our nature[2].

The nine sentences in ten which are metaphorical are borrowed from extraneous things to assist (the comprehension of) my argument. (When it is said, for instance), 'A father does not act the part of matchmaker for his own son,' (the meaning is that) 'it is better for another man to praise the son than for his father to do so.' The use of such metaphorical language is not my fault, but the fault of men (who would not otherwise readily understand me).

Men assent to views which agree with their own, and oppose those which do not so agree. Those which agree with their own they hold to be right, and those which do not so agree they hold to be wrong. The seven out of ten illustrations taken from valued writers are designed to put an end to disputations. Those writers are the men of hoary eld, my predecessors in time. But such as are un-

[1] See vol. xxxix, pp. 155, 156.

[2] See Bk. II, par. 10.

versed in the warp and woof, the beginning and end of the subject, cannot be set down as of venerable eld, and regarded as the predecessors of others. If men have not that in them which fits them to precede others, they are without the way proper to man, and they who are without the way proper to man can only be pronounced defunct monuments of antiquity.

Words like the water that daily issues from the cup, and are harmonised by the Heavenly Element (of our nature), may be carried on into the region of the unlimited, and employed to the end of our years. But without words there is an agreement (in principle). That agreement is not effected by words, and an agreement in words is not effected by it. Hence it is said, 'Let there be no words.' Speech does not need words. One may speak all his life, and not have spoken a (right) word; and one may not have spoken all his life, and yet all his life been giving utterance to the (right) words. There is that which makes a thing allowable, and that which makes a thing not allowable. There is that which makes a thing right, and that which makes a thing not right. How is a thing right? It is right because it is right. How is a thing wrong? It is wrong because it is wrong. How is a thing allowable? It is allowable because it is so. How is a thing not allowable? It is not allowable because it is not so. Things indeed have what makes them right, and what makes them allowable. There is nothing which has not its condition of right; nothing which has not its condition of allowability. But without the words of the (water-) cup in daily use, and harmonised by the Heavenly Element (in our nature), what one can continue long in the possession of these characteristics?

All things are divided into their several classes, and succeed to one another in the same way, though of different bodily forms. They begin and end as in an unbroken ring, though how it is they do so be not apprehended. This is what is called the Lathe of Heaven; and the Lathe of Heaven is the Heavenly Element in our nature.

2. *K*wang-ȝze said to Hui-ȝze, 'When Confucius was in his sixtieth year, in that year his views changed[1]. What he had before held to be right, he now ended by holding to be wrong; and he did not know whether the things which he now pronounced to be right were not those which he had for fifty-nine years held to be wrong.' Hui-ȝze replied, 'Confucius with an earnest will pursued the acquisition of knowledge, and acted accordingly.' *K*wang-ȝze rejoined, 'Confucius disowned such a course, and never said that it was his. He said, "Man receives his powers from the Great Source[2] (of his being), and he should restore them to their (original) intelligence in his life. His singing should be in accordance with the musical tubes, and his speech a model for imitation. When profit and righteousness are set before him, and his liking (for the latter) and dislike (of the

---

[1] Compare this with the same language about *K*ü Po-yü in Bk. XXV, par. 8. There is no proof to support our author's assertion that the views of Confucius underwent any change.

[2] 'The Great Source (Root)' here is generally explained by 'the Grand Beginning.' It is not easy to say whether we are to understand an ideal condition of man designed from the first, or the condition of every man as he is born into the world. On the 'powers' received by man, see Mencius VI, i, 6.

former), his approval and disapproval, are manifested, that only serves to direct the speech of men (about him). To make men in heart submit, and not dare to stand up in opposition to him; to establish the fixed law for all under heaven:—ah! ah! I have not attained to that."'

3. Ȝăng-ȝze twice took office, and on the two occasions his state of mind was different. He said, 'While my parents were alive I took office, and though my emolument was only three fû[1] (of grain), my mind was happy. Afterwards when I took office, my emolument was three thousand *k*ung[2]; but I could not share it with my parents, and my mind was sad.' The other disciples asked *K*ung-nî, saying, 'Such an one as Shăn may be pronounced free from all entanglement:—is he to be blamed for feeling as he did[3]?' The reply was, 'But he was subject to entanglement[4]. If he had been free from it, could he have had that sadness? He would have looked on his three fû and three thousand *k*ung no more than on a heron or a mosquito passing before him.'

4. Yen *Kh*ăng Ȝze-yû said to Tung-kwo Ȝze-*kh*î[5], 'When I (had begun to) hear your instructions, the first year, I continued a simple rustic; the second

---

[1] A fû = ten tâu and four shing, or sixty-four shing, the shing at present being rather less than an English pint.

[2] A *k*ung = sixty-four tâu; but there are various accounts of its size.

[3] This sentence is difficult to construe.

[4] But Confucius could not count his love for his parents an entanglement.

[5] We must suppose this master to be the same as the Nan-kwo Ȝze-*kh*î of Bk. II.

year, I became docile; the third year, I comprehended (your teaching); the fourth year, I was (plastic) as a thing; the fifth year, I made advances; the sixth year, the spirit entered (and dwelt in me); the seventh year, (my nature as designed by) Heaven was perfected; the eighth year, I knew no difference between death and life; the ninth year, I attained to the Great Mystery[1].

'Life has its work to do, and death ensues, (as if) the common character of each were a thing prescribed. Men consider that their death has its cause; but that life from (the operation of) the Yang has no cause. But is it really so? How does (the Yang) operate in this direction? Why does it not operate there?

'Heaven has its places and spaces which can be calculated; (the divisions of) the earth can be assigned by men. But how shall we search for and find out (the conditions of the Great Mystery)? We do not know when and how (life) will end, but how shall we conclude that it is not determined (from without)? and as we do not know when and how it begins, how should we conclude that it is not (so) determined?

'In regard to the issues of conduct which we deem appropriate, how should we conclude that there are no spirits presiding over them; and where those issues seem inappropriate, how should we conclude that there are spirits presiding over them?'

---

[1] In illustration of the text here Lû Shû-kih refers to the use of Miâo (妙), in the account of the term 'Spirit,' in the fifth Appendix to the Yî, par. 10, as meaning 'the subtle (presence and operation of God) with all things.' 3ze-yû's further exposition of his attainments is difficult to understand fully.

5. The penumbrae (once) asked the shadow[1], saying, 'Formerly you were looking down, and now you are looking up; formerly you had your hair tied up, and now it is dishevelled; formerly you were sitting, and now you have risen up; formerly you were walking, and now you have stopped:—how is all this?' The shadow said, 'Venerable Sirs, how do you ask me about such small matters? These things all belong to me, but I do not know how they do so. I am (like) the shell of a cicada or the cast-off skin of a snake[2];—like them, and yet not like them. With light and the sun I make my appearance; with darkness and the night I fade away. Am not I dependent on the substance from which I am thrown? And that substance is itself dependent on something else! When it comes, I come with it; when it goes, I go with it. When it comes under the influence of the strong Yang, I come under the same. Since we are both produced by that strong Yang, what occasion is there for you to question me?'

6. Yang Ȝze-*k*ü[3] had gone South to Phei[4], while Lâo Tan was travelling in the west in *Kh*in[5]. (He thereupon) asked (Lâo-ȝze) to come to the border (of Phei), and went himself to Liang, where he met him. Lâo-ȝze stood in the middle of the way, and, looking up to heaven, said with a sigh, 'At first I thought that you might be taught, but now I see that you cannot be.' Yang Ȝze-*k*ü made no reply;

[1] Compare Bk. II, par. 11.

[2] Such is the reading of Ȝiâo Hung.

[3] No doubt the Yang *K*û of Lieh-ȝze and Mencius.

[4] See in XIV, 26 b.

[5] In the borders of Phei; can hardly be the great State.

and when they came to their lodging-house, he brought in water for the master to wash his hands and rinse his mouth, along with a towel and comb. He then took off his shoes outside the door, went forward on his knees, and said, 'Formerly, your disciple wished to ask you, Master, (the reason of what you said); but you were walking, and there was no opportunity, and therefore I did not presume to speak. Now there is an opportunity, and I beg to ask why you spoke as you did.' Lâo-ȝze replied, 'Your eyes are lofty, and you stare;—who would live with you? The purest carries himself as if he were soiled; the most virtuous seems to feel himself defective.' Yang Ȝze-*k*ü looked abashed and changed countenance, saying, 'I receive your commands with reverence.'

When he first went to the lodging-house, the people of it met him and went before him. The master of it carried his mat for him, and the mistress brought the towel and comb. The lodgers left their mats, and the cook his fire-place (as he passed them). When he went away, the others in the house would have striven with him about (the places for) their mats[1].

[1] So had his arrogant superciliousness given place to humility.

BOOK XXVIII.

PART III. SECTION VI.

*Z*ang Wang, or 'Kings who have wished to resign the Throne[1].'

1. Yâo proposed to resign the throne to Hsü Yû, who would not accept it. He then offered it to Ȝze-*k*âu *K*ih-fû[2], but he said, 'It is not unreasonable to propose that I should occupy the throne, but I happen to be suffering under a painful sorrow and illness. While I am engaged in dealing with it, I have not leisure to govern the kingdom.' Now the throne is the most important of all positions, and yet this man would not occupy it to the injury of his life; how much less would he have allowed any other thing to do so! But only he who does not care to rule the kingdom is fit to be entrusted with it.

Shun proposed to resign the throne to Ȝze-*k*âu *K*ih-po[2], who declined in the very same terms as *K*ih-fû had done. Now the kingdom is the greatest of all concerns, and yet this man would not give his life in exchange for the throne. This shows how they who possess the Tâo differ from common men.

---

[1] See vol. xxxix, pp. 156, 157.

[2] We know nothing of this man but what is related here. He is, no doubt, a fictitious character. *K*ih-fû and *K*ih-po are supposed to be the same individual. See Hwang-fû Mî, I, 7.

Shun proposed to resign the throne to Shan *K*üan[1], who said, 'I am a unit in the midst of space and time. In winter I wear skins and furs; in summer, grass-cloth and linen; in spring I plough and sow, my strength being equal to the toil; in autumn I gather in my harvest, and am prepared to cease from labour and eat. At sunrise I get up and work; at sunset I rest. So do I enjoy myself between heaven and earth, and my mind is content:—why should I have anything to do with the throne? Alas! that you, Sir, do not know me better!' Thereupon he declined the proffer, and went away, deep among the hills, no man knew where.

Shun proposed to resign the throne to his friend, a farmer of Shih-hû[2]. The farmer, however, said (to himself), 'How full of vigour does our lord show himself, and how exuberant is his strength! If Shun with all his powers be not equal (to the task of government, how should I be so?).' On this he took his wife on his back, led his son by the hand, and went away to the sea-coast, from which to the end of his life he did not come back.

When Thâi-wang Than-fû[3] was dwelling in Pin[3], the wild tribes of the North attacked him. He tried to serve them with skins and silks, but they were not satisfied. He tried to serve them with dogs and horses, but they were not satisfied, and then

---

[1] Nor do we know more of Shan *K*üan, though Mî relates a visit of Yâo to him.

[2] Name of a place; where it was is very uncertain.

[3] An ancestor of the House of *K*âu, who about B.C. 1325 removed from Pin (in the present small department so called of Shen-hsî), and settled in the district of *Kh*î-shan, department of Făng-ʒhiang. He was the grandfather of king Wăn.

with pearls and jade, but they were not satisfied. What they sought was his territory. Thâi-wang Than-fû said (to his people), 'To dwell with the elder brother and cause the younger brother to be killed, or with the father and cause the son to be killed,—this is what I cannot bear to do. Make an effort, my children, to remain here. What difference is there between being my subjects, or the subjects of those wild people? And I have heard that a man does not use that which he employs for nourishing his people to injure them.' Thereupon he took his staff and switch and left, but the people followed him in an unbroken train, and he established a (new) state at the foot of mount *Kh*î[1]. Thus Thâi-wang Than-fû might be pronounced one who could give its (due) honour to life. Those who are able to do so, though they may be rich and noble, will not, for that which nourishes them, injure their persons; and though they may be poor and mean, will not, for the sake of gain, involve their bodies (in danger). The men of the present age who occupy high offices and are of honourable rank all lose these (advantages) again, and in the prospect of gain lightly expose their persons to ruin:—is it not a case of delusion?

The people of Yüeh three times in succession killed their ruler, and the prince Sâu[2], distressed by it, made his escape to the caves of Tan, so that Yüeh was left without a ruler. The people sought

[1] See note 3, p. 150.

[2] Sze-mâ *Kh*ien takes up the history of Yüeh at a later period, and we have from him no details of this prince Sâu. Tan-hsüeh was the name of a district in the south of Yüeh, in which was a valley with caves containing cinnabar;—the fabled home of the phœnix.

for the prince, but could not find him, till (at last) they followed him to the cave of Tan. The prince was not willing to come out to them, but they smoked him out with moxa, and made him mount the royal chariot. As he took hold of the strap, and mounted the carriage, he looked up to heaven, and called out, 'O Ruler, O Ruler, could you not have spared me this?' Prince Sâu did not dislike being ruler;—he disliked the evil inseparable from being so. It may be said of him that he would not for the sake of a kingdom endanger his life; and this indeed was the reason why the people of Yüeh wanted to get him for their ruler.

2. Han[1] and Wei[1] were contending about some territory which one of them had wrested from the other. Ȝze-hwâ Ȝze[2] went to see the marquis *K*âo-hsî (of Han)[3], and, finding him looking sorrowful, said, 'Suppose now that all the states were to sign an agreement before you to the effect that "Whoever should with his left hand carry off (the territory in dispute) should lose his right hand, and whoever should do so with his right hand should lose his left hand, but that, nevertheless, he who should carry it off was sure to obtain the whole kingdom;" would your lordship feel yourself able to carry it off?' The marquis said, 'I would not carry it off,' and Ȝze-hwâ rejoined, 'Very good. Looking at the thing from this point of view, your two arms are of more value to you than the whole kingdom. But

[1] Two of the three states into which the great state of Ȝin was divided about the beginning of the fifth century B.C.

[2] A native, we may call him a philosopher, of Wei.

[3] Began his rule in B.C. 359.

your body is of more value than your two arms, and Han is of much less value than the whole kingdom. The territory for which you are now contending is further much less important than Han:—your lordship, since you feel so much concern for your body, should not be endangering your life by indulging your sorrow.'

The marquis *K*âo-hsî said, 'Good! Many have given me their counsel about this matter; but I never heard what you have said.' Ȝze-hwâ Ȝze may be said to have known well what was of great importance and what was of little.

3. The ruler of Lû, having heard that Yen Ho[1] had attained to the Tâo, sent a messenger, with a gift of silks, to prepare the way for further communication with him. Yen Ho was waiting at the door of a mean house, in a dress of coarse hempen cloth, and himself feeding a cow[2]. When the messenger arrived, Yen Ho himself confronted him. 'Is this,' said the messenger, 'the house of Yen Ho?' 'It is,' was the reply; and the other was presenting the silks to him, when he said, 'I am afraid you heard (your instructions) wrongly, and that he who sent you will blame you. You had better make sure.' The messenger on this returned, and made sure that he was right; but when he came back, and sought for Yen Ho, he was not to be found.

Yes; men like Yen Ho do of a truth dislike riches and honours. Hence it is said, 'The true

[1] Perhaps the Yen Ho of IV, 5.

[2] The same thing is often seen at the present day. The party in charge of the cow pours its prepared food down its throat from a joint of bamboo.

object of the Tâo is the regulation of the person. Quite subordinate to this is its use in the management of the state and the clan; while the government of the kingdom is but the dust and refuse of it.' From this we may see that the services of the Tîs and Kings are but a surplusage of the work of the sages, and do not contribute to complete the person or nourish the life. Yet the superior men of the present age will, most of them, throw away their lives for the sake of their persons, in pursuing their (material) objects;—is it not cause for grief? Whenever a sage is initiating any movement, he is sure to examine the motive which influences him, and what he is about to do. Here, however, is a man, who uses a pearl like that of the marquis of Sui [1] to shoot a bird at a distance of 10,000 feet. All men will laugh at him; and why? Because the thing which he uses is of great value, and what he wishes to get is of little. And is not life of more value than the pearl of the marquis of Sui?

4. 3ze [2] Lieh-ȝze [2] was reduced to extreme poverty, and his person had a hungry look. A visitor mentioned the case to 3ze-yang, (the premier) of *K*ăng, saying, 'Lieh Yü-khâu, I believe, is a scholar who has attained to the Tâo. Is it because our ruler does not love (such) scholars, that he should be living in his state in such poverty?' 3ze-yang immediately ordered an officer to send to him a supply of grain.

---

[1] Sui was a small feudal state, a dependency of Wei. Its name remains in the Sui-*k*âu, Teh-an department, Hû-pei. The story is that one of its lords having healed a wounded snake, the creature one night brought him a large pearl in its mouth.

[2] The phraseology is peculiar. See Introductory Note on Bk. XXXII.

When Lieh-ȝze saw the messenger, he bowed to him twice, and declined the gift, on which the messenger went away. On Lieh-ȝze's going into the house, his wife looked to him and beat her breast, saying, 'I have heard that the wife and children of a possessor of the Tâo all enjoy plenty and ease, but now we look starved. The ruler has seen his error, and sent you a present of food, but you would not receive it; —is it appointed (for us to suffer thus)?' Ȝze Lieh-ȝze laughed and said to her, 'The ruler does not himself know me. Because of what some one said to him, he sent me the grain; but if another speak (differently) of me to him, he may look on me as a criminal. This was why I did not receive the grain.'

In the end it did come about, that the people, on an occasion of trouble and disorder, put Ȝze-yang to death.

5. When king *K*âo of *Kh*û[1] lost his kingdom, the sheep-butcher Yüeh followed him in his flight. When the king (recovered) his kingdom and returned to it, and was going to reward those who had followed him, on coming to the sheep-butcher Yüeh, that personage said, 'When our Great King lost his kingdom, I lost my sheep-killing. When his majesty got back his kingdom, I also got back my sheep-killing. My income and rank have been recovered: why speak further of rewarding me?' The king, (on hearing of this reply), said, 'Force him (to take the reward);' but Yüeh said, 'It was not through any crime of mine that the king lost his kingdom,

[1] B.C. 515–489. He was driven from his capital by an invasion of Wû, directed by Wû Ȝze-hsü.

and therefore I did not dare to submit to the death (which would have been mine if I had remained in the capital). And it was not through any service of mine that he recovered his kingdom, and therefore I do not dare to count myself worthy of any reward from him.'

The king (now) asked that the butcher should be introduced to him, but Yüeh said, 'According to the law of *Kh*û, great reward ought to be given to great service, and the recipient then be introduced to the king; but now my wisdom was not sufficient to preserve the kingdom, nor my courage sufficient to die at the hands of the invaders. When the army of Wû entered, I was afraid of the danger, and got out of the way of the thieves;—it was not with a distinct purpose (of loyalty) that I followed the king. And now he wishes, in disregard of the law, and violations of the conditions of our social compact, to see me in court;—this is not what I would like to be talked of through the kingdom.' The king said to 3ze-*kh*î, the Minister of War, 'The position of the sheep-butcher Yüeh is low and mean, but his setting forth of what is right is very high; do you ask him for me to accept the place of one of my three most distinguished nobles[1].' (This being communicated to Yüeh), he said, 'I know that the place of such a distinguished noble is nobler than a sheep-butcher's stall, and that the salary of 10,000 *k*ung is more than its profits. But how should I, through my greed of rank and emolument, bring on our ruler the name of an unlawful dispensation of his gifts? I dare not

[1] Literally, 'My three banners or flags,' emblems of the favour of the sovereign.

respond to your wishes, but desire to return to my stall as the sheep-butcher.' Accordingly he did not accept (the proffered reward).

6. Yüan Hsien[1] was living in Lû. His house, whose walls were only a few paces round, looked as if it were thatched with a crop of growing grass; its door of brushwood was incomplete, with branches of a mulberry tree for its side-posts; the window of each of its two apartments was formed by an earthenware jar (in the wall), which was stuffed with some coarse serge. It leaked above, and was damp on the ground beneath; but there he sat composedly, playing on his guitar. Ȝze-kung, in an inner robe of purple and an outer one of pure white, riding in a carriage drawn by two large horses, the hood of which was too high to get into the lane (leading to the house), went to see him. Yüan Hsien, in a cap made of bark, and slippers without heels, and with a stalk of hellebore for a staff, met him at the door. 'Alas! Master,' said Ȝze-kung, 'that you should be in such distress!' Yüan Hsien answered him, 'I have heard that to have no money is to be poor, and that not to be able to carry one's learning into practice is to be distressed. I am poor but not in distress.' Ȝze-kung shrank back, and looked ashamed, on which the other laughed and said, 'To act with a view to the world's (praise); to pretend to be public-spirited and yet be a partisan; to learn in order to please men; to teach for the sake of one's own gain; to conceal one's wickedness under the garb of

---

[1] A disciple of Confucius, called also Yüan Sze;—see Confucian Analects VI, iii, 3. With the description of his house or hut, compare in the Lî *K*î, XXVIII, 10.

benevolence and righteousness; and to be fond of the show of chariots and horses:—these are things which Hsien cannot bear to do.'

Ȝăng-ȝze was residing in Wei. He wore a robe quilted with hemp, and had no outer garment; his countenance looked rough and emaciated; his hands and feet were horny and callous; he would be three days without lighting a fire; in ten years he did not have a new suit; if he put his cap on straight, the strings would break; if he drew tight the overlap of his robe, his elbow would be seen; in putting on his shoes, the heels would burst them. Yet dragging his shoes along, he sang the 'Sacrificial Odes of Shang' with a voice that filled heaven and earth as if it came from a bell or a sounding stone. The Son of Heaven could not get him to be a minister; no feudal prince could get him for his friend. So it is that he who is nourishing his mind's aim forgets his body, and he who is nourishing his body discards all thoughts of gain, and he who is carrying out the Tâo forgets his own mind.

Confucius said to Yen Hui, 'Come here, Hui. Your family is poor, and your position is low; why should you not take office?' Hui replied, 'I have no wish to be in office. Outside the suburban district I possess fields to the extent of fifty acres, which are sufficient to supply me with congee; and inside it I have ten acres, which are sufficient to supply me with silk and flax. I find my pleasure in playing on my lute, and your doctrines, Master, which I study, are sufficient for my enjoyment; I do not wish to take office.' Confucius looked sad, changed countenance, and said, 'How good is the mind of Hui! I have heard that he who is contented will not entangle himself with the pursuit of gain, that he who is conscious of having gained (the truth) in himself is not afraid of losing other things, and that he who cultivates the path of inward rectification is not ashamed though he may have no official position. I have long been preaching this; but to-day I see it realised in Hui:—this is what I have gained.'

7. Prince Mâu[1] of *K*ung-shan[1] spoke to *K*an-ȝze[2], saying, 'My body has its place by the streams and near the sea, but my mind dwells at the court of Wei;—what have you to say to me in the circumstances?' *K*an-ȝze replied, 'Set the proper value on your life. When one sets the proper value on his life, gain seems to him unimportant.' The prince rejoined, 'I know that, but I am not able to overcome (my wishes).' The reply was, 'If you cannot master yourself (in the matter), follow (your inclinations so that) your spirit may not be dissatisfied. When you cannot master yourself, and try to force yourself where your spirit does not follow, this is what is called doing yourself a double injury; and those who so injure themselves are not among the long-lived.'

Mâu of Wei was the son of a lord of ten thousand chariots. For him to live in retirement among crags and caves was more difficult than for a scholar who had not worn the dress of office. Although he

[1] Prince Mâu was a son of the marquis of Wei, and had been appointed to the appanage of *K*ung-shan,—corresponding to part of the present Ting *K*âu in Pei *K*ih-lî.

[2] A worthy officer or thinker of Wei. One is not sure that his advice was altogether good.

had not attained to the Tâo, he may be said to have had some idea of it.

8. When Confucius was reduced to extreme distress between *Kh*ăn and ʒhâi, for seven days he had no cooked meat to eat, but only some soup of coarse vegetables without any rice in it. His countenance wore the appearance of great exhaustion, and yet he kept playing on his lute and singing inside the house. Yen Hui (was outside), selecting the vegetables, while ʒze-lû and ʒze-kung were talking together, and said to him, 'The Master has twice been driven from Lû; he had to flee from Wei; the tree (beneath which he rested) was cut down in Sung; he was reduced to extreme distress in Shang and *K*âu; he is held in a state of siege here between *Kh*ăn and ʒhâi; any one who kills him will be held guiltless; there is no prohibition against making him a prisoner. And yet he keeps playing and singing, thrumming his lute without ceasing. Can a superior man be without the feeling of shame to such an extent as this?' Yen Hui gave them no reply, but went in and told (their words) to Confucius, who pushed aside his lute, and said, 'Yû and ʒhze are small men. Call them here, and I will explain the thing to them.'

When they came in, ʒze-lû said, 'Your present condition may be called one of extreme distress.' Confucius replied, 'What words are these! When the Superior man has free course with his principles, that is what we call his success; when such course is denied, that is what we call his failure. Now I hold in my embrace the principles of benevolence and righteousness, and with them meet the evils of a disordered age;—where is the proof of my being in extreme distress? Therefore looking inwards and examining myself, I have no difficulties about my principles; though I encounter such difficulties (as the present), I do not lose my virtue. It is when winter's cold is come, and the hoar-frost and snow are falling, that we know the vegetative power of the pine and cypress. This strait between *Kh*ăn and Ȝhâi is fortunate for me.' He then took back his lute so that it emitted a twanging sound, and began to play and sing. (At the same time) Ȝze-lû, hurriedly, seized a shield, and began to dance, while Ȝze-kung said, 'I did not know (before) the height of heaven nor the depth of the earth.'

The ancients who had got the Tâo were happy when reduced to extremity, and happy when having free course. Their happiness was independent of both these conditions. The Tâo and its characteristics!—let them have these and distress and success come to them as cold and heat, as wind and rain in the natural order of things. Thus it was that Hsü Yû found pleasure on the north of the river Ying, and that the earl of Kung enjoyed himself on the top of mount (Kung)[1].

9. Shun proposed to resign the throne to his friend, the Northerner Wû-*k*âi[2], who said, 'A strange man you are, O sovereign! You (first) lived among the channeled fields, and then your

[1] This takes us to the famous Kung-ho period (B.C. 842–828), but our author evidently follows the account of it found in the 'Bamboo Books;'—see the prolegomena to the Shû King, p. 154.

[2] We found, in Book XXI (see vol. xxxix, p. 133), Wû-*k*âi as the name of Thien Ȝze-fang. Here is the same name belonging to a much earlier man, 'a man of the north.'

place was in the palace of Yâo. And not only so:—you now further wish to extend to me the stain of your disgraceful doings. I am ashamed to see you.' And on this he threw himself into the abyss of *Kh*ing-lăng[1].

When Thang was about to attack *K*ieh, he took counsel with Pien Sui, who said, 'It is no business of mine.' Thang then said, 'To whom should I apply?' And the other said, 'I do not know.' Thang then took counsel with Wû Kwang, who gave the same answer as Pien Sui; and when asked to whom he should apply, said in the same way, 'I do not know.' 'Suppose,' Thang then said, 'I apply to Î Yin, what do you say about him?' The reply was, 'He has a wonderful power in doing what is disgraceful, and I know nothing more about him!'

Thang thereupon took counsel with Î Yin, attacked *K*ieh, and overcame him, after which he proposed to resign the throne to Pien Sui, who declined it, saying, 'When you were about to attack *K*ieh, and sought counsel from me, you must have supposed me to be prepared to be a robber. Now that you have conquered *K*ieh, and propose to resign the throne to me, you must consider me to be greedy. I have been born in an age of disorder, and a man without principle twice comes, and tries to extend to me the stain of his disgraceful proceedings!—I cannot bear to hear the repetition of his proposals.' With this he threw himself into the *K*âu[2] water and died.

---

[1] At the foot of a hill in the present department of Nan-yang, Ho-nan.

[2] The reading uncertain.

Thang further made proffer of the throne to Wû Kwang[1], saying, 'The wise man has planned it; the martial man has carried it through; and the benevolent man should occupy it:—this was the method of antiquity. Why should you, Sir, not take the position?' Wû Kwang refused the proffer, saying, 'To depose the sovereign is contrary to right; to kill the people is contrary to benevolence. When another has encountered the risks, if I should accept the gain of his adventure, I should violate my disinterestedness. I have heard it said, "If it be not right for him to do so, one should not accept the emolument; in an age of unprincipled (government), one should not put foot on the soil (of the) country:"—how much less should I accept this position of honour! I cannot bear to see you any longer.' And with this he took a stone on his back, and drowned himself in the Lü water[2].

10. Formerly, at the rise of the *K*âu dynasty, there were two brothers who lived in Kû-*k*û[3], and were named Po-î and Shû-*kh*î. They spoke together and said, 'We have heard that in the west there is one who seems to rule according to the Right Way; let us go and see.' (Accordingly) they came to the south of (mount) *Kh*î; and when king Wû heard of them, he sent (his brother) Shû Tan to see them, and make a covenant with them, engaging that their wealth should be second (only to that of the king), and that their offices should be of the first rank.

[1] Not elsewhere heard of, save in the same connexion.

[2] In the west of Liâo-tung.

[3] A small principality, in the present Lwan-*k*âu, department of Yung-phing *K*ih-lî.

and instructing him to bury the covenant with the blood of the victim after they had smeared the corners of their mouths with it[1]. The brothers looked at each other and laughed, saying, 'Ah! How strange! This is not what we call the Right Way. Formerly, when Shăn Năng had the kingdom, he offered his sacrifices at the proper seasons and with the utmost reverence, but without praying for any blessing. Towards men he was leal-hearted and sincere, doing his utmost in governing them, but without seeking anything for himself. When it was his pleasure to use administrative measures, he did so; and a sterner rule when he thought that would be better. He did not by the ruin of others establish his own power; he did not exalt himself by bringing others low; he did not, when the time was opportune, seek his own profit. But now *K*âu, seeing the disorder of Yin, has suddenly taken the government into its hands; with the high it has taken counsel, and with those below employed bribes; it relies on its troops to maintain the terror of its might; it makes covenants over victims to prove its good faith; it vaunts its proceedings to please the masses; it kills and attacks for the sake of gain:—this is simply overthrowing disorder and changing it for tyranny. We have heard that the officers of old, in an age of good government, did not shrink from their duties, and in an age of disorder did not recklessly seek to remain in office. Now the kingdom is in a state of darkness; the virtue of *K*âu is decayed. Than to join with it and

[1] According to the usual forms in which a covenant was made and established. The translation is free and diffuse.

lay our persons in the dust, it is better for us to abandon it, and maintain the purity of our conduct.'

The two princes then went north to the hill of Shâu-yang[1], where they died of starvation. If men such as they, in the matter of riches and honours, can manage to avoid them, (let them do so); but they must not depend on their lofty virtue to pursue any perverse course, only gratifying their own tendencies, and not doing service in their time:—this was the style of these two princes.

---

[1] In the present department of Phû-*k*au, Shan-hsî.

BOOK XXIX.

Part III. Section VII.

Tâo *K*ih, or 'The Robber *K*ih[1].'

1. Confucius was on terms of friendship with Liû-hsiâ *K*î[2], who had a brother named Tâo *K*ih. This Tâo *K*ih had 9,000 followers, who marched at their will through the kingdom, assailing and oppressing the different princes. They dug through walls and broke into houses; they drove away people's cattle and horses; they carried off people's wives and daughters. In their greed to get, they forgot the claims of kinship, and paid no regard to their parents and brethren. They did not sacrifice to their ancestors. Wherever they passed through the country, in the larger states the people guarded their city walls, and in the smaller the people took to their strongholds. All were distressed by them.

Confucius spoke to Liû-hsiâ *K*î, saying, 'Fathers should be able to lay down the law to their sons,

[1] See vol. xxxix, pp. 157, 158.

[2] Better known as Liû-hsiâ Hui, under which designation he is mentioned both in the Confucian Analects and in Mencius, but it is an anachronism to say that Confucius was on terms of friendship with him. He was a scion of the distinguished family of *K*an in Lû, and was called *K*an Hwo and *K*an *Kh*in. We find, in the Ȝo *K*wan, a son of his employed in an important expedition in B.C. 634, so that he, probably, had passed away before Confucius was born in B.C. 551, and must certainly have deceased before the death of Ȝze-lû (480), which is mentioned in the Book.

and elder to instruct their younger brothers. If they are unable to do so, they do not fulfil the duties of the relationships which they sustain. You, Sir, are one of the most talented officers of the age, and your younger brother is this Robber *K*ih. He is a pest in the kingdom, and you are not able to instruct him better; I cannot but be ashamed of you, and I beg to go for you and give him counsel.' Liû-hsiâ *K*î replied, 'You say, Sir, that fathers must be able to lay down the law to their sons, and elder to instruct their younger brothers, but if sons will not listen to the orders of their fathers, nor the younger receive the lessons of their elder brothers, though one may have your powers of persuasion, what is to be done? And, moreover, *K*ih is a man whose mind is like a gushing fountain, and his will like a whirlwind; he is strong enough to resist all enemies, and clever enough to gloss over his wrong-doings. If you agree with him, he is glad; if you oppose him, he is enraged; and he readily meets men with the language of abuse. You must not go to him.'

Confucius, however, did not attend to this advice. With Yen Hui as his charioteer, and Ȝze-kung seated on the right, he went to see Tâo *K*ih, whom he found with his followers halted on the south of Thâi-shan, and mincing men's livers, which he gave them to eat. Confucius alighted from his carriage, and went forward, till he saw the usher, to whom he said, 'I, Khung *Kh*iû of Lû, have heard of the general's lofty righteousness,' bowing twice respectfully to the man as he said so. The usher went in and announced the visitor. But when Tâo *K*ih heard of the arrival, he flew into a great rage; his eyes became like blazing stars, and his hair rose up and touched his cap. 'Is not this fellow,' said he, 'Khung *Kh*iû, that artful hypocrite of Lû? Tell him from me, "You invent speeches and babble away, appealing without ground to (the examples of) Wăn and Wû. The ornaments on your cap are as many as the branches of a tree, and your girdle is (a piece of skin) from the ribs of a dead ox. The more you talk, the more nonsense you utter. You get your food without (the labour of) ploughing, and your clothes without (that of) weaving. You wag your lips and make your tongue a drum-stick. You arbitrarily decide what is right and what is wrong, thereby leading astray the princes throughout the kingdom, and making its learned scholars not occupy their thoughts with their proper business. You recklessly set up your filial piety and fraternal duty, and curry favour with the feudal princes, the wealthy and the noble. Your offence is great; your crime is very heavy. Take yourself off home at once. If you do not do so, I will take your liver, and add it to the provision for to-day's food."'

But Confucius sent in another message, saying, 'I enjoy the good will of (your brother) *K*î, and I wish and hope to tread the ground beneath your tent[1].' When the usher had communicated this message, Tâo *K*ih said, 'Make him come forward.' On this Confucius hastened forwards. Declining to take a mat, he drew hastily back, and bowed twice to Tâo *K*ih, who in a great rage stretched

[1] That is, I wish to have an interview with you, to see and speak to you face to face.

his legs apart, laid his hand on his sword, and with glaring eyes and a voice like the growl of a nursing tigress, said, 'Come forwards, *Kh*iû. If what you say be in accordance with my mind, you shall live; but, if it be contrary to it, you shall die.' Confucius replied, 'I have heard that everywhere under the sky there are three (most excellent) qualities. To be naturally tall and large, to be elegant and handsome without a peer, so that young and old, noble and mean, are pleased to look upon him;—this is the highest of those qualities. To comprehend both heaven and earth in his wisdom, and to be able to speak eloquently on all subjects;—this is the middle one of them. To be brave and courageous, resolute and daring, gathering the multitudes round him, and leading on his troops;—this is the lowest of them. Whoever possesses one of these qualities is fit to stand with his face to the south[1], and style himself a Prince. But you, General, unite in yourself all the three. Your person is eight cubits and two inches in height; there is a brightness about your face and a light in your eyes; your lips look as if stained with vermilion; your teeth are like rows of precious shells; your voice is attuned to the musical tubes, and yet you are named "The Robber *K*ih." I am ashamed of you, General, and cannot approve of you. If you are inclined to listen to me, I should like to go as your commissioner to Wû and Yüeh in the south; to *Kh*î and Lû in the north; to Sung and Wei in the east; and to 3in and *Kh*û in the west. I will get them to build for you a great city several hundred lî in size, to

[1] To take the position of a ruler in his court.

establish under it towns containing several hundred thousands of inhabitants, and honour you there as a feudal lord. The kingdom will see you begin your career afresh; you will cease from your wars and disband your soldiers; you will collect and nourish your brethren, and along with them offer the sacrifices to your ancestors[1]:—this will be a course befitting a sage and an officer of ability, and will fulfil the wishes of the whole kingdom.'

'Come forward, *Kh*iû,' said Tâo *K*ih, greatly enraged. 'Those who can be persuaded by considerations of gain, and to whom remonstrances may be addressed with success, are all ignorant, low, and ordinary people. That I am tall and large, elegant and handsome, so that all who see me are pleased with me;—this is an effect of the body left me by my parents. Though you were not to praise me for it, do I not know it myself? And I have heard that he who likes to praise men to their face will also like to speak ill of them behind their back. And when you tell me of a great wall and a multitudinous people, this is to try to persuade me by considerations of gain, and to cocker me as one of the ordinary people. But how could such advantages last for long? Of all great cities there is none so great as the whole kingdom, which was possessed by Yâo and Shun, while their descendants (now) have not so much territory as would admit an awl[2]. Thang and Wû were both set up as the Sons of Heaven, but in after ages (their posterity) were cut

[1] It is said near the beginning that *K*ih and his followers had ceased to offer such sacrifices;—they had no religion.

[2] The descendants of those worthies were greatly reduced; but they still had a name and a place.

off and extinguished;—was not this because the gain of their position was so great a prize[1]?

'And moreover I have heard that anciently birds and beasts were numerous, and men were few, so that they lived in nests in order to avoid the animals. In the daytime they gathered acorns and chestnuts, and in the night they roosted on the trees; and on account of this they are called the people of the Nest-builder. Anciently the people did not know the use of clothes. In summer they collected great stores of faggots, and in winter kept themselves warm by means of them; and on account of this they are called the people who knew how to take care of their lives. In the age of Shăn Năng, the people lay down in simple innocence, and rose up in quiet security. They knew their mothers, but did not know their fathers. They dwelt along with the elks and deer. They ploughed and ate; they wove and made clothes; they had no idea of injuring one another:—this was the grand time of Perfect virtue[2]. Hwang-Tî, however, was not able to perpetuate this virtuous state. He fought with *Kh*ih-yû[3] in the wild of *K*o-lû[4] till the blood flowed over a hundred lî. When Yâo and Shun arose, they instituted their crowd of ministers. Thang banished his lord. King Wû killed *K*âu. Since that time the strong have oppressed the weak, and the many tyrannised over the few. From Thang and Wû downwards, (the

---

[1] See note 2, p. 170.

[2] Compare the description of this primeval time in Book X, par. 4.

[3] Commonly spoken of as 'the first rebel.' See Mayers's Manual, p. 36.

[4] Perhaps in the present Pâo-an *K*âu, department of Hsüan-hwâ, *K*ih-lî.

rulers) have all been promoters of disorder and confusion. You yourself now cultivate and inculcate the ways of Wăn and Wû; you handle whatever subjects are anywhere discussed for the instruction of future ages. With your peculiar robe and narrow girdle, with your deceitful speech and hypocritical conduct, you delude the lords of the different states, and are seeking for riches and honours. There is no greater robber than you are;—why does not all the world call you the Robber *Kh*iû, instead of styling me the Robber *K*ih?

'You prevailed by your sweet speeches on 3ze-lû, and made him your follower; you made him put away his high cap, lay aside his long sword, and receive your instructions, so that all the world said, "Khung *Kh*iû is able to arrest violence and repress the wrong-doer;" but in the end, when 3ze-lû wished to slay the ruler of Wei, and the affair proved unsuccessful, his body was exhibited in pickle over the eastern gate of the capital;—so did your teaching of him come to nothing.

'Do you call yourself a scholar of talent, a sage? Why, you were twice driven out of Lû; you had to run away from Wei; you were reduced to extremity in *Kh*î; you were held in a state of siege between *Kh*ăn and 3hâi; there is no resting-place for your person in the kingdom; your instructions brought 3ze-lû to pickle. Such have been the misfortunes (attending your course). You have done no good either for yourself or for others;—how can your doctrines be worth being thought much of?

'There is no one whom the world exalts so much as it does Hwang-Tî, and still he was not able to perfect his virtue, but fought in the wilderness of

*K*o-lû, till the blood flowed over a hundred lî. Yâo was not kind to his son[1]. Shun was not filial[2]. Yü was paralysed on one side[3]. Thang banished his sovereign. King Wû smote *K*âu. King Wăn was imprisoned in Yû-lî[4]. These are the six men of whom the world thinks the most highly, yet when we accurately consider their history, we see that for the sake of gain they all disallowed their true (nature), and did violence to its proper qualities and tendencies:—their conduct cannot be thought of but with deep shame.

'Among those whom the world calls men of ability and virtue were (the brothers) Po-Î and Shû-*kh*î. They declined the rule of Kû-*k*û, and died of starvation on the hill of Shâu-yang, leaving their bones and flesh unburied. Pâo Ʒiâo vaunted his conduct, and condemned the world, but he died with his arms round a tree[5]. When Shăn-thû Tî's remonstrances were not listened to, he fastened a stone on his back, and threw himself into the Ho, where he was eaten by the fishes and turtles[6]. *K*ieh Ʒze-thui was the most devoted (of followers), and cut a piece from his thigh as food for duke Wăn. But when the duke afterwards overlooked him (in

[1] Referring to his setting aside his unworthy son, Tan-*k*û, and giving the throne to Shun.

[2] See in Mencius, V, i, 1. 3, 4.

[3] This, I think, is the meaning; the fact was highly honourable to Yü, and brought on by his devotion to his labours.

[4] In the present district of Thang-yin, department *Kh*ang-teh, Ho-nan. There king Wăn pursued his labours on the Yî King.

[5] A recluse of the time of Confucius, according to Han Ying (I, art. 27). After a dispute with Ʒze-kung, he committed suicide in the way described.

[6] See art. 26, in the same Book of Han Ying.

his distribution of favours), he was angry, and went away, and was burned to death with a tree in his arms[1]. Wei Shăng had made an appointment with a girl to meet him under a bridge; but when she did not come, and the water rose around him, he would not go away, and died with his arms round one of the pillars[2]. (The deaths of) these four men were not different from those of the dog that is torn in pieces, the pig that is borne away by a current, or the beggar (drowned in a ditch) with his alms-gourd in his hand. They were all caught as in a net by their (desire for) fame, not caring to nourish their life to its end, as they were bound to do.

'Among those whom the world calls faithful ministers there have been none like the prince Pî-kan and Wû ʒze-hsü. But ʒze-hsü's (dead) body was cast into the *K*iang, and the heart of Pî-kan was cut out. These two were what the world calls loyal ministers, but the end has been that everybody laughs at them. Looking at all the above cases, down to those of ʒze-hsü and Pî-kan, there is not one worthy to be honoured; and as to the admonitions which you, *Kh*iû, wish to impress on me, if you tell me about the state of the dead, I am unable to know anything about it; if you tell me about the things of men (alive), they are only such as I have stated, what I have heard and know all about. I will now tell you, Sir, my views about the condition of man. The eyes wish to look on beauty; the ears to hear music; the mouth to enjoy flavours; the will to be gratified. The greatest longevity man

[1] See Mayers's Manual, p. 80.

[2] Supposed to be the same with the Wei-shăng Kâo, mentioned in Analects, V, 23;—see Mayers's Manual, p. 251.

can reach is a hundred years; a medium longevity is eighty years; the lowest longevity is sixty. Take away sickness, pining, bereavement, mourning, anxieties, and calamities, the times when, in any of these, one can open his mouth and laugh, are only four or five days in a month. Heaven and earth have no limit of duration, but the death of man has its (appointed) time. Take the longest amount of a limited time, and compare it with what is unlimited, its brief existence is not different from the passing of a crevice by one of king Mû's horses[1]. Those who cannot gratify their will and natural aims, and nourish their appointed longevity, are all unacquainted with the (right) Way (of life). I cast from me, *Kh*iû, all that you say. Be quick and go. Hurry back and say not a word more. Your Way is only a wild recklessness, deceitful, artful, vain, and hypocritical. It is not available to complete the true (nature of man); it is not worth talking about!'

Confucius bowed twice, and hurried away. He went out at the door, and mounted his carriage. Thrice he missed the reins as he tried to take hold of them. His eyes were dazed, and he could not see; and his colour was that of slaked lime. He laid hold of the cross-bar, holding his head down, and unable to draw his breath. When he got back, outside the east gate of (the capital of) Lû, he encountered Liû-hsiâ *K*î, who said to him, 'Here you are, right in the gate. For some days I have not seen you. Your carriage and horses are travel-stained;—have you not been to see Tâo *K*ih?' Con-

[1] King Mû had eight famous horses, each having its own name. The name of only one—*Kh*ih-*k*i—is given here. See Bk. XVII, par. 5.

fucius looked up to heaven, sighed, and said, 'Yes.' The other went on, 'And did he not set himself in opposition to all your views, as I said he would do?' 'He did. My case has been that of the man who cauterised himself without being ill. I rushed away, stroked the tiger's head, played with his whiskers, and narrowly escaped his mouth.'

2. Ȝze-*k*ang[1] asked Mân Kâu-teh[2], saying, 'Why do you not pursue a (righteous) course? Without such a course you will not be believed in; unless you are believed in, you will not be employed in office; and if not employed in office, you will not acquire gain. Thus, if you look at the matter from the point of reputation, or estimate it from the point of gain, a righteous course is truly the right thing. If you discard the thought of reputation and gain, yet when you think over the thing in your own mind, you will see that the scholar should not be a single day without pursuing a (righteous) course.' Mân Kâu-teh said, 'He who has no shame becomes rich, and he in whom many believe becomes illustrious. Thus the greatest fame and gain would seem to spring from being without shame and being believed in. Therefore if you look at the matter from the point of reputation, or estimate it from the point of gain, to be believed in is the right thing. If you discard the thought of fame and gain, and think over the thing in your own mind, you will see that the scholar in the course which he pursues is (simply) holding fast his Heavenly (nature, and gaining nothing).'

[1] We are told (Analects, II, 18) that Ȝze-*k*ang 'studied with a view to official emolument.' This is, probably, the reason why he appears as interlocutor in this paragraph.

[2] A fictitious name, meaning, 'Full of gain recklessly got.'

3ze-*k*ang said, 'Formerly *K*ieh and *K*âu each enjoyed the honour of being the sovereign, and all the wealth of the kingdom was his; but if you now say to a (mere) money-grabber, "Your conduct is like that of *K*ieh or *K*âu," he will look ashamed, and resent the imputation:—(these two sovereigns) are despised by the smallest men. *K*ung-nî and Mo Tî (on the other hand) were poor, and common men; but if you say to a Prime Minister that his conduct is like that of *K*ung-nî or Mo Tî, then he will be put out and change countenance, and protest that he is not worthy (to be so spoken of):—(these two philosophers) are held to be truly noble by (all) scholars. Thus it is that the position of sovereign does not necessarily connect with being thought noble, nor the condition of being poor and of common rank with being thought mean. The difference of being thought noble or mean arises from the conduct being good or bad.' Mân Kâu-teh replied, 'Small robbers are put in prison; a great robber becomes a feudal lord; and in the gate of the feudal lord your righteous scholars will be found. For instance, Hsiâo-po[1], the duke Hwan, killed his elder brother, and took his sister-in-law to himself, and yet Kwan *K*ung became his minister; and Thien *Kh*ang, styled *Kh*ăng-3ze, killed his ruler, and usurped the state[2], and yet Confucius received a present of silks from him. In their discussions they would condemn the men, but

[1] The name of duke Hwan.

[2] Compare the account of the same transaction in Book X, par. 1. See also Analects, XIV, 22. But there is no evidence but rather the contrary, that Confucius ever received a gift from Thien or *Kh*ăn Hăng.

in their conduct they abased themselves before them. In this way their words and actions must have been at war together in their breasts;—was it not a contradiction and perversity? As it is said in a book, "Who is bad? and who is good? The successful is regarded as the Head, and the unsuccessful as the Tail."'

Ʒze-*k*ang said, 'If you do not follow the usual course of what is held to be right, but observe no distinction between the near and remote degrees of kin, no difference between the noble and the mean, no order between the old and the young, then how shall a separation be made of the fivefold arrangement (of the virtues), and the six parties (in the social organisation)?' Mân Kâu-teh replied, 'Yâo killed his eldest son, and Shun banished his half-brother[1]:—did they observe the rules about the different degrees of kin? Thang deposed *K*ieh; king Wû overthrew *K*âu:—did they observe the righteousness that should obtain between the noble and the mean? King *K*î took the place of his elder brother[2], and the duke of *K*âu killed his[3]:—did they observe the order that should obtain between the elder and the younger? The Literati make hypocritical speeches; the followers of Mo hold that all should be loved equally:—do we find in them the separation of the fivefold arrangement (of the

[1] Exaggerations or misrepresentations.

[2] King *K*î was the so-called king *K*î-lî, the father of king Wăn. His elder brother, that the state of *K*âu might descend to him, left it, and withdrew south to what was then the wild region of Wû. See Analects, VIII, 1; the Shih King, III, i, Ode 7. 3, 4.

[3] Who had joined with Wû-kăng, son of the tyrant of Yin, in rebellion, thus threatening the stability of the new dynasty of *K*âu.

virtues)[1], and the six parties (in the social organisation)[2]? And further, you, Sir, are all for reputation, and I am all for gain; but where the actual search for reputation and gain may not be in accordance with principle and will not bear to be examined in the light of the right way, let me and you refer the matter to-morrow[3] to the decision of Wû-yo[4].'

(This Wû-yo) said, 'The small man pursues after wealth; the superior man pursues after reputation. The way in which they change their feelings and alter their nature is different; but if they were to cast away what they do, and replace it with doing nothing, they would be the same. Hence it is said, "Do not be a small man;—return and pursue after the Heavenly in you. Do not be a superior man;—follow the rule of the Heavenly in you. Be it crooked, be it straight, view the thing in the light of Heaven as revealed in you. Look all round on every side of it, and as the time indicates, cease your endeavours. Be it right, be it wrong, hold fast the ring in yourself in which all conditions converge. Alone by yourself, carry out your idea; ponder over the right way. Do not turn your course; do not try to complete your righteousness. You will fail in what you do. Do not haste to be rich; do not follow after your perfection. If you do, you will lose the heavenly in you."

1 Probably what are called 'the five constant virtues.'

2 The parties in the 'Three Bonds of Society,' or Three Cardinal Objects of Duty.

3 So Lû Shû-kih (日 = 明日).

4 If we take Wû-yo as a name, which is the simplest construction, we must still recognise its meaning as denoting 'one who is unbound by the conventionalities of opinion.' Much of what he is made to say is in rhyme, and might also be so translated.

'Pi-kan had his heart cut out; 3ze-hsü had his eyes gouged out:—such were the evil consequences of their loyalty. The upright person[1] bore witness against his father; Wei Shăng was drowned:—such were the misfortunes of good faith. Pao-ȝze stood till he was dried up; Shăn-ȝze would not defend himself[2]:—such were the injuries brought on by disinterestedness. Confucius did not see his mother[3]; Khwang-ȝze[4] did not see his father:—such were the failures of the righteous. These are instances handed down from former ages, and talked about in these later times. They show us how superior men, in their determination to be correct in their words and resolute in their conduct, paid the penalty of these misfortunes, and were involved in these distresses.'

3. Mr. Dissatisfied[5] asked Mr. Know-the-Mean[5], saying, 'There is no man after all who does not strive for reputation and pursue after gain. When men are rich, then others go to them. Going to them, they put themselves beneath them. In that position they do honour to them as nobler than themselves. But to

---

[1] See the Analects, XIII, 18.

[2] The reading of the name here is not certain. The best identification perhaps is with Shan Shăng (申生), the eldest son of duke Hsien of 3in, who was put to death on a false charge of having put poison into his father's food, from which he would not defend himself.

[3] A false charge.

[4] The Khwang *K*ang of Mencius, IV, ii, 30, q.v.

[5] Both of these names are fictitious. About the meaning of the first, there can be no difference of opinion. I have given that of the second according to my understanding of it,—see in the Lî *K*î, Book XXVIII, section I.

see others taking that position and doing honour to us is the way to prolong life, and to secure the rest of the body and the satisfaction of the mind. You alone, Sir, however, have no idea of this. Is it that your knowledge is deficient? Is it that you have the knowledge, but want the strength to carry it into practice? Or is it that your mind is made up to do what you consider right, and never allow yourself to forget it?' Know-the-Mean replied, 'Here now is this man judging of us, his contemporaries, and living in the same neighbourhood as himself, that we consider ourselves scholars who have abjured all vulgar ways and risen above the world. He is entirely without the thought of submitting to the rule of what is right. He therefore studies ancient times and the present, and the differing questions about the right and wrong, and agrees with the vulgar ideas and influences of the age, abandoning what is most important and discarding what is most honourable, in order to be free to act as he does. But is he not wide of the mark when he thinks that this is the way to promote long life, and to secure the rest of the body and the satisfaction of the mind? He has his painful afflictions and his quiet repose, but he does not inquire how his body is so variously affected; he has his apprehensive terrors, and his happy joys, but he does not inquire how his mind has such different experiences. He knows how to pursue his course, but he does not know why he does so. Even if he had the dignity of the Son of Heaven, and all the wealth of the kingdom were his, he would not be beyond the reach of misfortunes and evils.' Dissatisfied rejoined, 'But riches are in every way advantageous to man.

With them his attainment of the beautiful and mastery of every art become what the perfect man cannot obtain nor the sagely man reach to; his appropriation of the bravery and strength of others enables him to exercise a powerful sway; his availing himself of the wisdom and plans of others makes him be accounted intelligent and discriminating; his taking advantage of the virtues of others makes him be esteemed able and good. Though he may not be the holder of a state, he is looked to with awe as a ruler and father. Moreover, music, beauty, with the pleasures of the taste and of power, are appreciated by men's minds and rejoiced in without any previous learning of them; the body reposes in them without waiting for the example of others. Desire and dislike, avoidance and pursuit, do not require any master;—this is the nature of man. Though the world may condemn one's indulgence of them, who can refrain from it?' Know-the-Mean replied, 'The action of the wise is directed for the good of the people, but they do not go against the (proper) rule and degree. Therefore when they have enough, they do not strive (for more); they have no further object, and so they do not seek for one. When they have not enough, they will seek for it; they will strive for it in every quarter, and yet not think of themselves as greedy. If they have (already) a superfluity, they will decline (any more); they will decline the throne, and yet not think of themselves as disinterested:—the conditions of disinterestedness and greediness are (with them) not from the constraint of anything external. Through their exercise of introspection, their power may be that of the sovereign, but they will not in their nobility be arrogant to others; their wealth may be that of the whole kingdom, but they will not in their possession of it make a mock of others. They estimate the evils to which they are exposed, and are anxious about the reverses which they may experience. They think how their possessions may be injurious to their nature, and therefore they will decline and not accept them;—but not because they seek for reputation and praise.

'Yâo and Shun were the sovereigns, and harmony prevailed. It did so, not because of their benevolence towards the people;—they would not, for what was (deemed) admirable, injure their lives. Shan *K*üan and Hsü Yû might have been the sovereigns, but they would not receive the throne;—not that they declined it without purpose, but they would not by its occupancy injure themselves. These all followed after what was advantageous to them, and declined what was injurious, and all the world celebrates their superiority. Thus, though they enjoy the distinction, they did what they did, not for the sake of the reputation and praise.'

Dissatisfied (continued his argument), saying, 'In thus thinking it necessary for their reputation, they bitterly distressed their bodies, denied themselves what was pleasant, and restricted themselves to a bare sustenance in order to sustain their life; but so they had life-long distress, and long-continued pressure till their death arrived.' Know-the-Mean replied, 'Tranquil ease is happiness; a superfluity is injurious:—so it is with all things, and especially it is so, where the superfluity is of wealth. The ears of the rich are provided with the music of bells, drums, flageolets and flutes; and their mouths are stuffed with the flesh of fed beasts and with wine of the richest flavour; so are their desires satisfied, till they forget their proper business:—theirs may be pronounced a condition of disorder. Sunk deeply in their self-sufficiency, they resemble individuals ascending a height with a heavy burden on their backs:—their condition may be pronounced one of bitter suffering. They covet riches, thinking to derive comfort from them; they covet power, and would fain monopolise it; when quiet and retired, they are drowned in luxurious indulgence; their persons seem to shine, and they are full of boasting:—they may be said to be in a state of disease. In their desire to be rich and striving for gain, they fill their stores, and, deaf to all admonition, refuse to desist from their course. They are even more elated, and hold on their way:—their conduct may be pronounced disgraceful. When their wealth is amassed till they cannot use it, they clasp it to their breasts and will not part with it; when their hearts are distressed with their very fulness, they still seek for more and will not desist:—their condition may be said to be sad. In-doors they are apprehensive of pilfering and begging thieves, and out-of-doors they are afraid of being injured by plundering robbers; in-doors they have many chambers and partitions, and out-of-doors they do not dare to go alone:—they may be said to be in a state of (constant) alarm.

'These six conditions are the most deplorable in the world, but they forget them all, and have lost their faculty of judgment. When the evil comes, though they begged it with all the powers of their nature, and by the sacrifice of all their wealth, they could not bring back one day of untroubled peace. When they look for their reputation, it is not to be seen; when they seek for their wealth, it is not to be got. To task their thoughts, and destroy their bodies, striving for (such an end as) this;—is it not a case of great delusion?'

BOOK XXX.

Part III. Section VIII.

Yüeh *K*ien, or 'Delight in the Sword-fight[1].'

Formerly, king Wăn of *K*âo[2] delighted in the sword-fight. More than three thousand men, masters of the weapon, appeared as his guests, lining the way on either side of his gate, and fighting together before him day and night. Over a hundred of them would die or be (severely) wounded in the course of a year, but he was never weary of looking on (at their engagements), so fond was he of them. The thing continued for three years, when the kingdom began to decay, and other states to plan measures against it.

The crown-prince Khwei[3] was distressed, and laid the case before his attendants, saying, 'If any one can persuade the king, and put an end to these swordsmen, I will give him a thousand ounces of

---

[1] See vol. xxxix, pp. 158, 159.

[2] Probably king Hui-wăn (B.C. 298–265) of *K*âo, one of the states into which the great state of ȝin was subdivided, and which afterwards all claimed the sovereignty of the kingdom. In this Book *K*wang-ȝze appears as a contemporary of king Wăn, which makes the 'formerly' with which the paragraph commences seem strange.

[3] Sze-mâ *Kh*ien says nothing of king Wăn's love of the sword-fight, nor of this son Khwei. He says that in 265 Wăn was succeeded by his son Tan (丹), who appears to have been quite young.

silver.' His attendants said, '(Only) *K*wang-ȝze is able to do this.' Thereupon the prince sent men with a thousand ounces of silver to offer to *K*wang-ȝze, who, however, would not accept them, but went with the messengers. When he saw the prince, he said, 'O prince, what have you to say to *K*âu, and why would you give me the silver?' The prince replied, 'I have heard that you, master, are sagacious and sage. I sent you respectfully the thousand ounces of silver, as a prelude to the silks and other gifts[1]. But as you decline to receive them, how dare I now tell you (what I wished from you)?' *K*wang-ȝze rejoined, 'I have heard, O prince, that what you wanted me for was to wean the king from what is his delight. Suppose that in trying to persuade his Majesty I should offend him, and not fulfil your expectation, I shall be punished with death;—and could I then enjoy this silver? Or suppose that I shall succeed in persuading his Majesty, and accomplish what you desire, what is there in the kingdom of *K*âo that I might ask for which I would not get?'

The crown-prince said, 'Yes; but my (father), the king, will see none but swordsmen.' *K*wang-ȝze replied, 'I know; but I am expert in the use of the sword.' 'That is well,' observed the prince; 'but the swordsmen whom his Majesty sees all have their hair in a tangle, with whiskers projecting out. They wear slouching caps with coarse and unornamented tassels, and their coats are cut short behind. They have staring eyes, and talk about the hazards of

[1] This, I think, is the meaning. It may possibly mean 'for presents to your followers in attendance on you.'

their game. The king is delighted with all this; but now you are sure to present yourself to him in your scholar's dress, and this will stand greatly in the way of your success.'

*K*wang-ȝze said, 'I will then, with your leave, get me a swordsman's dress.' This was ready in three days, and when he appeared in it before the prince, the latter went with him to introduce him to the king, who then drew his sword from its scabbard and waited for him. When *K*wang-ȝze entered the door of the hall, he did not hurry forward, nor, when he saw the king, did he bow. The king asked him, 'What do you want to teach me, Sir, that you have got the prince to mention you beforehand?' The reply was, 'I have heard that your Majesty is fond of the sword-fight, and therefore I have sought an interview with you on the ground of (my skill in the use of) the sword.' 'What can you do with your sword against an opponent?' 'Let me meet with an opponent every ten paces, my sword would deal with him, so that I should not be stopped in a march of a thousand lî.' The king was delighted with him, and said, 'You have not your match in the kingdom.' *K*wang-ȝze replied, 'A good swordsman first makes a feint (against his opponent), then seems to give him an advantage, and finally gives his thrust, reaching him before he can return the blow. I should like to have an opportunity to show you my skill.' The king said, 'Stop (for a little), Master. Go to your lodging, and wait for my orders. I will make arrangements for the play, and then call you.'

The king accordingly made trial of his swordsmen for seven days, till more than sixty of them were killed, or (severely) wounded. He then selected five or six men, and made them bring their swords and take their places beneath the hall, after which he called *K*wang-ȝze, and said to him, 'To-day I am going to make (you and) these men show what you can do with your swords.' 'I have long been looking for the opportunity,' replied *K*wang-ȝze. The king then asked him what would be the length of the sword which he would use; and he said, 'Any length will suit me, but I have three swords, any one of which I will use, as may please your Majesty. Let me first tell you of them, and then go to the arena.' 'I should like to hear about the three swords,' said the king; and *K*wang-ȝze went on, 'There is the sword of the Son of Heaven; the sword of a feudal prince; and the sword of a common man.'

'What about the sword of the Son of Heaven?'

'This sword has Yen-*kh*î[1] and Shih-*kh*ang[2] for its point; *Kh*î and (Mount) Tâi[3] for its edge; Ȝin and Wei for its back; *K*âu and Sung for its hilt; Han and Wei for its sheath. It is embraced by the wild tribes all around; it is wrapped up in the four seasons; it is bound round by the Sea of Po[4]; and its girdle is the enduring hills. It is regulated by the five elements; its wielding is by means of Punishments and Kindness; its unsheathing is like that of

---

[1] Some noted place in the state of Yen, the capital of which was near the site of the present Peking.

[2] A wall, north of Yen, built as a barrier of defence against the northern tribes.

[3] Mount Thâi.

[4] A region lying along the present gulf of *K*ih-lî, between the Pei-ho and the *Kh*ing-ho in Shan-tung.

the Yin and Yang; it is held fast in the spring and summer; it is put in action in the autumn and winter. When it is thrust forward, there is nothing in front of it; when lifted up, there is nothing above it; when laid down, there is nothing below it; when wheeled round, there is nothing left on any side of it; above, it cleaves the floating clouds; and below, it penetrates to every division of the earth. Let this sword be once used, and the princes are all reformed, and the whole kingdom submits. This is the sword of the Son of Heaven [1].'

King Wăn looked lost in amazement, and said again, 'And what about the sword of a feudal lord?' (*K*wang-ȝze) replied, 'This sword has wise and brave officers for its point; pure and disinterested officers for its edge; able and honourable officers for its back; loyal and sage officers for its hilt; valiant and eminent officers for its sheath. When this sword is thrust directly forward, as in the former case, there is nothing in front of it; when directed upwards, there is nothing above it; when laid down, there is nothing below it; when wheeled round, there is nothing on any side of it. Above, its law is taken from the round heaven, and is in accordance with the three luminaries; below, its law is taken from the square earth, and is in accordance with the four seasons; between, it is in harmony with the minds of the people, and in all the parts of the state there is peace. Let this sword be once used, and you seem to hear the crash of the thunder-peal. Within

[1] By this sword *K*wang-ȝze evidently means the power of the sovereign, supported by the strength of the kingdom, and directed by good government.

the four borders there are none who do not respectfully submit, and obey the orders of the ruler. This is the sword of the feudal lord.'

'And what about the sword of the common man?' asked the king (once more). (*K*wang-ȝze) replied, 'The sword of the common man (is wielded by) those who have their hair in a tangle, with whiskers projecting out; who wear slouching caps with coarse and unornamented tassels, and have their coats cut short behind; who have staring eyes, and talk (only) about the hazards (of their game). They hit at one another before you. Above, the sword slashes through the neck; and below, it scoops out the liver and lungs. This is the sword of the common man. (The users of it) are not different from fighting cocks; any morning their lives are brought to an end; they are of no use in the affairs of the state. Your Majesty occupies the seat of the Son of Heaven, and that you should be so fond of the swordsmanship of such common men, is unworthy, as I venture to think, of your Majesty.'

On this the king drew *K*wang-ȝze with him, and went up to the top of the hall, where the cook set forth a meal, which the king walked round three times (unable to sit down to it). *K*wang-ȝze said to him, 'Sit down quietly, Great King, and calm yourself. I have said all I wished to say about swords.' King Wăn, thereafter, did not quit the palace for three months, and the swordsmen all killed themselves in their own rooms[1].

[1] *K*wang-ȝze's parables had had their intended effect. It was not in his mind to do anything for the swordsmen. The commentators say:—'Indignant at not being treated as they had been before, they all killed themselves.'

BOOK XXXI.

PART III. SECTION IX.

Yü-fû, or 'The Old Fisherman[1].'

Confucius, rambling in the forest of Ȝze-wei[2], stopped and sat down by the Apricot altar. The disciples began to read their books, while he proceeded to play on his lute, singing as he did so. He had not half finished his ditty when an old fisherman stepped

[1] See vol. xxxix, p. 159.

[2] A forest or grove in the neighbourhood of the capital of Lû. Ȝze-wei means 'black silken curtains;' and I do not know why the forest was so denominated. That I have correctly determined its position, however, may be inferred from a quotation in the Khang-hsî dictionary under the character thân (='altar') to the effect that 'Confucius, leaving (the capital of) Lû by the eastern gate, on passing the old apricot altar, said, "This is the altar reared by Ȝang Wăn-*k*ung to solemnise covenants."' Dr. Morrison under the same thân defines the second phrase—hsing thân—as 'The place where Confucius taught,' which Dr. Williams, under hsing, has amplified into 'The place where Confucius had his school.' But the text does not justify so definite a conclusion. The picture which the Book raises before my mind is that of a forest, with a row or clump of apricot trees, along which was a terrace, having on it the altar of Ȝang Wăn-*k*ung, and with a lake or at least a stream near to it, to which the ground sloped down. Here the writer introduces us to the sage and some of his disciples, on one occasion, when they were attracted from their books and music by the appearance of the old fisherman. I visited in 1873, not far from the Confucian cemetery, a ruined building called 'the College of *K*û-Sze,' which was pointed out as the site of the School of Confucius. The place would suit all the demands of the situation in this Book.

down from his boat, and came towards them. His beard and eyebrows were turning white; his hair was all uncombed; and his sleeves hung idly down. He walked thus up from the bank, till he got to the dry ground, when he stopped, and, with his left hand holding one of his knees, and the right hand at his chin, listened. When the ditty was finished, he beckoned to Ȝze-kung and Ȝze-lû, who both responded and went to him. Pointing to Confucius, he said, 'Who is he?' Ȝze-lû replied, 'He is the Superior Man of Lû.' 'And of what family is he?' 'He is of the Khung family.' 'And what is the occupation of this Mr. Khung?' To this question Ȝze-lû gave no reply, but Ȝze-kung replied, 'This scion of the Khung family devotes himself in his own nature to leal-heartedness and sincerity; in his conduct he manifests benevolence and righteousness; he cultivates the ornaments of ceremonies and music; he pays special attention to the relationships of society; above, he would promote loyalty to the hereditary lords; below, he seeks the transformation of all classes of the people; his object being to benefit the kingdom:—this is what Mr. Khung devotes himself to.'

The stranger further asked, 'Is he a ruler possessed of territory?' 'No,' was Ȝze-kung's reply. 'Is he the assistant of any prince or king?' 'No;' and on this the other began to laugh and to retrace his steps, saying as he went, 'Yes, benevolence is benevolence! But I am afraid he will not escape (the evils incident to humanity). By embittering his mind and toiling his body, he is imperilling his true (nature)! Alas! how far removed is he from the proper way (of life)!'

Ȝze-kung returned, and reported (what the man had said) to Confucius, who pushed his lute aside, and arose, saying, 'Is he not a sage?' and down the slope he went in search of him. When he reached the edge of the lake, there was the fisherman with his pole, dragging the boat towards him. Turning round and seeing Confucius, he came back towards him and stood up. Confucius then drew back, bowed to him twice, and went forward. 'What do you want with me, Sir?' asked the stranger. The reply was, 'A little while ago, my Master, you broke off the thread of your remarks and went away. Inferior to you, I do not know what you wished to say, and have ventured here to wait for your instructions, fortunate if I may but hear the sound of your words to complete the assistance that you can give me!' 'Ah!' responded the stranger, 'how great is your love of learning!'

Confucius bowed twice, and then rose up, and said, 'Since I was young, I have cultivated learning till I am now sixty-nine years old; but I have not had an opportunity of hearing the perfect teaching;—dare I but listen to you with a humble and unprejudiced mind?' The stranger replied, 'Like seeks to like, and (birds) of the same note respond to one another;—this is a rule of Heaven. Allow me to explain what I am in possession of, and to pass over (from its standpoint) to the things which occupy you. What you occupy yourself with are the affairs of men. When the sovereign, the feudal lords, the great officers, and the common people, these four classes, do what is correct (in their several positions), we have the beauty of good order; and when they leave their proper duties, there ensues the greatest disorder. When the officials attend to their duties, and the common people are anxiously concerned about their business, there is no encroachment on one another's rights.

'Fields running to waste; leaking rooms; insufficiency of food and clothing; taxes unprovided for; want of harmony among wives and concubines; and want of order between old and young;—these are the troubles of the common people.

'Incompetency for their charges; inattention to their official business; want of probity in conduct; carelessness and idleness in subordinates; failure of merit and excellence; and uncertainty of rank and emolument:—these are the troubles of great officers.

'No loyal ministers at their courts; the clans in their states rebellious; want of skill in their mechanics; articles of tribute of bad quality; late appearances at court in spring and autumn; and the dissatisfaction of the sovereign:—these are the troubles of the feudal lords.

'Want of harmony between the Yin and Yang; unseasonableness of cold and heat, affecting all things injuriously; oppression and disorder among the feudal princes, their presuming to plunder and attack one another, to the injury of the people; ceremonies and music ill-regulated; the resources for expenditure exhausted or deficient; the social relationships uncared for; and the people abandoned to licentious disorder:—these are the troubles of the Son of Heaven and his ministers.

'Now, Sir, you have not the high rank of a ruler, a feudal lord, or a minister of the royal court, nor are you in the inferior position of a great minister, with his departments of business, and yet you take it on you to regulate ceremonies and music, and to give special attention to the relationships of society, with a view to transform the various classes of the people:—is it not an excessive multiplication of your business?

'And moreover men are liable to eight defects, and (the conduct of) affairs to four evils; of which we must by all means take account.

'To take the management of affairs which do not concern him is called monopolising. To bring forward a subject which no one regards is called loquacity. To lead men on by speeches made to please them is called sycophancy. To praise men without regard to right or wrong is called flattery. To be fond of speaking of men's wickedness is called calumny. To part friends and separate relatives is called mischievousness. To praise a man deceitfully, or in the same way fix on him the character of being bad, is called depravity. Without reference to their being good or bad, to agree with men with double face, in order to steal a knowledge of what they wish, is called being dangerous. Those eight defects produce disorder among other men and injury to one's self. A superior man will not make a friend of one who has them, nor will an intelligent ruler make him his minister.

'To speak of what I called the four evils:—To be fond of conducting great affairs, changing and altering what is of long-standing, to obtain for one's self the reputation of meritorious service, is called ambition; to claim all wisdom and intrude into affairs, encroaching on the work of others, and representing it as one's own, is called greediness; to see his errors without changing them, and to go on more resolutely in his own way when remonstrated with, is called obstinacy; when another agrees with himself, to approve of him, and, however good he may be, when he disagrees, to disapprove of him, is called boastful conceit. These are the four evils. When one can put away the eight defects, and allow no course to the four evils, he begins to be capable of being taught.'

Confucius looked sorrowful and sighed. (Again) he bowed twice, and then rose up and said, 'I was twice driven from Lû. I had to flee from Wei; the tree under which I rested was cut down in Sung; I was kept in a state of siege between *Kh*ăn and Ȝhâi. I do not know what errors I had committed that I came to be misrepresented on these four occasions (and suffered as I did).' The stranger looked grieved (at these words), changed countenance, and said, 'Very difficult it is, Sir, to make you understand. There was a man who was frightened at his shadow and disliked to see his footsteps, so that he ran to escape from them. But the more frequently he lifted his feet, the more numerous his footprints were; and however fast he ran, his shadow did not leave him. He thought he was going too slow, and ran on with all his speed without stopping, till his strength was exhausted and he died. He did not know that, if he had stayed in a shady place, his shadow would have disappeared, and that if he had remained still, he would have lost his footprints:—his stupidity was excessive! And you, Sir, exercise your judgment on the questions about benevolence and righteousness; you investigate the points where agreement and difference touch; you look at the changes from movement to rest and from rest to movement; you have mastered the rules of receiving and giving; you have defined the feelings of liking and disliking; you have harmonised the limits of joy and anger:—and yet you have hardly been able to escape (the troubles of which you speak). If you earnestly cultivated your own person, and carefully guarded your (proper) truth, simply rendering to others what was due to them, then you would have escaped such entanglements. But now, when you do not cultivate your own person, and make the cultivation of others your object, are you not occupying yourself with what is external?'

Confucius with an air of sadness said, 'Allow me to ask what it is that you call my proper Truth.' The stranger replied, 'A man's proper Truth is pure sincerity in its highest degree;—without this pure sincerity one cannot move others. Hence if one (only) forces himself to wail, however sadly he may do so, it is not (real) sorrow; if he forces himself to be angry, however he may seem to be severe, he excites no awe; if he forces himself to show affection, however he may smile, he awakens no harmonious reciprocation. True grief, without a sound, is yet sorrowful; true anger, without any demonstration, yet awakens awe; true affection, without a smile, yet produces a harmonious reciprocation. Given this truth within, it exercises a spiritual efficacy without, and this is why we count it so valuable. In our relations with others, it appears according to the requirements of each case:—in the service of parents, as gentle, filial duty; in the service of rulers, as loyalty and integrity; in festive drinking, as pleasant enjoyment; in the performance of the mourning rites, as sadness and sorrow. In loyalty and integrity, good service is the principal thing; in festive drinking, the enjoyment; in the mourning rites, the sorrow; in the service of parents, the giving them pleasure. The beauty of the service rendered (to a ruler) does not require that it always be performed in one way; the service of parents so as to give them pleasure takes no account of how it is done; the festive drinking which ministers enjoyment does not depend on the appliances for it; the observance of the mourning rites with the proper sorrow asks no questions about the rites themselves. Rites are prescribed for the practice of the common people; man's proper Truth is what he has received from Heaven, operating spontaneously, and unchangeable. Therefore the sages take their law from Heaven, and prize their (proper) Truth, without submitting to the restrictions of custom. The stupid do the reverse of this. They are unable to take their law from Heaven, and are influenced by other men; they do not know how to prize the proper Truth (of their nature), but are under the dominion of ordinary things, and change according to the customs (around them):—always, consequently, incomplete. Alas for you, Sir, that you were early steeped in the hypocrisies of men, and have been so late in hearing about the Great Way!'

(Once more), Confucius bowed twice (to the fisherman), then rose again, and said, 'That I have met you to-day is as if I had the happiness of getting to heaven. If you, Master, are not ashamed, but will let me be as your servant, and continue to teach me, let me venture to ask where your dwelling is. I will then beg to receive your instructions there, and finish my learning of the Great Way.' The stranger replied, 'I have heard the saying, "If it be one with whom you can walk together, go with him to the subtlest mysteries of the Tâo. If it be one with whom you cannot walk together and he do not know the Tâo, take care that you do not associate with him, and you will yourself incur no responsibility." Do your utmost, Sir. I must leave you,—I must leave you!' With this he shoved off his boat, and went away among the green reeds.

Yen Yüan (now) returned to the carriage, where Ȝze-lû handed to him the strap; but Confucius did not look round, (continuing where he was), till the wavelets were stilled, and he did not hear the sound of the pole, when at last he ventured to (return and) take his seat. Ȝze-lû, by his side in the carriage, asked him, saying, 'I have been your servant for a long time, but I have never seen you, Master, treat another with the awe and reverence which you have now shown. I have seen you in the presence of a Lord of ten thousand chariots or a Ruler of a thousand, and they have never received you in a different audience-room, or treated you but with the courtesies due to an equal, while you have still carried yourself with a reserved and haughty air; but to-day this old fisherman has stood erect in front of you with his pole in his hand, while you, bent from your loins in the form of a sounding-stone, would bow twice before you answered him;—was not your reverence of him excessive? Your disciples will all think it strange in you, Master. Why did the old fisherman receive such homage from you?'

Confucius leant forward on the cross-bar of the

carriage, heaved a sigh, and said, 'Difficult indeed is it to change you, O Yû! You have been trained in propriety and righteousness for long, and yet your servile and mean heart has not been taken from you. Come nearer, that I may speak fully to you. If you meet one older than yourself, and do not show him respect, you fail in propriety. If you see a man of superior wisdom and goodness, and do not honour him, you want the great characteristic of humanity. If that (fisherman) did not possess it in the highest degree, how could he make others submit to him? And if their submission to him be not sincere, they do not attain to the truth (of their nature), and inflict a lasting injury on their persons. Alas! there is no greater calamity to man than the want of this characteristic; and you, O Yû, you alone, would take such want on yourself.

'Moreover, the Tâo is the course by which all things should proceed. For things to fail in this is death; to observe it, is life. To oppose it in practice is ruin; to conform it, is success. Therefore wherever the sagely man finds the Tâo, he honours it. And that old fisherman to-day might be said to possess it;—dared I presume not to show him reverence?'

BOOK XXXII.

PART III. SECTION X.

Lieh Yü-khâu[1].

1. Lieh Yü-khâu had started to go to *Kh*î, but came back when he was half-way to it. He met Po-hwăn Wû-žăn[2], who said, 'Why have you come back?' His reply was, 'I was frightened.' 'What frightened you?' 'I went into ten soup-shops[3] to get a meal, and in five of them the soup was set before me before (I had paid for it)[4].' 'But what was there in that to frighten you?' (Lieh-ȝze) said, 'Though the inward and true purpose be not set forth, the body like a spy gives some bright display of it. And this outward demonstration overawes men's minds, and makes men on light grounds treat one as noble or as aged, from which evil to him will be produced. Now vendors of soup supply their commodity simply as a matter of business, and however much they may dispose of, their profit is but little,

---

[1] See vol. xxxix, pp. 160–162.

[2] The same teacher, no doubt, who is mentioned in II, par. 2, and XXI, par. 2, though the Wû in Wû-žăn is here 瞀, and there 無.

[3] Like the tea and congee shanties, I suppose, which a traveller in China finds still on the road-side.

[4] The meaning is not plain. There must have been something in the respect and generosity of the attendants which made Lieh-ȝze feel that his manner was inconsistent with his profession of Tâoism.

and their power is but slight; and yet they treated me as I have said:—how much more would the lord of ten thousand chariots do so! His body burdened with (the cares of his) kingdom, and his knowledge overtasked by its affairs, he would entrust those affairs to me, and exact from me the successful conduct (of its government). It was this which frightened me.' Po-hwăn Wû-žăn replied, 'Admirable perspicacity! But if you carry yourself as you do, men will flock to you for protection.'

Not long after, Po-hwăn Wû-žăn went (to visit Lieh-ȝze), and found the space outside his door full of shoes[1]. There he stood with his face to the north, holding his staff upright, and leaning his chin on it till the skin was wrinkled. After standing so for some time, and without saying a word, he was going away, when the door-keeper[2] went in, and told Lieh-ȝze. The latter (immediately) took up his shoes, and ran barefoot after the visitor. When he overtook him at the (outer) gate, he said, 'Since you, Sir, have come, are you going away without giving me some medicine[3]?' The other replied, 'It is of no use. I did tell you that men would flock to you, and they do indeed do so. It is not that you can cause men to flock to you, but you cannot keep them from not so coming;—of what use is (all my warning)? What influences them and makes them glad is the display of your extraordinary (qualities); but you must also be influ-

[1] See the Lî Kî (vol. xxvii, pp. 70, 71). It is still the custom in Japan for visitors to leave their shoes outside, in order not to soil the mats.

[2] Whose business it was to receive and announce the guests.

[3] Good advice.

enced in your turn, and your proper nature be shaken, and no warning can be addressed to you. Those who associate with you do not admonish you of this. The small words which they speak are poison to a man. You perceive it not; you understand it not;—how can you separate yourself from them?

'The clever toil on, and the wise are sad. Those who are without ability seek for nothing. They eat to the full, and wander idly about. They drift like a vessel loosed from its moorings, and aimlessly wander about[1].'

2. A man of *K*ăng, called Hwan, learned[2] his books in the neighbourhood of *Kh*iû-shih[3], and in no longer time than three years became a Confucian scholar, benefiting the three classes of his kindred[4] as the Ho extends its enriching influence for nine lî. He made his younger brother study (the principles of) Mo[5], and then they two—the scholar and the Mohist—disputed together (about their respective systems), and the father took the side of the younger[6]. After ten years Hwan killed himself. (By and by) he appeared to his father in a dream, saying, 'It was I who made your son become a

[1] Was this then Wû-*z*ăn's idea of how the Tâoist should carry himself? From 'those who associate with you' Wû-*z*ăn's address might be rhymed.

[2] Read them aloud, and so committed them to memory;—as Chinese schoolboys do still.

[3] The name of a place, or, perhaps, of Hwan's schoolmaster.

[4] Probably, the kindred of his father, mother, and wife;—through his getting office as a scholar.

[5] Or Mih Tî;—Mencius's heresiarch.

[6] Literally, 'of Tî,' as if that had been the name of the younger brother, as it was that of the heresiarch.

Mohist; why did you not recognise that good service[1]? I am become (but) the fruit of a cypress in autumn[2].' But the Creator[3], in apportioning the awards of men, does not recompense them for their own doings, but recompenses them for the (use of the) Heavenly in them. It was thus that Hwan's brother was led to learn Mohism. When this Hwan thought that it was he who had made his brother different from what he would have been, and proceeded to despise his father, he was like the people of *K*hî, who, while they drank from a well, tried to keep one another from it. Hence it is said, 'Now-a-days all men are Hwans[4].' From this we perceive that those who possess the characteristics (of the Tâo) consider that they do not know them; how much more is it so with those who possess the Tâo itself! The ancients called such (as Hwan) 'men who had escaped the punishment of Heaven.'

3. The sagely man rests in what is his proper rest; he does not rest in what is not so;—the multitude of men rest in what is not their proper rest; they do not rest in their proper rest[5].

4. *K*wang-ȝze said, 'To know the Tâo is easy; not to say (that you know it) is difficult. To know it and not to speak of it is the way to attain to the

[1] The character for this in the text (甚) is explained as meaning 'a grave,' with special reference to this passage, in the Khang-hsî dictionary.

[2] The idea of a grave is suggested by the 'cypress,' and we need not try to find it in 甚.

[3] The creator was, in *K*wang-ȝze's mind, the Tâo.

[4] Arrogating to themselves what was the work of the Tâo.

[5] The best editions make this sentence a paragraph by itself.

Heavenly; to know and to speak of it, is the way to show the Human. The ancients pursued the Heavenly (belonging to them), and not the Human.'

5. *K*û Phing-man[1] learned how to slaughter the dragon[2] from *K*ih-lî Yî, expending (in doing so) all his wealth of a thousand ounces of silver. In three years he became perfect in the art, but he never exercised his skill.

6. The sage looks on what is deemed necessary as unnecessary, and therefore is not at war[3] (in himself). The mass of men deem what is unnecessary to be necessary, and therefore they are often at war (in themselves). Therefore those who pursue this method of (internal) war, resort to it in whatever they seek for. But reliance on such war leads to ruin.

7. The wisdom of the small man does not go beyond (the minutiae of) making presents and writing memoranda, wearying his spirits out in what is trivial and mean. But at the same time he wishes to aid in guiding to (the secret of) the Tâo and of (all) things in the incorporeity of the Grand Unity. In this way he goes all astray in regard to (the mysteries of) space and time. The fetters of embodied matter keep him from the knowledge of the Grand Beginning. (On the other hand), the perfect man directs the energy of his spirit to what was before the Beginning, and finds pleasure in the mysteriousness

[1] These are names fashioned by our author.

[2] 'Slaughtering the dragon' means 'learning the Tâo,' by expending or putting away all doing and knowledge, till one comes to the perfect state of knowing the Tâo and not speaking of it.

[3] Being 'at war' here is not the conflict of arms, but of joy, anger, and desire in one's breast. See ȝiâo Hung in loc.

belonging to the region of nothingness. He is like the water which flows on without the obstruction of matter, and expands into the Grand Purity.

Alas for what you do, (O men)! You occupy yourselves with things trivial as a hair, and remain ignorant of the Grand Rest!

8. There was a man of Sung, called Ȝhâo Shang, who was sent by the king of Sung on a mission to *Kh*in. On setting out, he had several carriages with him; and the king (of *Kh*in) was so pleased with him that he gave him another hundred. When he returned to Sung, he saw *K*wang-ȝze, and said to him, 'To live in a narrow lane of a poor mean hamlet, wearing sandals amid distress of poverty, with a weazen neck and yellow face[1];—that is what I should find it difficult to do. But as soon as I come to an understanding with the Lord of a myriad carriages, to find myself with a retinue of a hundred carriages,—that is wherein I excel.' *K*wang-ȝze replied, 'When the king of *Kh*ăn is ill, the doctor whom he calls to open an ulcer or squeeze a boil receives a carriage; and he who licks his piles receives five. The lower the service, the more are the carriages given. Did you, Sir, lick his piles? How else should you have got so many carriages? Begone!'

9. Duke Âi of Lû asked Yen Ho, saying, 'If I employ *K*ung-nî as the support of my government, will the evils of the state be thereby cured?' The

[1] The character for 'face' generally means 'ears;' but the Khang-hsî dictionary, with special reference to this paragraph, explains it by 'face.'—The whole paragraph is smart and bitter, but Lin Hsî-*k*ung thinks it too coarse to be from *K*wang-ȝze's pencil.

reply was, '(Such a measure) would be perilous! It would be full of hazard! *K*ung-nî, moreover, will try to ornament a feather and paint it; in the conduct of affairs he uses flowery speeches. A (mere) branch is to him more admirable (than the root); he can bear to misrepresent their nature in instructing the people, and is not conscious of the unreality of his words. He receives (his inspiration) from his own mind, and rules his course from his own spirit:—what fitness has he to be set over the people? Is such a man suitable for you (as your minister)? Could you give to him the nourishment (of the people)? You would do so by mistake (but not on purpose, for a time, but not as a permanency). To make the people leave what is real, and learn what is hypocritical—that is not the proper thing to be shown to them; if you take thought for future ages, your better plan will be to give up (the idea of employing Confucius). What makes government difficult, is the dealing with men without forgetting yourself; this is not according to the example of Heaven in diffusing its benefits. Merchants and traffickers are not to be ranked (with administrative officers); if on an occasion you so rank them, the spirits (of the people) do not acquiesce in your doing so. The instruments of external punishment are made of metal and wood; those of internal punishment are agitation (of the mind) and (the sense of) transgression. When small men become subject to the external punishment, the (instruments of) metal and wood deal with them; when they become liable to the internal punishments, the Yin and Yang[1] con-

[1] Compare the use of 'the Yin and the Yang' in XXIII, par. 8.—Yen Ho does not flatter Confucius in his description of him.

sume them. It is only the true man who can escape both from the external and internal punishment.'

10. Confucius said, 'The minds of men are more difficult of approach than (the position defended by) mountains and rivers, and more difficult to know than Heaven itself. Heaven has its periods of spring and autumn, of winter and summer, and of morning and evening; but man's exterior is thickly veiled, and his feelings lie deep. Thus the demeanour of some is honest-like, and yet they go to excess (in what is mean); others are really gifted, and yet look to be without ability; some seem docile and impressible, but yet they have far-reaching schemes; others look firm, and yet may be twisted about; others look slow, and yet they are hasty. In this way those who hasten to do what is right as if they were thirsty will anon hurry away from it as if it were fire. Hence the superior man looks at them when employed at a distance to test their fidelity, and when employed near at hand to test their reverence. By employing them on difficult services, he tests their ability; by questioning them suddenly, he tests their knowledge; by appointing them a fixed time, he tests their good faith; by entrusting them with wealth, he tests their benevolence; by telling them of danger, he tests their self-command in emergencies; by making them drunk, he tests their tendencies[1]; by placing them in a variety of society, he tests their chastity:—by these nine tests the inferior man is discovered.'

11. When Khâo-fû, the Correct[2], received the first

[1] Is this equivalent to the adage 'In vino veritas?'

[2] A famous ancestor of Confucius in the eighth century B.C.,

grade of official rank, he walked with head bowed down; on receiving the second, with bent back; on receiving the third, with body stooping, he ran and hurried along the wall:—who would presume not to take him as a model? But one of those ordinary men, on receiving his first appointment, goes along with a haughty stride; on receiving his second, he looks quite elated in his chariot; and on receiving the third, he calls his uncles by their personal names;—how very different from Hsü (Yû) in the time (of Yâo of) Thang!

Of all things that injure (men) there is none greater than the practising of virtue with the purpose of the mind, till the mind becomes supercilious. When it becomes so, the mind (only) looks inwards (on itself), and such looking into itself leads to its ruin. This evil quality has five forms, and the chief of them is that which is the central. What do we mean by the central quality? It is that which appears in a man's loving (only) his own views, and reviling whatever he does not do (himself).

Limiting (men's advance), there are eight extreme conditions; securing (that advance), there are three things necessary; and the person has its six repositories. Elegance; a (fine) beard; tallness; size; strength; beauty; bravery; daring; and in all these excelling others:—(these are the eight extreme conditions) by which advance is limited. Depending on and copying others; stooping in order to rise; and being straitened by the fear of not equalling others:—

before the Khung family fled from Sung. See the account of him, with some verbal alterations, in the 3o *Kh*wan, under the seventh year of duke *K*âo.

these are the three things that lead to advancing. Knowledge seeking to reach to all that is external; bold movement producing many resentments; benevolence and righteousness leading to many requisitions; understanding the phenomena of life in an extraordinary degree; understanding all knowledge so as to possess an approach to it; understanding the great condition appointed for him, and following it, and the smaller conditions, and meeting them as they occur:—(these are the six repositories of the person)[1].

12. There was a man who, having had an interview with the king of Sung, and been presented by him with ten carriages, showed them boastfully to *K*wang-ȝze, as if the latter had been a boy. *K*wang-ȝze said to him, 'Near the Ho there was a poor man who supported his family by weaving rushes (to form screens). His son, when diving in a deep pool, found a pearl worth a thousand ounces of silver. The father said, "Bring a stone, and break it in pieces. A pearl of this value must have been in a pool nine *kh*ung deep[2], and under the chin of the Black Dragon. That you were able to get it must have been owing to your finding him asleep. Let him awake, and the consequences to you will not be small!" Now the kingdom of Sung is deeper than any pool of nine *kh*ung, and its king is fiercer than the Black Dragon. That you were able to get the

[1] These eight words are supplied to complete the structure of the paragraph; but I cannot well say what they mean, nor in what way the predicates in the six clauses that precede can be called 'the stores, or repositories of the body or person.'

[2] = in a pool deeper than any nine pools. Compare the expression 九重天.

chariots must have been owing to your finding him asleep. Let him awake, and you will be ground to powder[1].'

13. Some (ruler) having sent a message of invitation to him, *K*wang-ʒze replied to the messenger, 'Have you seen, Sir, a sacrificial ox? It is robed with ornamental embroidery, and feasted on fresh grass and beans. But when it is led into the grand ancestral temple, though it wished to be (again) a solitary calf, would that be possible for it[2]?'

14. When *K*wang-ʒze was about to die, his disciples signified their wish to give him a grand burial. 'I shall have heaven and earth,' said he, 'for my coffin and its shell; the sun and moon for my two round symbols of jade; the stars and constellations for my pearls and jewels; and all things assisting as the mourners. Will not the provisions for my burial be complete? What could you add to them?' The disciples replied, 'We are afraid that the crows and kites will eat our master.' *K*wang-ʒze rejoined, 'Above, the crows and kites will eat me; below, the mole-crickets and ants will eat me:—to take from those and give to these would only show your partiality[3].'

The attempt, with what is not even, to produce what is even will only produce an uneven result; the attempt, with what is uncertain, to make the uncertain certain will leave the uncertainty as it

---

[1] Compare paragraph 8. But Lin again denies the genuineness of this.

[2] Compare XVII, par. 11.

[3] We do not know whether *K*wang-ʒze was buried according to his own ideal or not. In the concluding sentences we have a strange descent from the grandiloquence of what precedes.

was. He who uses only the sight of his eyes is acted on by what he sees; it is the (intuition of the) spirit, that gives the assurance of certainty. That the sight of the eyes is not equal to that intuition of the spirit is a thing long acknowledged. And yet stupid people rely on what they see, and will have it to be the sentiment of all men;—all their success being with what is external:—is it not sad?

BOOK XXXIII.

PART III. SECTION XI.

Thien Hsiâ[1].

1. The methods employed in the regulation of the world[2] are many; and (the employers of them) think each that the efficiency of his own method leaves nothing to be added to it.

But where is what was called of old 'the method of the Tâo[2]?' We must reply, 'It is everywhere.' But then whence does the spiritual[3] in it come down? and whence does the intelligence[4] in it come forth? There is that which gives birth to the Sage, and that which gives his perfection to the King:—the origin of both is the One[5].

Not to be separate from his primal source constitutes what we call the Heavenly man; not to be separate from the essential nature thereof constitutes what we call the Spirit-like man; not to be separate from its real truth constitutes what we call the Perfect man[6].

---

[1] See vol. xxxix, pp. 162, 163.

[2] All the methods of educational training and schemes of governmental policy, advocated by 'the hundred schools' of human wisdom in contradistinction from the method or art of the Tâo. Fang Shû has little more meaning than our word 'nostrum.'

[3] Which forms the sage.

[4] Which forms the sage king.

[5] Or, one and the same.

[6] Compare the three definitions in Book I, par. 3.

To regard Heaven as his primal Source, Its Attributes as the Root (of his nature), and the Tâo as the Gate (by which he enters into this inheritance), (knowing also) the prognostics given in change and transformation, constitutes what we call the Sagely man[1].

To regard benevolence as (the source of all) kindness, righteousness as (the source of all) distinctions, propriety as (the rule of) all conduct, and music as (the idea of) all harmony, thus diffusing a fragrance of gentleness and goodness, constitutes what we call the Superior man[2].

To regard laws as assigning the different (social) conditions, their names as the outward expression (of the social duties), the comparison of subjects as supplying the grounds of evidence, investigation as conducting to certainty, so that things can be numbered as first, second, third, fourth (and so on): —(this is the basis of government). Its hundred offices are thus arranged; business has its regular course; the great matters of clothes and food are provided for; cattle are fattened and looked after; the (government) stores are filled; the old and weak, orphans and solitaries, receive anxious consideration:—in all these ways is provision made for the nourishment of the people.

How complete was (the operation of the Tâo) in the men of old! It made them the equals of spiritual beings, and subtle and all-embracing as heaven and earth. They nourished all things, and produced

---

[1] Here we have five definitions of the 'Man of Tâo.'

[2] Still within the circle of the Tâo, but inferior to the five above.

harmony all under heaven. Their beneficent influence reached to all classes of the people. They understood all fundamental principles, and followed them out to their graduated issues; in all the six directions went their penetration, and in the four quarters all things were open to them. Great and small, fine and coarse;—all felt their presence and operation. Their intelligence, as seen in all their regulations, was handed down from age to age in their old laws, and much of it was still to be found in the Historians. What of it was in the Shih, the Shû, the Lî, and the Yo, might be learned from the scholars of Ȝâu[1] and Lû[1], and the girdled members of the various courts. The Shih describes what should be the aim of the mind; the Shû, the course of events; the Lî is intended to direct the conduct; the Yo, to set forth harmony; the Yî, to show the action of the Yin and Yang; and the *Kh*un *Kh*iû, to display names and the duties belonging to them.

Some of the regulations (of these men of old), scattered all under heaven, and established in our Middle states, are (also) occasionally mentioned and described in the writings of the different schools.

There ensued great disorder in the world, and sages and worthies no longer shed their light on it. The Tâo and its characteristics ceased to be regarded as uniform. Many in different places got

[1] These scholars were pre-eminently Confucius and Mencius. In this brief phrase is the one recognition, by our author, of the existence and work of Mencius, who was 'the scholar of Ȝâu.' But one is not prepared for the comparatively favourable judgment passed on those scholars, and on what we call the Confucian classics. The reading Ȝâu has not been challenged, and can only be understood of Mencius.

one glimpse of it, and plumed themselves on possessing it as a whole. They might be compared to the ear, the eye, the nose, or the mouth. Each sense has its own faculty, but their different faculties cannot be interchanged. So it was with the many branches of the various schools. Each had its peculiar excellence, and there was the time for the use of it; but notwithstanding no one covered or extended over the whole (range of truth). The case was that of the scholar of a corner who passes his judgment on all the beautiful in heaven and earth, discriminates the principles that underlie all things, and attempts to estimate the success arrived at by the ancients. Seldom is it that such an one can embrace all the beautiful in heaven and earth, or rightly estimate the ways of the spiritual and intelligent; and thus it was that the Tâo, which inwardly forms the sage and externally the king[1], became obscured and lost its clearness, became repressed and lost its development. Every one in the world did whatever he wished, and was the rule to himself. Alas! the various schools held on their several ways, and could not come back to the same point, nor agree together. The students of that later age unfortunately did not see the undivided purity of heaven and earth, and the great scheme of truth held by the ancients. The system of the Tâo was about to be torn in fragments all under the sky.

2. To leave no example of extravagance to future generations; to show no wastefulness in the use of

[1] Compare 'the spiritual' and 'the intelligence' near the commencement, and the notes 3 and 4.

anything; to make no display in the degree of their (ceremonial) observances; to keep themselves (in their expenditure) under the restraint of strict and exact rule, so as to be prepared for occurring emergencies;—such regulations formed part of the system of the Tâo in antiquity, and were appreciated by Mo Tî, and (his disciple) *Kh*in Hwa-lî[1]. When they heard of such ways, they were delighted with them; but they enjoined them in excess, and followed them themselves too strictly. (Mo) made the treatise 'Against Music,' and enjoined the subject of another, called 'Economy in Expenditure,' on his followers. He would have no singing in life, and no wearing of mourning on occasions of death. He inculcated Universal Love, and a Common Participation in all advantages, and condemned Fighting. His doctrine did not admit of Anger. He was fond also of Learning, and with it all strove not to appear different from others. Yet he did not agree with the former kings, but attacked the ceremonies and music of the ancients.

Hwang-Tî had his Hsien-*kh*ih; Yâo, his Tâ *K*ang; Shun, his Tâ Shâo; Yü, his Tâ Hsiâ; Thang, his Tâ Hû; king Wăn, his music of the Phi-yung[2]; and king Wû and the duke of *K*âu made the Wû.

---

[1] Thus Mohism appears as an imperfect Tâoism. Mo (or Meh) Tî was a great officer of the state of Sung, of the period between Confucius and Mencius. He left many treatises behind him, of which only a few, but the most important, survive. *Kh*in Hwa-lî seems to have been his chief disciple. He says, in one place, '*Kh*in Hwa-lî and my other disciples,—300 men.'

[2] The name of the great hall built by king Wăn, and still applied to the examination hall of the Han-lin graduates in Peking.

In the mourning rites of the ancients, the noble and mean had their several observances, the high and low their different degrees. The coffin of the Son of Heaven was sevenfold; of a feudal lord, fivefold; of a great officer, threefold; of other officers, twofold. But now Mo-ȝze alone, would have no singing during life, and no wearing of mourning after death. As the rule for all, he would have a coffin of elaeococca wood, three inches thick, and without any enclosing shell. The teaching of such lessons cannot be regarded as affording a proof of his love for men; his practising them in his own case would certainly show that he did not love himself; but this has not been sufficient to overthrow the views of Mo-ȝze. Notwithstanding, men will sing, and he condemns singing; men will wail, and he condemns wailing; men will express their joy, and he condemns such expression:—is this truly in accordance with man's nature? Through life toil, and at death niggardliness:—his way is one of great unkindliness. Causing men sorrow and melancholy, and difficult to be carried into practice, I fear it cannot be regarded as the way of a sage. Contrary to the minds of men everywhere, men will not endure it. Though Mo-ȝze himself might be able to endure it, how can the aversion of the world to it be overcome? The world averse to it, it must be far from the way of the (ancient) kings.

Mo-ȝze, in praise of his views, said, 'Anciently, when Yü was draining off the waters of the flood, he set free the channels of the *K*iang and the Ho, and opened communications with them from the

What the special music made for it by Wăn was called, I do not know.

regions of the four Î and the nine provinces. The famous hills with which he dealt were 300, the branch streams were 3000, and the smaller ones innumerable. With his own hands he carried the sack and wielded the spade, till he had united all the streams of the country (conducting them to the sea). There was no hair left on his legs from the knee to the ankle. He bathed his hair in the violent wind, and combed it in the pelting rain, thus marking out the myriad states. Yü was a great sage, and thus he toiled in the service of the world.' The effect of this is that in this later time most of the Mohists wear skins and dolychos cloth, with shoes of wood or twisted hemp, not stopping day or night, but considering such toiling on their part as their highest achievement. They say that he who cannot do this is acting contrary to the way of Yü, and not fit to be a Mohist.

The disciples of *Kh*in of Hsiang-lî [1], the followers of the various feudal lords [2]; and Mohists of the south, such as Khû Hu [3], *K*i *Kh*ih [3], and Tăng Ling-ȝze [3], all repeated the texts of Mo, but they differed in the objections which they offered to them, and in their deceitful glosses they called one another Mohists of different schools. They had their disputations, turning on 'what was hard,' and 'what was white,' what constituted 'sameness' and what 'difference,' and their expressions about the difference between 'the odd' and 'the even,' with which they answered one another. They regarded

[1] Some say this *Kh*in was the preceptor of Mo Tî.

[2] Easily translated; but the statement has not been historically illustrated.

[3] Known only by the mention of them here.

their most distinguished member as a sage, and wished to make him their chief, hoping that he would be handed down as such to future ages. To the present day these controversies are not determined.

The idea of Mo Tî and *Kh*in Hwa-lî was good, but their practice was wrong. They would have made the Mohists of future ages feel it necessary to toil themselves, till there was not a hair on their legs, and still be urging one another on; (thus producing a condition) superior indeed to disorder, but inferior to the result of good government. Nevertheless, Mo-ȝze was indeed one of the best men in the world, which you may search without finding his equal. Decayed and worn (his person) might be, but he is not to be rejected,—a scholar of ability indeed!

3. To keep from being entangled by prevailing customs; to shun all ornamental attractions in one's self; not to be reckless in his conduct to others; not to set himself stubbornly against a multitude; to desire the peace and repose of the world in order to preserve the lives of the people; and to cease his action when enough had been obtained for the nourishment of others and himself, showing that this was the aim of his mind;—such a scheme belonged to the system of the Tâo in antiquity [1], and it was appreciated by Sung Hsing [2] and Yin Wăn [2].

---

[1] It is difficult to understand the phases of the Tâo here referred to.

[2] Both these men are said to have been of the time of king Hsüan of *Kh*î. In the Catalogue of the Imperial Library of Han, Yin Wăn appears, but not among the Tâoist writers, as the author

When they heard of such ways, they were delighted with them. They made the Hwa-shan cap, and wore it as their distinguishing badge[1]. In their intercourse with others, whatever their differences might be, they began by being indulgent to them. Their name for 'the Forbearance of the Mind' was 'the Action of the Mind.' By the warmth of affection they sought the harmony of joy, and to blend together all within the four seas; and their wish was to plant this everywhere as the chief thing to be pursued. They endured insult without feeling it a disgrace; they sought to save the people from fighting; they forbade aggression and sought to hush the weapons of strife, to save their age from war. In this way they went everywhere, counselling the high and instructing the low. Though the world might not receive them, they only insisted on their object the more strongly, and would not abandon it. Hence it is said, 'The high and the low might be weary of them, but they were strong to show themselves.'

Notwithstanding all this, they acted too much out of regard to others, and too little for themselves. It was as if they said, 'What we request and wish is simply that there may be set down for us five pints of rice;—that will be enough.' But I fear the Master would not get his fill from this; and the disciples, though famishing, would still have to be mindful of the world, and, never stopping day or night, have to say, 'Is it necessary I should preserve

of 'one Treatise.' He is said also to have been the preceptor of Kung-sun Lung.

[1] I cannot fashion the shape of this cap or of the Hwa mountain in my own mind,—'flat both above and below.'

my life? Shall I scheme how to exalt myself above the master, the saviour of the age?'

It was moreover as if they said, 'The superior man does not censoriously scrutinize (the faults of others); he does not borrow from others to supersede his own endeavours; when any think that he is of no use to the world, he knows that their intelligence is inferior to his own; he considers the prohibition of aggression and causing the disuse of arms to be an external achievement, and the making his own desires to be few and slight to be the internal triumph.' Such was their discrimination between the great and the small, the subtle and the coarse; and with the attainment of this they stopped.

4. Public-spirited, and with nothing of the partizan; easy and compliant, without any selfish partialities; capable of being led, without any positive tendencies; following in the wake of others, without any double mind; not looking round because of anxious thoughts; not scheming in the exercise of their wisdom; not choosing between parties, but going along with all;—all such courses belonged to the Tâoists of antiquity, and they were appreciated by Phăng Măng[1], Thien Phien[1], and Shăn Tâo[1]. When they heard of such ways, they were delighted with them. They considered that the first thing for them to do was to adjust the controversies about different things. They said, 'Heaven can cover, but it cannot sustain; Earth can contain, but it can-

[1] Thien Phien is mentioned in the Han Catalogue, among the Tâoist writers, as a native of *Kh*î, and an author of twenty-five phien. Shăn Tâo also appears among the legal writers, as author of forty-two phien. He is mentioned by Han Fei.

not cover. The Great Tâo embraces all things, but It does not discriminate between them.'

They knew that all things have what they can do and what they cannot do. Hence it is said, 'If you select, you do not reach all; if you teach some things, you must omit the others; but the Tâo neglects none.' Therefore Shăn Tâo discarded his knowledge and also all thought of himself, acting only where he had no alternative, and pursued it as his course to be indifferent and pure in his dealings with others. He said that the best knowledge was to have no knowledge, and that if we had a little knowledge it was likely to prove a dangerous thing. Conscious of his unfitness, he undertook no charge, and laughed at those who valued ability and virtue. Remiss and evasive, he did nothing, and disallowed the greatest sages which the world had known. Now with a hammer, now with his hand, smoothing all corners, and breaking all bonds, he accommodated himself to all conditions. He disregarded right and wrong, his only concern being to avoid trouble; he learned nothing from the wise and thoughtful, and took no note of the succession of events, thinking only of carrying himself with a lofty disregard of everything. He went where he was pushed, and followed where he was led, like a whirling wind, like a feather tossed about, like the revolutions of a grindstone.

What was the reason that he appeared thus complete, doing nothing wrong? that, whether in motion or at rest, he committed no error, and could be charged with no transgression? Creatures that have no knowledge are free from the troubles that arise from self-assertion and the entanglements that spring from the use of knowledge. Moving and at rest, they do not depart from their proper course, and all their life long they do not receive any praise. Hence (Shăn Tâo) said, 'Let me come to be like a creature without knowledge. Of what use are the (teachings of the) sages and worthies?' But a clod of earth never fails in the course (proper for it), and men of spirit and eminence laughed together at him, and said, 'The way of Shăn Tâo does not describe the conduct of living men; that it should be predicable only of the dead is strange indeed!'

It was just the same with Thien Phien. He learned under Phăng Măng, but it was as if he were not taught at all. The master of Phăng Măng said, 'The Tâoist professors of old came no farther than to say that nothing was absolutely right and nothing absolutely wrong.' His spirit was like the breath of an opposing wind; how can it be described in words? But he was always contrary to (the views of) other men, which he would not bring together to view, and he did not escape shaving the corners and bonds (of which I have spoken). What he called the Tâo was not the true Tâo, and what he called the right was really the wrong.

Phăng Măng, Thien Phien, and Shăn Tâo did not in fact know the Tâo; but nevertheless they had heard in a general way about it.

5. To take the root (from which things spring) as the essential (part), and the things as its coarse (embodiment); to see deficiency in accumulation; and in the solitude of one's individuality to dwell with the spirit-like and intelligent;—such a course belonged to the Tâo of antiquity, and it was appre-

ciated by Kwan Yin[1] and Lâo Tan[2]. When they heard of such ways, they were delighted with them. They built their system on the assumption of an eternal non-existence, and made the ruling idea in it that of the Grand Unity. They made weakness and humility their mark of distinction, and considered that by empty vacuity no injury could be sustained, but all things be preserved in their substantiality.

Kwan Yin[1] says, 'To him who does not dwell in himself the forms of things show themselves as they are. His movement is like that of water; his stillness is like that of a mirror; his response is like that of the echo. His tenuity makes him seem to be disappearing altogether; he is still as a clear (lake), harmonious in his association with others, and he counts gain as loss. He does not take precedence of others, but follows them.' Lâo Tan[2] says, 'He knows his masculine power, but maintains his female weakness,—becoming the channel into which all streams flow. He knows his white purity, but keeps his disgrace,—becoming the valley of the world. Men all prefer to be first; he alone chooses to be last, saying, "I will receive the offscourings of the world." Men all choose fulness; he alone chooses emptiness. He does not store, and therefore he has a superabundance; he looks solitary, but has a multitude around him. In his conducting

[1] Kwan Yin;—see Book XIX, par. 2, and vol. xxxix, p. 35. In the Catalogue of the Han Library there is an entry of a work by Kwan Yin in nine phien; and there is still a work current in China, called *K*wan Yin-ʒze in one *k*üan, but it is not generally received as genuine.

[2] See the account of Lâo-ʒze in vol. xxxix, pp. 34–36.

of himself he is easy and leisurely and wastes nothing. He does nothing, and laughs at the clever and ingenious. Men all seek for happiness, but he feels complete in his imperfect condition, and says, "Let me only escape blame." He regards what is deepest as his root, and what is most restrictive as his rule; and says, "The strong is broken; the sharp and pointed is blunted[1]." He is always generous and forbearing with others, and does not encroach on any man;—this may be pronounced the height (of perfection).'

O Kwan Yin, and Lâo Tan, ye were among the greatest men of antiquity; True men indeed!

6. That the shadowy and still is without bodily form; that change and transformation are ever proceeding, but incapable of being determined. What is death? What is life? What is meant by the union of Heaven and Earth? Does the spiritual intelligence go away? Shadowy, where does it go? Subtle, whither does it proceed? All things being arranged as they are, there is no one place which can be fitly ascribed to it. Such were the questions belonging to the scheme of Tâo in antiquity, and they were appreciated by *K*wang *K*âu. When he heard of such subjects, he was delighted with them. (He discussed them), using strange and mystical expressions, wild and extravagant words, and phrases to which no definite meaning could be assigned. He constantly indulged his own wayward ideas, but did not make himself a partisan, nor look at them as peculiar to himself. Considering that men were

[1] From the 'Lâo Tan says' down to this, may be said to be all quotation, with more or less exactness, from the Tâo Teh *K*ing. See chaps. 28, 22, et al.

sunk in stupidity and could not be talked to in dignified style, he employed the words of the cup of endless application, with important quotations to substantiate the truth, and an abundance of corroborative illustrations. He chiefly cared to occupy himself with the spirit-like operation of heaven and earth, and did not try to rise above the myriads of things. He did not condemn the agreements and differences of others, so that he might live in peace with the prevalent views. Though his writings may seem to be sparkling trifles, there is no harm in amusing one's self with them; though his phraseology be ever-varying, its turns and changes are worth being looked at;—the fulness and completeness of his ideas cannot be exhausted. Above he seeks delight in the Maker; below, he has a friendly regard to those who consider life and death as having neither beginning nor end. As regards his dealing with the Root (origin of all things), he is comprehensive and great, opening up new views, deep, vast, and free. As regards the Author and Master (the Great Tâo Itself), he may be pronounced exact and correct, carrying our thoughts to range and play on high. Nevertheless on the subject of transformation, and the emancipation of that from (the thraldom of) things, his principles are inexhaustible, and are not derived from his predecessors. They are subtle and obscure, and cannot be fully explained [1].

---

[1] The question of the genuineness of this paragraph has been touched on in vol. xxxix, p. 163. Whether from himself or from some disciple, it celebrates *K*wang-ʒze as the chief and most interesting of all ancient Tâoist writers.

7. Hui Shih[1] had many ingenious notions. His writings would fill five carriages; but his doctrines were erroneous and contradictory, and his words were wide of their mark. Taking up one thing after another, he would say:—'That which is so great that there is nothing outside it may be called the Great One; and that which is so small that there is nothing inside it may be called the Small One.' 'What has no thickness and will not admit of being repeated is 1000 lî in size[2].' 'Heaven may be as low as the earth.' 'A mountain may be as level as a marsh.' 'The sun in the meridian may be the sun declining.' 'A creature may be born to life and may die at the same time.' '(When it is said that) things greatly alike are different from things a little alike, this is what is called making little of agreements and differences; (when it is said that) all things are entirely alike or entirely different, this is what is called making much of agreements and differences.' 'The south is unlimited and yet has a limit.' 'I proceed to Yueh to-day and came to it yesterday.' 'Things which are joined together can be separated.' 'I know the centre of the world;—it is north of Yen or south of Yueh.' 'If all things be regarded with love, heaven and earth are of one body (with me).'

Hui Shih by such sayings as these made himself

[1] Introduced to us in the first Book of our author, and often mentioned in the intervening Books. He was not a Tâoist, but we are glad to have the account of him here given, as enabling us to understand better the intellectual life of China in *K*wang-ȝze's time.

[2] It is of little use trying to find the answers to these sayings of Hui Shih and others. They are only riddles or paradoxes.

very conspicuous throughout the kingdom, and was considered an able debater. All other debaters vied with one another and delighted in similar exhibitions. (They would say), 'There are feathers in an egg.' 'A fowl has three feet.' 'The kingdom belongs to Ying.' 'A dog might have been (called) a sheep.' 'A tadpole has a tail.' 'Fire is not hot.' 'A mountain gives forth a voice.' 'A wheel does not tread on the ground.' 'The eye does not see.' 'The finger indicates, but needs not touch, (the object).' 'Where you come to may not be the end.' 'The tortoise is longer than the snake.' 'The carpenter's square is not square.' 'A compass should not itself be round.' 'A chisel does not surround its handle.' 'The shadow of a flying bird does not (itself) move.' 'Swift as the arrowhead is, there is a time when it is neither flying nor at rest.' 'A dog is not a hound.' 'A bay horse and a black ox are three.' 'A white dog is black.' 'A motherless colt never had a mother.' 'If from a stick a foot long you every day take the half of it, in a myriad ages it will not be exhausted.'—It was in this way that the debaters responded to Hui Shih, all their lifetime, without coming to an end.

Hwan Twan[1] and Kung-sun Lung[2] were true members of this class. By their specious representations they threw a glamour over men's minds and altered their ideas. They vanquished men in argument, but could not subdue their minds, only keeping them in the enclosure of their sophistry. Hui Shih daily used his own knowledge and the arguments of others to propose strange theses to all debaters;—

[1] Elsewhere unknown.

[2] See Book XVII, par. 10.

such was his practice. At the same time he would talk freely of himself, thinking himself the ablest among them, and saying, 'In heaven or earth who is my match?' Shih maintained indeed his masculine energy, but he had not the art (of controversy).

In the south there was a man of extraordinary views, named Hwang Liâo[1], who asked him how it was that the sky did not fall nor the earth sink, and what was the cause of wind, rain, and the thunder's roll and crash. Shih made no attempt to evade the questions, and answered him without any exercise of thought, talking about all things, without pause, on and on without end; yet still thinking that his words were few, and adding to them the strangest observations. He thought that to contradict others was a real triumph, and wished to make himself famous by overcoming them; and on this account he was not liked by the multitude of debaters. He was weak in real attainment, though he might seem strong in comparison with others, and his way was narrow and dark. If we look at Hui Shih's ability from the standpoint of Heaven and Earth, it was only like the restless activity of a mosquito or gadfly; of what service was it to anything? To give its full development to any one capacity is a good thing, and he who does so is in the way to a higher estimation of the Tâo; but Hui Shih could find no rest for himself in doing this. He diffused himself over the world of things without satiety, till in the end he had only the reputation of being a skilful debater. Alas! Hui Shih, with

[1] Elsewhere unknown.

all his talents, vast as they were, made nothing out; he pursued all subjects and never came back (with success). It was like silencing an echo by his shouting, or running a race with his shadow. Alas!

THE THÂI-SHANG

TRACTATE OF ACTIONS AND THEIR RETRIBUTIONS.

THE THÂI-SHANG

TRACTATE OF ACTIONS AND THEIR RETRIBUTIONS[1].

1. The Thâi-Shang (Tractate) says, 'There are no special doors for calamity and happiness (in men's lot); they come as men themselves call them. Their recompenses follow good and evil as the shadow follows the substance[2].

The Thesis.

2. 'Accordingly, in heaven and earth[3] there are spirits that take account of men's transgressions, and, according to the lightness or gravity of their offences, take away from their term of life[4]. When that term is curtailed, men become poor and reduced, and meet with many sorrows and afflictions. All (other) men hate them; punishments and calamities attend them; good luck and occasions for felicitation shun them;

Machinery to secure retribution.

---

[1] See vol. xxxix, pp. 38–40.

[2] This paragraph, after the first three characters, is found in the Ȝo *Kh*wan, under the tenth and eleventh notices in the twenty-third year of duke Hsiang (B.C. 549),—part of an address to a young nobleman by the officer Min Ȝze-mâ. The only difference in the two texts is in one character which does not affect the meaning. Thus the text of this Tâoist treatise is taken from a source which cannot be regarded as Tâoistic.

[3] This seems equivalent to 'all through space.'

[4] The swan in the text here seems to mean 'the whole of the allotted term of life.' Further on, the same character has the special meaning of 'a period of a hundred days.'

evil stars send down misfortunes on them[1]. When their term of life is exhausted they die.

'There also are the Spirit-rulers in the three pairs of the Thâi stars of the Northern Bushel[2] over men's heads, which record their acts of guilt and wickedness, and take away (from their term of life) periods of twelve years or of a hundred days.

'There also are the three Spirits of the recumbent body which reside within a man's person[3]. As each kăng-shăn[4] day comes round, they forthwith ascend to the court of Heaven, and report men's deeds of guilt and transgression. On the last day of the moon, the spirit of the Hearth does the same[5].

'In the case of every man's transgressions, when they are great, twelve years are taken from his term of life; when they are small, a hundred days.

'Transgressions, great and small, are seen in several hundred things. He who wishes to seek for long life[6] must first avoid these.

---

[1] This and other passages show how Tâoism pressed astrology into its service.

[2] The Northern Peck or Bushel is the Chinese name of our constellation of the Great Bear, 'the Chariot of the Supreme Ruler.' The three pairs of stars, ι, κ; λ, μ; ν, ξ, are called the upper, middle, and lower Thâi, or 'their three Eminences:'—see Reeves's Names of Stars and Constellations, appended to Morrison's Dictionary, part ii, vol. i.

[3] The Khang-hsî Dictionary simply explains san shîh as 'the name of a spirit;' but the phrase is evidently plural. The names and places of the three spirits are given, and given differently. Why should we look for anything definite and satisfactory in a notion which is merely an absurd superstition?

[4] Kăng-shăn is the name of the fifty-seventh term of the cycle, indicating every fifty-seventh day, or year. Here it indicates the day.

[5] The name of this spirit of the fire-place is given by commentators with many absurd details which need not be touched on.

[6] Long life is still the great quest of the Tâoist.

3. 'Is his way right, he should go forward in it; is it wrong, he should withdraw from it.

The way of a good man.

'He will not tread in devious by-ways; he will not impose on himself in any secret apartment. He will amass virtue and accumulate deeds of merit. He will feel kindly towards (all) creatures[1]. He will be loyal, filial, loving to his younger brothers, and submissive to his elder. He will make himself correct and (so) transform others. He will pity orphans, and compassionate widows; he will respect the old and cherish the young. Even the insect tribes, grass, and trees he should not hurt.

'He ought to pity the malignant tendencies of others; to rejoice over their excellences; to help them in their straits; to rescue them from their perils; to regard their gains as if they were his own, and their losses in the same way; not to publish their shortcomings; not to vaunt his own superiorities; to put a stop to what is evil, and exalt and display what is good; to yield much, and take little for himself; to receive insult without resenting it, and honour with an appearance of apprehension; to bestow favours without seeking for a return, and give to others without any subsequent regret:—this is what is called a good man. All other men respect him; Heaven in its course protects him; happiness and emolument follow him; all evil things keep far from him; the spiritual Intelligences defend him; what he does is sure to succeed[2];

---

[1] In its widest meaning:—Men, creatures, and all living things.

[2] Here are the happy issues of doing good in addition to long life;—compare the Tâo Teh *K*ing, ch. 50, et al.

he may hope to become Immaterial and Immortal[1].

Happy issues of his course.

He who would seek to become an Immortal of Heaven[1] ought to give the proof of 1300 good deeds; and he who would seek to become an Immortal of Earth[1] should give the proof of three hundred.

4. 'But if the movements (of a man's heart) are contrary to righteousness, and the (actions of his) conduct are in opposition to reason; if he regard his wickedness as a proof of his ability, and can bear to do what is cruel and injurious; if he secretly harms the honest and good; if he treats with clandestine slight his ruler or parents; if he is disrespectful to his elders and teachers[2]; if he disregards the authority of those whom he should serve; if he deceives the simple; if he calumniates his fellow-learners; if he vent baseless slanders, practise deception and hypocrisy,

The way of a bad man.

[1] Here there appears the influence of Buddhism on the doctrine of the Tâo. The *Ri*shis of Buddhism are denoted in Chinese by Hsien *Z*ăn (仙人), which, for want of a better term, we translate by 'Immortals.' The famous Nâgâr*g*una, the fourteenth Buddhist patriarch, counts ten classes of these *Ri*shis, and ascribes to them only a temporary exemption for a million years from transmigration, but Chinese Buddhists and Tâoists view them as absolutely immortal, and distinguish five classes:—first, Deva *Ri*shis, or Heavenly Hsien, residing on the seven concentric rocks round Meru; second, Purusha, or Spirit-like Hsien, roaming through the air; third, Nara, or Human Hsien, dwelling among men; fourth, Bhûmi, or Earth Hsien, residing on earth in caves; and fifth, Preta, or Demon Hsien, roving demons. See Eitel's Handbook to Chinese Buddhism, second edition, p. 130. In this place three out of the five classes are specified, each having its own price in good deeds.

[2] Literally, 'those born before himself,' but generally used as a designation of teachers.

and attack and expose his kindred by consanguinity and affinity; if he is hard, violent, and without humanity; if he is ruthlessly cruel in taking his own way; if his judgments of right and wrong are incorrect; and his likings and aversions are in despite of what is proper; if he oppresses inferiors, and claims merit (for doing so); courts superiors by gratifying their (evil) desires; receives favours without feeling grateful for them; broods over resentments without ceasing; if he slights and makes no account of Heaven's people[1]; if he trouble and throw into disorder the government of the state; bestows rewards on the unrighteous and inflicts punishments on the guiltless; kills men in order to get their wealth, and overthrows men to get their offices; slays those who have surrendered, and massacres those who have made their submission; throws censure on the upright, and overthrows the worthy; maltreats the orphan and oppresses the widow; if he casts the laws aside and receives bribes; holds the right to be wrong and the wrong to be right; enters light offences as heavy; and the sight of an execution makes him more enraged (with the criminal); if he knows his faults and does not change them, or knows what is good and does not do it; throws the guilt of his crimes on others; if he tries to hinder the exercise of an art (for a living); reviles and slanders the sage and worthy; and assails and oppresses (the principles of) reason and virtue[2];

---

[1] A Confucian phrase. See the Lî *K*î, III, v, 13.

[2] One is sorry not to see his way to translate here—'Assails and oppresses those who pursue the Tâo and its characteristics.' Julien gives for it—'Insulter et traiter avec cruauté ceux qui se livrent à l'étude de la Raison et de la Vertu.' Watters

if he shoots birds and hunts beasts, unearths the burrowing insects and frightens roosting birds, blocks up the dens of animals and overturns nests, hurts the pregnant womb and breaks eggs; if he wishes others to have misfortunes and losses; and defames the merit achieved by others; if he imperils others to secure his own safety; diminishes the property of others to increase his own; exchanges bad things for good [1]; and sacrifices the public weal to his private advantage; if he takes credit to himself for the ability of others; conceals the excellences of others; publishes the things discreditable to others; and searches out the private affairs of others; leads others to waste their property and wealth; and causes the separation of near relatives [2]; encroaches on what others love; and assists others in doing wrong; gives the reins to his will and puts on airs of majesty; puts others to shame in seeking victory for himself; injures or destroys the growing crops of others; and breaks up projected marriages; if becoming rich by improper means makes him proud; and by a peradventure escaping the consequences of his misconduct, he yet feels no shame; if he owns to favours (which he did not confer), and puts off his errors (on others); marries away (his own) calamity to another, and sells (for gain) his own wickedness; purchases for himself empty praise; and keeps hidden dangerous purposes in his heart; detracts from the excel-

has—'Insults and oppresses (those who have attained to the practice of) Truth and Virtue.'

[1] It is a serious mistranslation of this which Mr. Balfour gives:—'returns evil for good,' as if it were the golden rule in its highest expression.

[2] Literally, 'separates men's bones and flesh.'

lences of others, and screens his own shortcomings; if he takes advantage of his dignity to practise intimidation, and indulges his cruelty to kill and wound; if without cause he (wastes cloth) in clipping and shaping it; cooks animals for food, when no rites require it; scatters and throws away the five grains; and burdens and vexes all living creatures; if he ruins the families of others, and gets possession of their money and valuables; admits the water or raises fire in order to injure their dwellings; if he throws into confusion the established rules in order to defeat the services of others; and injures the implements of others to deprive them of the things they require to use; if, seeing others in glory and honour, he wishes them to be banished or degraded; or seeing them wealthy and prosperous, he wishes them to be broken and scattered; if he sees a beautiful woman and forms the thought of illicit intercourse with her; is indebted to men for goods or money, and wishes them to die; if, when his requests and applications are not complied with, his anger vents itself in imprecations; if he sees others meeting with misfortune, and begins to speak of their misdeeds; or seeing them with bodily imperfections he laughs at them; or when their abilities are worthy of praise, he endeavours to keep them back; if he buries the image of another to obtain an injurious power over him[1]; or employs poison to kill trees; if he is indignant and angry with his instructors; or opposes and thwarts his

[1] The crimes indicated here are said to have become rife under the Han dynasty, when the arts of sorcery and witchcraft were largely employed to the injury of men.

father and elder brother; if he takes things by violence or vehemently demands them; if he loves secretly to pilfer, and openly to snatch; makes himself rich by plunder and rapine; or by artifice and deceit seeks for promotion; if he rewards and punishes unfairly; if he indulges in idleness and pleasure to excess; is exacting and oppressive to his inferiors; and tries to frighten other men; if he murmurs against Heaven and finds fault with men; reproaches the wind and reviles the rain; if he fights and joins in quarrels; strives and raises litigations; recklessly hurries to join associate fraternities; is led by the words of his wife or concubine to disobey the instructions of his parents; if, on getting what is new, he forgets the old; and agrees with his mouth, while he dissents in his heart; if he is covetous and greedy after wealth, and deceives and befools his superiors (to get it); if he invents wicked speeches to calumniate and overthrow the innocent; defames others and calls it being straightforward; reviles the Spirits and styles himself correct; if he casts aside what is according to right, and imitates what is against it; turns his back on his near relatives, and his face to those who are distant; if he appeals to Heaven and Earth to witness to the mean thoughts of his mind; or calls in the spiritual Intelligences to mark the filthy affairs of his life; if he gives and afterwards repents that he has done so; or borrows and does not return; if he plans and seeks for what is beyond his lot; or lays tasks (on people) beyond their strength; if he indulges his lustful desires without measure; if there be poison in his heart and mildness in his face; if he gives others filthy food to eat; or by corrupt doctrines deludes the multitude; if he uses a short cubit, a narrow measure, light weights, and a small pint; mixes spurious articles with the genuine; and (thus) amasses illicit gain; if he degrades (children or others of) decent condition to mean positions; or deceives and ensnares simple people; if he is insatiably covetous and greedy; tries by oaths and imprecations to prove himself correct; and in his liking for drink is rude and disorderly; if he quarrels angrily with his nearest relatives; and as a man he is not loyal and honourable; if a woman is not gentle and obedient; if (the husband) is not harmonious with his wife; if the wife does not reverence her husband; if he is always fond of boasting and bragging; if she is constantly jealous and envious; if he is guilty of improper conduct to his wife or sons; if she fails to behave properly to her parents-in-law; if he treats with slight and disrespect the spirits of his ancestors; if he opposes and rebels against the charge of his sovereign; if he occupies himself in doing what is of no use; and cherishes and keeps concealed a purpose other than what appears; if he utter imprecations against himself and against others (in the assertion of his innocence)[1]; or is partial in his likes and dislikes; if he strides over the well or the hearth; leaps over the food, or over a man[2]; kills newly-born children or brings about abortions[2]; if he does many actions of secret depravity; if he sings and dances on the

[1] The one illustrative story given by Julien under this clause shows clearly that I have rightly supplemented it. He translates it:—'Faire des imprécations contre soi-même et contre les autres.'

[2] Trifling acts and villainous crimes are here mixed together.

last day of the moon or of the year; bawls out or gets angry on the first day of the moon or in the early dawn; weeps, spits, or urinates, when fronting the north; sighs, sings, or wails, when fronting the fire-place; and moreover, if he takes fire from the hearth to burn incense; or uses dirty firewood to cook with; if he rises at night and shows his person naked; if at the eight terms of the year[1] he inflicts punishments; if he spits at a shooting star; points at a rainbow; suddenly points to the three luminaries; looks long at the sun and moon; in the months of spring burns the thickets in hunting; with his face to the north angrily reviles others; and without reason kills tortoises and smites snakes[2]:—

'In the case of crimes such as these, (the Spirits) presiding over the Life, according to their lightness or gravity, take away the culprit's periods of twelve years or of one hundred days. When his term of life is exhausted, death ensues. If at death there remains guilt unpunished, judgment extends to his posterity[3].

[1] The commencements of the four seasons, the equinoxes and solstices.

[2] Many of the deeds condemned in this long paragraph have a ground of reason for their condemnation; others are merely offences against prevailing superstitions.

[3] The principle enunciated here is very ancient in the history of the ethical teaching of China. It appears in one of the Appendixes to the Yî *K*ing (Sacred Books of the East, vol. xvi, p. 419), 'The family that accumulates goodness is sure to have superabundant happiness; the family that accumulates evil is sure to have superabundant misery.' We know also that the same view prevailed in the time of Confucius, though the sage himself does not expressly sanction it. This Tractate does not go for the issues of Retribution beyond the present life.

5. 'Moreover, when parties by wrong and violence take the money of others, an account is taken, and set against its amount, of their wives and children, and all the members of their families, when these gradually die. If they do not die, there are the disasters from water, fire, thieves, and robbers, from losses of property, illnesses, and (evil) tongues to balance the value of their wicked appropriations[1]. Further, those who wrongfully kill men are (only) putting their weapons into the hands of others who will in their turn kill them[2].

Conclusion of the whole matter.

'To take to one's self unrighteous wealth is like satisfying one's hunger with putrid food[3], or one's thirst with poisoned wine. It gives a temporary relief, indeed, but death also follows it.

'Now when the thought of doing good has arisen in a man's mind, though the good be not yet done, the good Spirits are in attendance on him. Or, if the thought of doing evil has arisen, though the evil be not yet done, the bad Spirits are in attendance on him.

'If one have, indeed, done deeds of wickedness, but afterwards alters his way and repents, resolved not to do anything wicked, but to practise reverently

[1] These sentences are rather weak. Nothing is said of any recompense to the parties who have been robbed. The thief is punished by the death of others, or the loss of property.

[2] A somewhat perplexing sentence. Julien gives for it:—'Ceux qui font périr des hommes innocens ressemblent à des ennemis qui échangent leurs armes et se tuent les uns les autres;' and Watters:—'Those who put others to death wrongly are like men who exchange arms and slay each other.'

[3] Literally, 'soaked food that has been spoiled by dripping water.'

all that is good, he is sure in the long-run to obtain good fortune :—this is called changing calamity into blessing. Therefore the good man speaks what is good, contemplates what is good, and does what is good; every day he has these three virtues :—at the end of three years Heaven is sure to send down blessing on him[1]. The bad man speaks what is wicked, contemplates what is wicked, and does what is wicked; every day he has these three vices :—at the end of three years, Heaven is sure to send down misery on him[1].—How is it that men will not exert themselves to do what is good?'

[1] The effect of repentance and reformation is well set forth; but the specification of three years, as the period within which the recompense or retribution will occur, is again an indication of the weakness in this concluding paragraph.

APPENDIXES.

APPENDIX I.

Khing Kăng King, or 'The Classic of Purity[1].'

So I must translate the title of this brochure, as it appears in the 'Collection of the Most Important Treatises of the Tâoist Fathers' (vol. xxxix, p. xvii), in which alone I have had an opportunity of perusing and studying the Text. The name, as given by Wylie (Notes, p. 178), Balfour (Tâoist Texts), and Faber (China Review, vol. xiii, p. 246), is *Khing King King*[2], and signifies 'The Classic of Purity and Rest.' The difference is in the second character, but both *Khing Kăng* and *Khing King* are well-known combinations in Tâoist writings; and it will be seen, as the translation of the Text is pursued, that neither of them is unsuitable as the title of the little Book.

It is, as Dr. Faber says, one of the 'mystical canons' of Tâoism; but the mysticism of Tâoism is of a nature peculiar to itself, and different from any mental exercises which have been called by that name in connexion with Christianity or Mohammedanism. It is more vague and shadowy than any theosophy or Sûfism, just as the idea of the Tâo differs from the apprehension of a personal God, however uncertain and indefinite that apprehension may be. Mr. Wylie says the work 'treats under very moderate limits of the subjection of the mental faculties.' This indeed is the consummation to which it conducts the student; a

---

[1] 清淨經. [2] 清靜經.

condition corresponding to the nothingness which Lâo-ȝze contended for as antecedent to all positive existence, and out of which he said that all existing being came, though he does not indicate how.

I give to the Treatise the first place among our appendixes here because of the early origin ascribed to it. It is attributed to Ko Yüan (or Hsüan)[1], a Tâoist of the Wû dynasty (A. D. 222–277), who is fabled to have attained to the state of an Immortal, and is generally so denominated[2]. He is represented as a worker of miracles; as addicted to intemperance, and very eccentric in his ways. When shipwrecked on one occasion, he emerged from beneath the water with his clothes unwet, and walked freely on its surface. Finally he ascended to the sky in bright day[3]. All these accounts may safely be put down as the figments of a later time.

It will be seen that the Text ascribes the work to Lâo-ȝze himself, and I find it impossible to accept the account of its origin which is assigned by Lî Hsî-yüeh to Ko Hsüan. As quoted by Lî in the first of some notes subjoined to his Commentary, Ko is made to say, 'When I obtained the true Tâo, I had recited this *K*ing ten thousand times. It is what the Spirits of heaven practise, and had not been communicated to scholars of this lower world. I got it from the Divine Ruler of the eastern Hwa; he received it from the Divine Ruler of the Golden Gate; he received it from the Royal-mother of the West. In all these cases it was transmitted from mouth to mouth, and was not committed to writing. I now, while I am in the world, have written it out in a book. Scholars of the highest order, understanding it, ascend and become officials of Heaven; those of the middle order, cultivating it, are ranked among the Immortals of the Southern Palace; those of the lowest order, possessing it, get long years of life in the world, roam

---

[1] 葛元 or 葛玄. [2] 葛仙公.

[3] See the Accounts of Ko in the Biographical Dictionary of Hsiâo *K*ih-han (1793), and Wang *Kh*î's supplement to the great work of Mâ Twan-lin, ch. 242.

through the Three Regions[1], and (finally) ascend to, and enter, the Golden Gate.'

This quotation would seem to be taken from the preface to our little classic by Ho Hsüan. If there were indeed such a preface during the time of the Wû dynasty, the corruption of the old Tâoism must have been rapid. The Hsî Wang-mû, or Royal-mother of the West, is mentioned once in *K*wang-ȝze (Bk. VI, par. 7); but no 'Divine Ruler' disfigures his pages. Every reader must feel that in the Classic of Purity he has got into a different region of thought from that which he has traversed in the Tâo Teh *K*ing and in the writings of *K*wang-ȝze.

With these remarks I now proceed to the translation and explanation of the text of our *K*ing.

Ch. 1. 1. Lâo the Master[1] said, The Great[2] Tâo has no bodily form, but It produced and nourishes heaven and earth[3]. The Great Tâo has no passions[4], but It causes the sun and moon to revolve as they do.

The Great[2] Tâo has no name[5], but It effects the growth and maintenance of all things[3].

I do not know its name, but I make an effort, and call It the Tâo[6].

[1] The name here is Lâo *K*ün (老君). I have stated (vol. xxxix, p. 40) that, with the addition of Thâi Shang, this is the common designation of Lâo-ȝze as the Father of Tâoism and deifying him, and that it originated probably in the Thang dynasty. It might seem to be used simply here by Ko Hsüan with the same high application; and since in his preface he refers to different 'Divine Rulers,' it may be contended that we ought to translate Lâo *K*ün by 'Lâo the Ruler.' But I am unwilling to think that the deification of Lâo-ȝze

[1] 'The three regions (三界)' here can hardly be the trilokya of the Buddhists, the ethical categories of desire, form, and formlessness. They are more akin to the Brahmanic bhuvanatraya, the physical or cosmological categories of bhûr or earth, bhuva*h* or heaven, and svar or atmosphere.

had taken place so early. The earliest occurrence of the combination Lâo *K*ün which has attracted my notice is in the history of Khung Yung, a descendant of Confucius in the twentieth generation,—the same who is celebrated in the San 3ze *K*ing, for his fraternal deference at the age of four, and who met with a violent death in A. D. 208. While still only a boy, wishing to obtain an interview with a representative of the Lâo family, he sent in this message to him, 'My honoured predecessor and the honoured Lâo, the predecessor of your Lî family, equally virtuous and righteous, were friends and teachers of each other.' The epithet *K*ün is equally applied to Confucius and Lâo-ȝze, and the combination Lâo *K*ün implies no exaltation of the latter above the other.

[2] See Tâo Teh *K*ing, chaps. 18, 25, 53.

[3] T. T. *K*., chaps. 1, 51, et al.

[4] See *K*wang-ȝze, Bk. II, par. 2. 'Passions,' that is, feelings, affections; as in the first of the thirty-nine Articles.

[5] T. T. *K*., chaps. 1, 25, 32, 51.

[6] T. T. *K*., ch. 25.

2. Now, the Tâo (shows itself in two forms); the Pure and the Turbid, and has (the two conditions of) Motion and Rest[1]. Heaven is pure and earth is turbid; heaven moves and earth is at rest. The masculine is pure and the feminine is turbid; the masculine moves and the feminine is still[2]. The radical (Purity) descended, and the (turbid) issue flowed abroad; and thus all things were produced[1].

The pure is the source of the turbid, and motion is the foundation of rest.

If man could always be pure and still, heaven and earth would both revert (to non-existence)[3].

[1] This paragraph is intended to set forth 'the production of all things;' but it does so in a way that is hardly intelligible. Comparing what is said here with the utterances in the former paragraph, Tâo would seem to be used in two

senses; first as an Immaterial Power or Force, and next as the Material Substance, out of which all things come. Lî Hsî-yüeh says that in the first member of par. 1 we have 'the Unlimited (or Infinite) producing the Grand (or Primal) Finite.' On the Tâo in par. 2 he says nothing. The fact is that the subject of creation in the deepest sense of the name is too high for the human mind.

[2] Compare T. T. *K.*, ch. 61.

[3] I do not understand this, but I cannot translate the Text otherwise. Mr. Balfour has:—'If a man is able to remain pure and motionless, Heaven and Earth will both at once come and dwell in him.' Lî explains thus:—天清地靜, 一齊返入於無矣. Compare T. T. *K.*, ch. 16, and especially Ho-shang Kung's title to it,—歸根.

3. Now the spirit of man loves Purity, but his mind[1] disturbs it. The mind of man loves stillness, but his desires draw it away[1]. If he could always send his desires away, his mind would of itself become still. Let his mind be made clean, and his spirit will of itself become pure.

As a matter of course the six desires[2] will not arise, and the three poisons[3] will be taken away and disappear.

[1] Tâoism thus recognises in man the spirit, the mind, and the body.

[2] 'The six desires' are those which have their inlets in the eyes, ears, nostrils, the tongue, the sense of touch, and the imagination. The two last are expressed in Chinese by shăn, 'the body,' and î, 'the idea, or thought.'

[3] 'The three poisons' are greed, anger, and stupidity;—see the Khang-hsî Thesaurus, under 毒.

4. The reason why men are not able to attain to this, is because their minds have not been cleansed, and their desires have not been sent away.

If one is able to send the desires away, when he then looks in at his mind, it is no longer his; when he looks out at his body, it is no longer his; and when he looks farther off at external things, they are things which he has nothing to do with.

When he understands these three things, there will appear to him only vacancy. This contemplation of vacancy will awaken the idea of vacuity. Without such vacuity there is no vacancy.

The idea of vacuous space having vanished, that of nothingness itself also disappears; and when the idea of nothingness has disappeared, there ensues serenely the condition of constant stillness.

In this paragraph we have what Mr. Wylie calls 'the subjection of the mental faculties;' and I must confess myself unable to understand what it is. It is probably another way of describing the Tâoist trance which we find once and again in *K*wang-ȝze, 'when the body becomes like a withered tree, and the mind like slaked lime' (Bk. II, par. 1, et al.). But such a sublimation of the being, as the characteristic of its serene stillness and rest, is to me inconceivable.

5. In that condition of rest independently of place how can any desire arise? And when no desire any longer arises, there is the True stillness and rest.

That True (stillness) becomes (a) constant quality, and responds to external things (without error); yea, that True and Constant quality holds possession of the nature.

In such constant response and constant stillness there is the constant Purity and Rest.

He who has this absolute Purity enters gradually into the (inspiration of the) True Tâo. And having entered thereinto, he is styled Possessor of the Tâo.

Although he is styled Possessor of the Tâo, in reality he does not think that he has become possessed of anything. It is as accomplishing the transformation of all living things, that he is styled Possessor of the Tâo.

He who is able to understand this may transmit to others the Sacred Tâo.

This is the consummation of the state of Purity. In explaining the former sentence of the fifth member, Lî Hsî-yüeh uses the characters of T. T. *K*., ch. 4, 道冲而用之或不盈, with some variation,—冲而用之, 不自滿假.

2. 1. Lâo the Master said, Scholars of the highest class do not strive (for anything); those of the lowest class are fond of striving[1]. Those who possess in the highest degree the attributes (of the Tâo) do not show them; those who possess them in a low degree hold them fast (and display them)[2]. Those who so hold them fast and display them are not styled (Possessors of) the Tâo and Its attributes[2].

[1] Compare the T. T. *K*., ch. 41, 1.
[2] Compare the T. T. *K*., ch. 38, 1.

2. The reason why all men do not obtain the True Tâo is because their minds are perverted. Their minds being perverted, their spirits become perturbed. Their minds being perturbed, they are attracted towards external things. Being attracted towards external things, they begin to seek for them greedily. This greedy quest leads to perplexities and annoyances; and these again result in disordered

thoughts, which cause anxiety and trouble to both body and mind. The parties then meet with foul disgraces, flow wildly on through the phases of life and death, are liable constantly to sink in the sea of bitterness, and for ever lose the True Tâo.

3. The True and Abiding Tâo! They who understand it naturally obtain it. And they who come to understand the Tâo abide in Purity and Stillness.

Our brief Classic thus concludes, and our commentator Lî thus sums up his remarks on it:—'The men who understand the Tâo do so simply by means of the Absolute Purity, and the acquiring this Absolute Purity depends entirely on the Putting away of Desire, which is the urgent practical lesson of the Treatise.'

I quoted in my introductory remarks Lî's account of the origin of the Classic by its reputed author Ko Hsüan. I will now conclude with the words which he subjoins from 'a True Man, Ʒo Hsüan:'—'Students of the Tâo, who keep this Classic in their hands and croon over its contents, will get good Spirits from the ten heavens to watch over and protect their bodies, after which their spirits will be preserved by the seal of jade, and their bodies refined by the elixir of gold. Both body and spirit will become exquisitely ethereal, and be in true union with the Tâo!'

Of this 'True Man, Ʒo Hsüan,' I have not been able to ascertain anything. The Divine Ruler of the eastern Hwa, referred to on p. 248, is mentioned in the work of Wang *Kh*î (ch. 241, p. 21b), but with no definite information about him. The author says his surname was Wang, but he knows neither his name nor when he lived.

APPENDIX II.

Yin Fû *K*ing, or 'Classic of the Harmony of the Seen and the Unseen.'

In the *Kh*ien-lung Catalogue of the Imperial Library, ch. 146, Part iii, this Book occupies the first place among all Tâoist works, with three notices, which all precede the account of Ho-shang Kung's Commentary on the Tâo Teh *K*ing. From the work of Lâo-ȝze we are conducted along the course of Tâoist literature to the year 1626, when the catalogue of what is called 'the Tâoist Canon[1]' appeared. Ch. 147 then returns to the Yin Fû *K*ing, and treats of nine other works upon it, the last being the Commentary of Lî Kwang-lî, one of the principal ministers and great scholars in the time of *Kh*ien-lung's grandfather, known as Khang-hsî from the name of his reign.

In the first of these many notices it is said that the preface of an old copy assigns the composition of the work to Hwang-Tî (in the 27th century B.C.), and says that commentaries on it had been made by Thâi-kung (12th century B.C.), Fan Lî (5th century B.C.), the Recluse of the Kwei Valley (4th century B.C.), *K*ang Liang (died B.C. 189), *K*û Ko Liang (A.D. 181–234), and Lî *Kh*wan of the Thang dynasty (about the middle of our 8th century)[2]. Some writers, going back to the time of Hwang-Tî for the composition of our small classic, attribute it not to that sovereign himself, but to his teacher Kwang *Kh*ăng-ȝze[3];

---

[1] 道藏目錄詳註.

[2] See also Mâ Twan-lin's great work, ch. 211, p. 18a.

[3] See *K*wang-ȝze, Bk. XI, par. 4.

and many of them hold that this Kwang *Kh*ăng-ȝze was an early incarnation of Lâo-ȝze himself, so that the Yin Fû might well be placed before the Tâo Teh *K*ing! Lî Hsî-yüeh is one of the scholars who adopt this view.

I will not say that under the *K*âu dynasty there was no book called Yin Fû, with a commentary ascribed to Thâi-kung[1], for Sze-mâ *Kh*ien, in his biography of Sû *Kh*in (Bk. lxix), relates how that adventurer obtained 'the Yin Fû book of *K*âu,' and a passage in the 'Plans of the Warring States' tells us that the book contained 'the schemes of Thâi-kung[1].' However this may have been, no such work is now extant. Of all the old commentaries on it mentioned in the *Kh*ien-lung Catalogue, the only one remaining is the last,—that of Lî *Kh*wan; and the account which we have of it is not to be readily accepted and relied on.

The story goes that in A. D. 441 Khâu *Kh*ien-*k*ih, who had usurped the dignity and title of Patriarch from the *K*ang family, deposited a copy of the Yin Fû *K*ing in a mountain cave. There it remained for about three centuries and a half, till it was discovered by Lî *Kh*wan, a Tâoist scholar, not a little damaged by its long exposure. He copied it out as well as he could, but could not understand it, till at last, wandering in the distant West, he met with an old woman, who made the meaning clear to him, at the foot of mount Lî; after which he published the Text with a Commentary, and finally died, a wanderer among the hills in quest of the Tâo; but the place of his death was never known[2].

The Classic, as it now exists, therefore cannot be traced higher than our eighth century; and many critics hold that, as the commentary was made by Lî *Kh*wan, so the text was forged by him. All that Hsî-yüeh has to say in reply to this is that, if the classic be the work of Lî *Kh*wan, then

[1] See the Khang-hsî Thesaurus under the combination Yin Fû.

[2] See the account of Lî *Kh*wan in Wang *Kh*î's continuation of Mâ Twan-lin's work, ch. 242; and various items in the *Kh*ien-lung Catalogue.

he must think of him as another Kwang *Kh*ăng-ʒze; but this is no answer to the charge of forgery.

As to the name of the Treatise, the force of Fû has been set forth in vol. xxxix, p. 133, in connexion with the title of *K*wang-ʒze's fifth Book. The meaning which I have given of the whole is substantially that of Lî Hsî-yüeh, who says that the Yin must be understood as including Yang, and grounds his criticism on the famous dictum in the Great Appendix to the Yî *K*ing (vol. xvi, p. 355), 'The successive movement of the Yin and Yang (their rest and active operation) constitutes what is called the course (of things).' Mr. Balfour translates the title by 'The Clue to the Unseen,' which is ingenious, but may be misleading. The writer reasons rather from the Unseen to the Seen than from the Seen to the Unseen.

Mr. Wylie gives his view of the object of the Treatise in these words:—'This short Treatise, which is not entirely free from the obscurity of Tâoist mysticism, professes to reconcile the decrees of Heaven with the current of mundane affairs.' To what extent the Book does this, and whether successfully or not, the reader will be able to judge for himself from the translation which will be immediately subjoined. Lî Hsî-yüeh, looking at it simply from its practical object, pronounces it 'hsiû lien *k*ih Shû, a Book of culture and refining[1].' This language suggests the idea of a Tâoist devotee, who has sublimated himself by the study of this Book till he is ready to pass into the state of an Immortal. I must be permitted to say, however, that the whole Treatise appears to me to have come down to us in a fragmentary condition, with passages that are incapable of any satisfactory explanation.

Ch. 1. 1. If one observes the Way of Heaven[1], and maintains Its doings (as his own)[2], all that he has to do is accomplished.

[1] Dr. Williams explains 'hsiû lien (修鍊 or 修煉)' as meaning 'becoming religious, as a recluse or ascetic.'

[1] To explain 'the Way of Heaven,' Lî Hsî-yüeh adduces the last sentence of the T. T. *K*., ch. 9, 'When the work is done, and one's name has become distinguished, to withdraw into obscurity is the Way of Heaven.'

[2] To explain 'the doings of Heaven,' he adduces the first paragraph of the symbolism of the first hexagram of the Yî, 'Heaven in its motion gives the idea of strength. In accordance with this, the superior man nerves himself to ceaseless activity.'

2. To Heaven there belong the five (mutual) foes [1], and he who sees them (and understands their operation) apprehends how they produce prosperity. The same five foes are in the mind of man, and when he can set them in action after the manner of Heaven, all space and time are at his disposal, and all things receive their transformations from his person [2].

[1] The startling name thieves (= foes, robbers) here is understood to mean the 'five elements,' which pervade and indeed make up the whole realm of nature, the heaven of the text including also earth, the other term in the binomial combination of 'heaven and earth.' According to the Tâoist teaching, the element of Earth generates Metal, and overcomes Water; Metal generates Water, and overcomes Wood; Water generates Wood, and overcomes Fire; Wood generates Fire, and overcomes Earth. These elements fight and strive together, now overcoming, now overcome, till by such interaction a harmony of their influences arises, and production goes on with vigour and beauty.

[2] It is more difficult to give an account of the operation of the five elements in the mind of man, though I have seen them distributed among the five viscera, and the five virtues of Benevolence, Righteousness, Propriety, Knowledge, and Faith. Granting, however, their presence and operation in the mind, what shall be said on the two concluding members of the paragraph? There underlies them

the doctrine of the three coordinate Powers;—Heaven, Earth, and Man, which I have never been able to comprehend clearly.

3. The nature of Heaven belongs (also) to Man; the mind of Man is a spring (of power). When the Way of Heaven is established, the (Course of) Man is thereby determined.

These short and enigmatic sentences seem merely to affirm the general subject of the Treatise,—the harmony between the unseen and the seen.

4. When Heaven puts forth its power of putting to death, the stars and constellations lie hidden in darkness. When Earth puts forth its power of putting to death, dragons and serpents appear on the dry ground. When Man puts forth his power of putting to death, Heaven and Earth resume their (proper course). When Heaven and Man exert their powers in concert, all transformations have their commencements determined.

'The power of putting to death here' seems merely to indicate the 'rest' which succeeds to movement. The paragraph is intended to show us the harmony of the Three Powers, but one only sees its meaning darkly. The language of the third sentence about the influence of Man on Heaven and Earth finds its explanation from the phraseology of the thwan of the twenty-fourth hexagram of the Yî (vol. xvi, pp. 107, 108).

5. The nature (of man) is here clever and there stupid; and the one of these qualities may lie hidden in the other. The abuse of the nine apertures is (chiefly) in the three most important, which may be now in movement and now at rest. When fire arises in wood, the evil, having once begun, is sure to go on to the destruction of the wood. When

calamity arises in a state, if thereafter movement ensue, it is sure to go to ruin.

When one conducts the work of culture and refining wisely we call him a Sage.

The constitution of man is twofold;—his mental constitution, quiet and restful, and his physical constitution, restless and fond of movement. The nine apertures are the eyes, ears, nostrils, mouth, and the lower parts, and of these the eyes, ears, and mouth are the most important; but they all need to be kept in subjection and under restraint. If indulged beyond reason, the ruin of themselves and of the mind and body to which they belong is sure to ensue.

2. 1. For Heaven now to give life and now to take it away is the method of the Tâo. Heaven and Earth are the despoilers of all things; all things are the despoilers of Man; and Man is the despoiler of all things. When the three despoilers act as they ought to do, as the three Powers, they are at rest. Hence it is said, 'During the time of nourishment, all the members are properly regulated; when the springs of motion come into play, all transformations quietly take place.'

Compare ch. 1, par. 2. The mutual contention of the five elements in nature only conduces to the nourishment of all its parts; and so man, as one of the three Powers, consumes only to increase his store, and throws down only to build up.

Where the concluding quotation is taken from is not known. Of course any quotation is inconsistent with the idea of the early origin of the Treatise.

2. Men know the mysteriousness of the Spirit's (action), but they do not know how what is not Spiritual comes to be so. The sun and moon have their definite times, and their exact measures as

large and small. The service of the sages hereupon arises, and the spiritual intelligence becomes apparent.

Compare par. 10 in the fifth Appendix to the Yî *K*ing.

3. The spring by which the despoilers are moved is invisible and unknown to all under the sky. When the superior man has got it, he strengthens his body by it; when the small man has got it, he makes light of his life.

The thing is good in itself, but its effect will be according to the character of its user, and of the use which is made of it.

3. 1. The blind hear well, and the deaf see well. To derive all that is advantageous from one source is ten times better than the employment of a host; to do this thrice in a day and night is a myriad times better.

That the loss of one sense may be in a manner compensated for by the greater cultivation of another,—in the case especially of the two senses specified,—is a fact; but I fail to perceive how this is illustrated by what follows in the rest of the paragraph. The illustration is taken from the seventh of the hexagrams in the Yî, but I have not discovered the nexus of it in the text of that classic or in the Appendixes on the thwan or hsiang of the hexagram.

It must be from this paragraph that the bearing of the Treatise on the conduct of military operations has been maintained.

2. The mind is quickened (to activity) by (external) things, and dies through (excessive pursuit of) them. The spring (of the mind's activity) is in the eyes.

Heaven has no (special feeling of) kindness, but so it is that the greatest kindness comes from It.

The crash of thunder and the blustering wind both come without design.

Mr. Balfour translates the first member here by—'The mind is produced from matter and dies with matter; the working faculty is in the eye;' and says that it embodies a bold denial of any future life, or the existence of spirit, apart from matter. The meaning of the Text, however, is only what I have given;—is moral and not metaphysical. The eye is singled out from the three most important apertures of the body in ch. 1, par. 5.

The rest of the paragraph has its parallelisms in Lâo-ʒze and *K*wang-ʒze.

3. Perfect enjoyment is the overflowing satisfaction of the nature. Perfect stillness is the entire disinterestedness of it. When Heaven seems to be most wrapt up in Itself, Its operation is universal in its character.

A sequel to the preceding paragraph. Lî Hsî-yüeh observes that the having no feeling of kindness is equivalent to Lâo-ʒze's 'doing nothing.' See the T. T. *K*., ch. 35, 'The Tâo does nothing, and so there is nothing which It does not do.'

4. It is by its breath that we control whatever creature we grasp. Life is the root of death, and death is the root of life. Kindness springs from injury, and injury springs from kindness. He who sinks himself in water or enters amidst fire brings destruction on himself.

The first member of this paragraph is very difficult to construe. Mr. Balfour gives for it:—'The Laws affecting the animal creation reside in the Breath or Vital Fluid.' The first character of it properly denotes 'birds.' It is often found with another denoting 'quadrupeds;' and again it is found alone denoting both birds and beasts. It is also interchanged with another of the same name, denoting 'to seize or grasp,' in which meaning I have taken it; but the bearing of the saying on the general meaning of the Treatise I have not apprehended.

The next four sayings are illustrations of Lâo-ȝze's 'contraries' of Tâoism. The final saying is a truism;—is it introduced here as illustrating that whatever is done with design is contrary to the Tâo?

5. The stupid man by studying the phenomena and laws of heaven and earth becomes sage; I by studying their times and productions become intelligent. He in his stupidity is perplexed about sageness; I in my freedom from stupidity am the same. He considers his sageness as being an extraordinary attainment; I do not consider mine so.

Some scholars have expunged this paragraph as not being genuine; it is certainly difficult to construe and to understand.

6. The method of spontaneity proceeds in stillness, and so it was that heaven, earth, and all things were produced. The method of heaven and earth proceeds gently and gradually, and thus it is that the Yin and Yang overcome (each other by turns). The one takes the place of the other, and so change and transformation proceed accordingly.

*K*û Hsî praises this paragraph as very good, and the use of the character Ȝin ('proceeds gently and gradually') as exquisite. After all, what do we learn from it? That Creation proceeded without striving or crying? And that the same Creative Power continues to act in the same way?

7. Therefore the sages, knowing that the method of spontaneity cannot be resisted, take action accordingly and regulate it (for the purpose of culture). The way of perfect stillness cannot be subjected to numerical calculations; but it would seem that there

is a wonderful machinery, by which all the heavenly bodies are produced, the eight diagrams, and the sexagenary cycle; spirit-like springs of power, and hidden ghostlinesses; the arts of the Yin and Yang in the victories of the one over the other:—all these come brightly forward into visibility.

I cannot say that I fully understand this concluding paragraph of the Yin Fû *K*ing. One thing is plain from it,—how the Yî *K*ing was pressed into the service of the Tâoism that prevailed when it was written. I leave it with the judgment on it, quoted by Lî Hsî-yüeh from a Lû Ȝhien-hsü. 'The subject-matter of the Yin Fû and Tâo Teh is all intended to set forth the action by contraries of the despoiling powers in nature and society. As to finding in them directions for the government of states, the conduct of war, and the mastery of the kingdom, with such expressions as those about a wonderful machinery by which the heavenly bodies are produced, the eight diagrams, the cycle, spirit-like springs, and hidden ghostlinesses:—they all have a deep meaning, but men do not know it. They who go to the Yin Fû for direction in war and use Lâo-ȝze for guidance in government go far astray from the meaning of both.'

APPENDIX III.

Yü Shû *K*ing, or 'The Classic of the Pivot of Jade.'

Mr. Wylie says (Notes, p. 179) that the Pivot of Jade is much used in the ritual services of Tâoism, meaning that it is frequently read in the assemblies of its monks. The object of the Treatise, according to Lî Hsî-yüeh, is 'to teach men to discipline and refine their spirit;' and he illustrates the name by referring to the North Star, which is called 'the Pivot of the Sky,' revolving in its place, and carrying round with it all the other heavenly bodies. So the body of man is carried round his spirit and by it, and when the spirit has been disciplined and refined, till it is freed from every obscuring influence, and becomes solid, soft, and strong as jade, the name, 'the Pivot of Jade,' is appropriate to it.

The name of the Treatise, when given at full length, is—'The True Classic of the Pivot of Jade, delivered by the Heaven-Honoured One, Who produces Universal Transformation by the Sound of His Thunder.' To this personage, as Wylie observes, the Tâoists attribute a fabulous antiquity, but there is little doubt that the author was a Hsüan-yang 3ze, about the time of the Yüan dynasty (A. D. 1280–1367). From the work of Wang *K*hî (ch. 243), we learn that this Hsüan-yang 3ze was the denomination of Âu-yang Yü-yüen, a scion of the famous Âu-yang family. What he says is to the following effect:—

1. The Heaven-honoured One says, 'All you, Heaven-endowed men, who wish to be instructed

about the Perfect Tâo, the Perfect Tâo is very recondite, and by nothing else but Itself can it be described. Since ye wish to hear about it, ye cannot do so by the hearing of the ear:—that which eludes both the ears and eyes is the True Tâo; what can be heard and seen perishes, and only this survives. There is (much) that you have not yet learned, and especially you have not acquired this! Till you have learned what the ears do not hear, how can the Tâo be spoken about at all?'

'Heaven-honoured (Thien Ȝun)' is a title given by the Tâoists to the highest objects of their reverence and worship. Chalmers translates it by 'Celestial Excellency,' and observes that it is given to 'all the Three Pure Ones;' but its application is much more extensive, as its use in this Treatise sufficiently proves. No doubt it was first adopted after the example of the Buddhists, by whom Buddha is styled 'World-honoured,' or 'Ever-honoured' (Shih Ȝun).

The phrase Thien *Z*ăn, which I have translated here 'Heaven-endowed Men,' is common to the three religions of China; but the meaning of it is very different in each. See the Confucian and the Tâoist significations of it in the Khang-hsî Thesaurus, under the phrase. Here it means 'the men possessed by the Tâo;—Tâo-*Z*ăn of the highest class.' In a Buddhist treatise the meaning would be 'Ye, devas and men.'

2. The Heaven-honoured One says, 'Sincerity is the first step towards (the knowledge of) the Tâo; it is by silence that that knowledge is maintained; it is with gentleness that (the Tâo) is employed. The employment of sincerity looks like stupidity; the employment of silence looks like difficulty of utterance; the employment of gentleness looks like want of ability. But having attained to this, you may

forget all bodily form; you may forget your personality; you may forget that you are forgetting.'

'All this,' says Lî Hsî-yüeh, 'is the achievement of vacuity, an illustration of the freedom from purpose which is characteristic of the Tâo.' Compare par. 14 in the sixth Book of *K*wang-ȝze.

3. 'He who has taken the first steps towards (the knowledge of) the Tâo knows where to stop; he who maintains the Tâo in himself knows how to be diligently vigilant; he who employs It knows what is most subtle.

'When one knows what is most subtle, the light of intelligence grows (around him); when he can know how to be diligently vigilant, his sage wisdom becomes complete; when he knows where to stop, he is grandly composed and restful.

'When he is grandly composed and restful, his sage wisdom becomes complete; when his sage wisdom becomes complete, the light of intelligence grows (around him); when the light of intelligence grows around him, he is one with the Tâo.

'This is the condition which is styled the True Forgetfulness;—a forgetting which does not forget; a forgetting of what cannot be forgotten.

'That which cannot be forgotten is the True Tâo. The Tâo is in heaven and earth, but heaven and earth are not conscious of It. Whether It seem to have feelings or to be without them, It is (always) one and the same.'

4. The Heaven-honoured One says, 'While I am in this world, what shall I do to benefit life? I occupy myself with this subtle and precious Treatise for the good of you, Heaven-endowed men. Those

who understand it will be allowed to ascend to the happy seats of the Immortals.

'Students of the Tâo believe that there are (the influences of) the ether and of destiny. But the (conditions of) climate being different, the constitutions received by men are naturally different, and hence they are ascribed to the ether. And the (conditions of) wisdom and stupidity being different, their constitutions as fine and coarse are naturally different, and hence they are ascribed to the destiny. The destiny depends on fate; the ether depends on Heaven.

'The restraints arising from the ether and destiny are the manacles decreed by Heaven. But if one acquire the True Tâo, though stupid, he may become wise; though coarse, he may become fine;—if there only be the decree of fate.

'Stupidity the darkest, and coarseness the densest, are consequences of climate; but the suffering of them and the changing of them may take place, when Heaven and Earth quicken the motive spring. When this is done without the knowledge of men, it is said to take place spontaneously. If it be done with a consciousness of that want of knowledge, it is still said to take place spontaneously. The mystery of spontaneity is greater than that of knowledge; but how it comes to be what it is remains a thing unknown. But as to the Tâo, It has not begun to come under the influence of what makes stupid and coarse. Hear this all ye Heaven (-endowed) men; and let all the multitude in all quarters rejoice.'

It may be considered as a proof of the difficulty of the Text that to this long paragraph Lî Hsî-yüeh does not subjoin a single explanatory remark.

APPENDIX IV.

*Z*ăh Yung *K*ing, or 'Classic of the Directory for a Day.'

I have nowhere found any mention of the author of this brief composition, or of its date. The use of Buddhistic expressions in it shows that it cannot have had a very early origin. It belongs to the same category of Tâoist writings as the *Kh*ing *K*ăng *K*ing, which is the first of these appendixes. Lî Hsî-yüeh says, 'The Treatise is called "the Directory for a Day," as showing that during all the hours (the Tâo) should not be left for a single instant (comp. the words of Confucius at the beginning of the *K*ung Yung). Let the work be done, and there is sure to be the result promised; only there must be the Purity insisted on both of body and mind. In the second paragraph it is said, "During the twelve hours of the day let the thoughts be constantly fixed on absolute Purity;" and in the last paragraph, "During the twelve hours be always pure and undefiled;"—thus showing what the main teaching of the Great Tâoistic system is, and the pre-eminent place which Purity occupies in the "Directory for a Day." The style is so clear and simple that I have left it without note or comment.'

1. As to what should be done in a day, when the eating and drinking has been arranged, let one sit straight with his mouth shut, and not allow a single thought to arise in his mind. Let him forget everything, and keep his spirit with settled purpose. Let

his lips be glued together, and his teeth be firmly pressed against one another. Let him not look at anything with his eyes, nor listen to a single sound with his ears. Let him with all his mind watch over his inward feelings. Let him draw long breaths, and gradually emit them, without a break, now seeming to breathe, and now not. In this way any excitement of the mind will naturally disappear, the water from the kidneys will rise up, the saliva will be produced in the mouth, and the real efficaciousness becomes attached to the body. It is thus that one acquires the way of prolonging life.

2. During the twelve hours of the day let one's thoughts be constantly fixed on absolute Purity. Where one thought (of a contrary kind) does not arise, we have what we call Purity; where nothing (of a contrary kind) enters the Tower of Intelligence (= the mind), we have what we call the Undefiled. The body is the house of the breath; the mind is the lodging of the spirit. As the thoughts move, the spirit moves; as the spirit moves, the breath is distributed. As the thoughts rest, the spirit rests; when the spirit rests, the breath is collected.

The true powers of the five elements unite and form the boat-like cup of jade, (after partaking of which), the body seems to be full of delicious harmony. This spreads like the unguent of the chrismal rite on the head. Walking, resting, sitting, sleeping, the man feels his body flexible as the wind, and in his belly a sound like that of thunder. His ears hear the songs of the Immortals, that need no aid from any instrument; vocal without words, and resounding without the drum. The spirit and the breath effect a union and the bloom of childhood returns. The man beholds scenes unfolded within him; Spirits of themselves speak to him; he sees the things of vacuity, and finds himself dwelling with the Immortals. He makes the Great Elixir, and his spirit goes out and in at its pleasure. He has the longevity of heaven and earth, and the brightness of the sun and moon. He has escaped from the toils of life and death.

Accustomed to the phraseology of the Text all his life, the commentator Lî, as has been seen, did not think it necessary to append here any notes of explanation. A few such notes, however, will be welcome to an English reader. 'The twelve hours of the day:'—a Chinese hour is equal to two of our hours, and their twelve to our twenty-four. The twelve hours are named by the twelve branch terms of the cycle.

'The boat-like cup of jade' seems to be a satisfactory rendering of the Chinese characters tâo kwei in the Text, which might be translated 'knife, and jade-symbol.' But tâo, commonly meaning 'knife,' is in the Shih *K*ing (I, v; VII, 2) used of 'a small boat.' In the Khang-hsî Thesaurus, under the phrase, we have the following quotation, as if from Ko Hung's Biographies of Immortals:—'*Kh*ăn Hsî, a native of the territory of Wû, was studying the Tâo in Shû, when the master Lâo sent a beautiful young lady to him with a tray of gold and a cup of jade filled with medicine, and the message, "This is the mysterious elixir; he who drinks it will not die." And on this he and his wife had each a tâo kwei.' See the account in Ko Hung's work, which is much more diffuse.

In the mention of 'the chrismal rite' there is a reference to what Dr. Williams calls 'a kind of Buddhist baptism or holy unction, by sprinkling, which confers goodness,' 'administered to children, idols, &c.' (See under the characters kwân and ting.)

3. Do not allow any relaxation of your efforts. During all the hours of the day strive always to be

pure and undefiled. The spirit is the child of the breath; the breath is the mother of the spirit.

As a fowl embraces its eggs, do you preserve the spirit and nourish the breath. Can you do this without intermission? Wonderful! wonderful! The mystery becomes still deeper!

In the body there are seven precious organs, which serve to enrich the state, to give rest to the people, and to make the vital force of the system full to overflowing. Hence we have the heart, the kidneys, the breath, the blood, the brains, the semen, and the marrow. These are the seven precious organs. They are not dispersed when the body returns (to the dust). Refined by the use of the Great Medicine, the myriad spirits all ascend among the Immortals.

If we were sure that we had exactly hit the meaning and spirit of every part of this paragraph, it would hardly be worth while to give more space to its illustration.

A sufficient number of the best of the Treatises of the later Tâoism have been placed before the reader to show him how different they are from the writings of Lâo and *K*wang, and how inferior to them. It might seem as if *K*wang-ȝze, when he ceased to write, had broken the staff of Tâoism and buried it many fathoms in the earth. We can hardly wonder that Confucianists, such as *K*û Hsî, should pronounce, 'What the sect of Tâo chiefly attend to is,—the preservation of the breath of life;' and that Buddhists, such as Liû Mî, should say of it, 'Long life being attained, its goal is reached.'

APPENDIX V.

Analyses by Lin Hsî-*k*ung of several of the Books of *K*wang-ȝze.

Book I.

The Hsiâo-yâo in the title of this Book denotes the appearance of perfect ease and satisfaction. The Yû, which conveys the idea of wandering or rambling about, is to be understood of the enjoyment of the mind. The three characters describe the chief characteristic of our 'Old *K*wang's' life, and therefore he placed the Book at the beginning of his more finished compositions or essays.

But when one wishes to enjoy himself in the fullest and freest way, he must first have before him a view like that of the wide sea or of the expanse of the air, in order that his mind may be free from all restraint, and from the entanglements of the world, and that it may respond in the fitting way to everything coming before it:—it is only what is Great that can enter into this enjoyment. Throughout the whole Book, the word Great has a significant force.

In paragraph 1 we are presented with the illustration of the phăng. Long was the journey which it would undertake, when it contemplated removing to the South. That it required a wind of 90,000 lî to support it, and even then only rested after a flight of six months, was owing to its own Great size, and also because the Southern Ocean was not to be easily reached by a single effort.

What is said, in paragraph 2, about men, when going anywhere, proportioning the provisions which they take with them to the length of the journey has the same meaning. How should such creatures as the cicada and the little dove be able to know this? Knowledge is great or small, because the years of the parties are many or few:—so it is that one is inferior to another. Have they not heard of the ming-ling and tâ-*kh*un, which make their spring and autumn for themselves? And so does the phăng, as we may understand. Its not resting till the end of six months is really not a long time to it. The case of Phăng 3û is not worth being taken into account.

This description of the greatness of the phăng is not any fabrication of our author's own, nor any statement peculiar to the *Kh*î Hsieh. The same things are told in the 'Questions of Thang to *K*î,' as in paragraph 3.

As to the long journey of the phăng and the marsh-quail's laughing at it, that is not different from what the other two little creatures said above;—arising simply from the difference between the great and the small. And what difference is there between this and the case of those who enjoy themselves for a season in the world? Yung-ȝze of Sung is introduced (and immediately dismissed), as not having planted himself in the right position, and not being Great. Then Lieh-ȝze is brought forward, and dismissed as not being Great, because he had something to wait for. It is only he who rides on the twofold primal ether of the Yin and Yang, driving along with the six elements through all their changes as they wax and wane, and enjoying himself at the gate of death, that can be pronounced Great. This is what is called the Perfect Man; the Spirit-like Man; and the Sage Man.

In illustration of this, as instances of the Great Man, we have, in paragraph 4, Hsü Yû, regardless of the name; the personage on the hill of Kû-shih, in paragraph 5, with no thought of the services he could perform; and Yâo with his deep-sunk eyes, in paragraph 6, no longer thinking much of his throne, and regardless of himself. All these characteristics could be used, and made their possessor great; but let not this lead to a suspicion of greatness as incompatible with usefulness. As a caution against this, we have, in paragraph 7, the salve to keep the hands from being chapped;—a Great thing when used properly, but of little value when not so used. Let those who exercise their minds look at this:—should they not seek to be useful, and so become Great? We have also the weasel and the yak, the one of which gets into trouble by its being of use, while the other escapes harm by its being of no use. Let those who have work to do in the world look at this. The Great calabash and the Great tree are, each of them, a phăng:—why may we not abandon ourselves to our natural feeling of enjoyment in connexion with them? Let men be satisfied with their Greatness and seek for nothing more.

As to the style of the Book, the sudden statement and the sudden proof; the sudden illustration and the sudden reasoning; the decision, made to appear as no decision; the connexion, now represented as no connexion; the repetition, turning out to be no repetition:—these features come and go on the paragraphs, like the clouds in the open firmament, changing every moment and delightful to behold.

Lû Fang-hû describes it well:—'The guiding thread in the unspun floss; the snake sleeping in the grass.'

Book II.

In writings intended to throw light on the Tâo we find many different views, affirmations on one side and denials on the other. These may be called Controversies, and the reason why they are not adjusted is that every one will hold fast to his own view. But every peculiar view arises from the holder's knowledge. Such knowledge, however, tends to the injury of his mind, and serves no purpose, good or bad, in illustrating the nature of the Tâo;—it only increases the confusion of controversy. Hence when we wish to adjust controversies, we must use our knowledge well; and to use our knowledge well, we must stop at the point beyond which it does not extend.

In this whole Book knowing and not knowing is the thread that runs through it, (and binds its parts together). The expressions about men's being 'in darkness,' in paragraph 2, and the Tâo's being 'obscure,' in paragraph 3, indicate the want of knowledge; those, also in paragraph 3, about 'the light of the mind,' and 'throwing that light on a subject,' indicate the good use of knowledge; those, in paragraph 5, about 'the scintillations of light from the midst of confusion and perplexity,' and 'the store of light,' in paragraph 7, indicate the stopping at the point to which our knowledge does not extend. And what is to be done when we stop at this point? Nothing more can be done; we have simply, as it is said in paragraph 6, to stop here.

When Nan-kwo Ʒze-*khî* says, in paragraph 1, 'I had lost myself,' he fully expresses the subject-matter of the Book. If we think that the affirmations and denials made by men's minds are fictions, made out from nothing to be something, that is like the myriad different sounds of the wind, suddenly appearing in their innumerable variations. But who is it that produces all these sounds? As is said in paragraph 2, they are 'the sounds of Earth which are really the notes of Heaven.' The minds of men speak from their possession of knowledge. However great or small their words may be, they are all of their own making. A discourse under a thousand Heads with a myriad Particulars, suddenly arising and as suddenly stopping, may suggest the idea of what we call 'a True Ruler.' But the idea is vague, and though our knowledge does not reach to such a subject, men toil their intelligence to the end of their lives, never stopping till both mind and body are exhausted. What is the reason of this? It is because they have their 'minds completely made up (par. 3).'

Now if words were like the chirpings of very young birds that come upon the ear, there would be no difference between them as regards truth or falsehood, right or wrong; but there is some obscuring influence, through which the different views of the Literati and Mohists are produced, with their confusion and uncertainty. All this is because the parties do not use their knowledge well. In their controversies each looks at the other's view only from his own standpoint, and throwing on the subject from that the light of Heaven, thus emptily replying to one another without end. And is this purposely intended to make a violent end of their disputations? (It is not so), for the Tâo is originally one. High and low, beautiful and ugly, ordinary and strange, success and overthrow, have nothing to do with it. The intelligent know this; those who weary their minds in trying to bring about a unity do not know it. At this point the sages throw on the subject the light of Heaven, also wishing to rest in Heaven, and so they come to a natural union:—this is how they use their knowledge well.

And what are we to consider the highest reach of knowledge (see par. 5)? The ancients thought it necessary to place this in the time before anything began to be. A second class would have it that there had (always) been (some) things; and a third class held that between those things (and men) there had been a relativity. Thus it was that gradually there came differences of opinion, in affirmations and denials; and when these once arose, there could not but be the experiences of success and failure.

But any one-sidedness in controversy is not sufficient to be accounted a proof of success or of failure. Not only is the Tâo radically one; but those who employ it, however they may seem to differ, will be found to be substantially one and the same. When the sages, in the midst of slippery confusion and doubtful perplexity, yet find the clearness of conviction, is it not because they place the controversies that we speak of among the things that are not to be used?

But if there were no affirmations and denials, there would be no words. And let me think here. Suppose there were no words of controversy, we must not infer from that that there were no words at all. Is this word correct? Then if I also employ it, I form one class with all who do so? Is it not correct? Then if I also deny it, I form another class with those who do the same. Formerly, when speaking of men's words, I said that they should change places, and look at things from the different standpoints of each other; so with reference to my own words, my holding my 'Yea,' does not interfere with my changing my place, and taking my position with those who say 'Nay' in the case. If indeed there be no words of affirmation and denial, what words will there be? We must go back to the beginning when there were no words. We must go back still farther,—to the vacuity before the beginning when there were no words. If we try to go back even farther still, then great and small, long life and short life, heaven and earth and all things, fade away, blending together in the One. But that ONE is also a word. In this way we go on without end, wishing to make an end of controversy, and instead of doing that, our endeavour only serves to increase it. The better plan is to stop, as is proposed in a former paragraph, to stop at this point.—Even this word about having no controversy may be spared.

The sage, by avoiding discussion, reasoning, and the drawing of distinctions, while he availed himself of words, yet retained the advantage of eschewing words, and was also afraid of calling the demarcations (of propositions) by their eight qualities (see par. 7). Still, however, the trace of the use of words remained with him. It is not so in the case of the Great Tâo and the Great Argument. The Tâo (which is displayed) is not the Tâo; the Argument (which is most subtle) does not reach the point; the degree of Non-action is very great; but notwithstanding it is difficult to speak of what is entirely empty of purpose. The way by which the knowledge of the ancients reached the highest point was their stopping when their knowledge extended no farther. If they could know what they did not know, it was by means of the Heavenly Treasure-house; it was thus they could take their place in the centre of the circle, to which all lines converged, and from which all questions could be answered. If they added what they did know to the sum of what they did not know, they then possessed the Store of Light; and it was thus that they made provision for the scintillations of slippery doubt.

To the same effect was what Shun told Yâo (end of par. 7). As to the referring what is advantageous and what is hurtful, and the mysteries of life and death, to the sphere of the unknown, that is set forth in the conversation between Nieh *Kh*üeh and Wang Î (par. 8).

As to how it is that rulers and grooms, other men and one's self, do not know each other, that is seen in the conversation between *Kh*ü Ȝhiâo-ȝze and *Kh*ang-wû Ȝze.

As to what is said about the substance and shadow waiting on each to make their manifestations, and not knowing how they were brought about, and about the dreamer and the man awake doubting about each other, and not knowing how to distinguish between them, we have knowledge stopping at the point to which it does not extend, and gradually entering into the region of transformation.

Is there anything still remaining to be done for the adjustment of controversy? One idea grows up out of another in the Book, and one expression gives rise to another apparently quite different. There is a mutual connexion and reference between its parts. Suddenly the style is difficult as the slope of Yang-*khh*ang, and vanishes like the path of a bird; suddenly it looks like so many steep cliffs and successive precipices. When ordinary scholars see this and cannot trace the connexion of thought, if they put it on one side, and did not venture to say anything about it, they might be forgiven. But when they dare to follow their prejudices, and to append their licentious explanations, breaking up the connexion of thought, and bringing down to the dust this wonderful composition, the admiration of thousands of years;—ah! when the old *K*wang took his pencil in hand, and proceeded to write down his thoughts, why should we be surprised that such men as these cannot easily understand him?

Book VI.

'The Great and most Honoured Master' is the Tâo. It appears separately in the Heavenly and Human elements (of our constitution), and exists alone and entire in what is beyond death and life; being, as we say, that which nothing can be without. To describe it as that which stands out superior and alone, we use for it the character *K*oh (卓) (par. 5); to describe it as abiding, we call it the True; to describe it as it vanishes from sight, we apply to it the names of Purity, Heaven, and Unity (par. 12).

When men value it, it is possible to get possession of it. But he who wishes to get it must, with the knowledge which he has attained to, proceed to nourish what that knowledge is still ignorant of. When both of these are (as it were) forgotten, and he comes under the transformation of the Tâo, he enters into the region in which there is neither life nor death;—to the Human element (in him) he has added the Heavenly.

Now what knowledge does not know is the time of birth and death, and what it does know is what comes after birth and precedes death. It would seem as if this could be nourished by the exercise of thought; but if we do this after birth and before death, we must wait for the time of birth and death to verify it. If we try to do so before that time, then the circumstances of the Human and the Heavenly have not yet become subject to their Ruler. It is this which makes the knowledge difficult, and it is only the True Man with the True Knowledge who has no anxiety about it.

In the position which the True man occupies, he has his adversities and prosperities, his successes and defeats, his gains and his losses, his seasons of security and of unrest,—all the changes of his circumstances; but his mind forgets them all, and this result is due to his possession of both the Knowledge and the Tâo.

As to his bodily conditions, he has his sleeping and

awaking, his eating and resting,—his constant experiences; but his mind (also) forgets them all. For the springs of action which move to the touch of Heaven, and the movements of desire are indeed different in men; but when we advance and examine the proper home of the mind, we find no difference between its place and nature at the time of birth and of death, and no complication in these after birth and before death:—so it is that the Mind, the Tâo, the Heavenly, and the Human are simply One. Is not the unconsciousness of the mind the way in which the True man exercises his knowledge and nourishes it? Carrying out this unconsciousness, from the mind to the body and from the body to the world, he comprehends the character of the time and the requirements of everything, without any further qualification. Hence, while the mind has not acquired this oblivion, the great work of life always suffers from some defect of the mind, and is not fit to be commended. But let the mind be able to exercise this quality, and it can be carried out with great and successful merit, and its admirable service be completed. This is the mind of the True man, never exercised one-sidedly in the world, and gaining no one-sided victory either Heavenward or Manward.

Given the True Man with the True Knowledge like this, the nature of death and life may begin to be fully described. Death and life are like the night and the dawn; —is there any power that can command them? Men cannot preside over them. This is what knowledge does not extend to; but within the sphere of knowledge, there is that which is dearer than a Father (par. 5), and more to be honoured than a Ruler; the Eminent, the True, and that moreover over which Heaven cannot preside. Valuable therefore is the nourishing of this Knowledge; and what other art in nourishing it is there but the unconsciousness of which we speak? Why do we say so? The body is born, grows old and dies. This is the common lot. However skilful one may be in hiding it away, it is sure to disappear. Men know that the body is not easily got, but they do not know that what might seem like man's body never comes to an end. Being hidden away in a place from which there is no escape for anything, it does not disappear. This takes place after birth and before death, and may be verified at the times of birth and death; but how much better it is to consider Heaven good, old age good, the beginning good and the end good, than vainly to think that the nourishing of knowledge is making the body good! The doing this is what is called the Tâo. And the sage enjoys himself in this; not only because the Tâo itself does not disappear, but also because of all who have got it not a single one has ever passed away from notice.

But it is not easy to describe the getting of the Tâo. In the case about which Nü Yü told Nan-po Ȝze-khwei (par. 8); the talents of a sage and the Tâo of a sage came together in the study of it; three, seven, and nine days are mentioned as the time of the several degrees of attainment; the learner went on from banishing all worldly matters from his mind as foreign to himself till he came to the utter disregard of time. In this way was he led from what was external, and brought inwards to himself; then again from the idea of the Tâo's being a thing, it was exhibited as Tranquillity amid all Disturbances, and he was carried out of himself till he understood that neither death nor life is more than a phenomenon. The narrator had learned all this from writings and from Lo-sung, searching them, and ever more the more remote they were. Truly great is the difficulty of getting the Tâo!

And yet it need not be difficult. It was not so with Ȝze-yü (par. 9), in whose words about one arm being transformed into a fowl, and the other into a cross-bow, we see its result, as also in what he said about his rump-bone being transformed into a wheel, his spirit into a horse, and one loosing the cord by which his life is suspended.

(Again) we have a similar accordance (with the Tâo) in Ȝze-lî's question to Ȝze-lâi (par. 10), about his being made the liver of a rat or the arm of an insect, with the latter's reply and his remark about the furnace of a founder.

These were men who had got the Tâo; as also were Ȝze-fan and *Kh*in *K*ang (par. 11), men after the Maker's mind, and who enjoyed themselves, disporting in the one vital ether of heaven and earth.

The same may be said of Măng-sun Ȝhâi (par. 12). If he had undergone a transformation, he would wait for the future transformation of which he did know. So it was that he obtained the Tâo. He and all the others were successful through the use of their mental unconsciousness; and they who pursue this method, must have the idea of I-*r* Ȝze, who wished to have his branding effaced, and his dismemberment removed by hearing the substance of the Tâo (par. 13).

Parties who have not lost the consciousness of their minds and wish to do so must become like Yen Hui (par. 14), who separated the connexion between his body and mind, and put away his knowledge, till he became one with the Great Pervader.

Of such as have lost (in part) the consciousness of their minds and wish to do so entirely, we have an instance in Ȝze-sang (par. 15), thinking of Heaven and Earth and of his parents as ignorant of his (miserable) condition, and then ascribing it to Destiny. He exhibited the highest obliviousness:—was he not, with the knowledge which he possessed, nourishing that of which he was ignorant? Such were the True Men, and such was the True Knowledge.

In this Book are to be found the roots of the ideas in the other six Books of this Part. In this they all unite. It exhibits the origin of all life, sets forth the reality of all cultivation, and shows the springs of all Making and Transformation, throwing open the door for the Immortals and Buddhas. Here is the wonderful Elixir produced by the pestle of Jade, the touch of which by a finger produces the feathers of Transformation. As to its style, a vast lake of innumerous wavelets, the mingling of a hundred sparkling eddies, a collection of the oldest achievements in composition, a granary filled with all woods;—it is only in the power of those who admire the leopard's spots to appreciate it!

Book IX.

Governing the world is like governing horses. There is the government, but the only effect of it is injury. Po-lâo's management of horses (par. 1) in a way contrary to their true nature was in no respect different from the way of the (first) potter and the (first) carpenter in dealing with their clay and wood in opposition to the nature of those substances, yet the world praises them all because of their skill, not knowing wherein the good government of the world consists.

Now the skilful governors of the world simply caused the people to fulfil the conditions of their regular nature (par. 2). It was their gifts which they possessed in common, and their Heaven-inspired instincts, which constituted the (Early) age of Perfect Virtue. When the sages fashioned their benevolence, righteousness, ceremonies, and music, and the people then began to lose their perfect virtue, it was not that they had themselves become different. For benevolence, righteousness, ceremonies, and music, are not endowments forming a part of their regular nature;—they are practised only after men have laid aside the Tâo and its characteristics, and abandoned the guidance of their nature and its feelings. This is what we say that the mechanic does when he hacks and cuts the raw materials to form his vessels. Why should we doubt that it was by Po-lâo's dealing with horses that they became wise enough to play the part of thieves (par. 3); and that it was by the sages' government of the people that their ability came to be devoted to the pursuit of gain? The error of the sages in this cannot be denied.

From beginning to end this Book is occupied with one idea. The great point in it grew out of the statement in paragraph 3 of the previous Book, that 'all men are furnished with certain regular principles,' and it is the easiest to construe of all *K*wang-ȝze's compositions; but the general style and illustrations are full of sparkling vigour. Some have thought that, where the ideas are so few, there is a waste of words about them, and they doubt therefore that the Book was written by some one imitating *K*wang-ȝze; but I apprehend no other hand could have shown such a mastery of his style.

Book XI.

That the world is not well governed is because there are those who try to govern it. When they try to govern it, they cannot but be 'doing' (to that end). Unable to keep from this 'doing,' they cause the world to be happy or to be miserable, both of which things the instincts of man's nature refuse to accept. Although the arts of governing are many, they only cause and increase disorder. Why so? Because they interfere with men's minds.

Now when men are made to be miserable or happy, they come to have great joy or great dissatisfaction. The condition ministers to the expansive or the opposite element (in nature), and the four seasons, the cold and the heat, all lose their regularity. This causes men everywhere in a contentious spirit to indulge their nature to excess, bringing about a change of its attributes, and originating the practice of good and evil. All unite in bringing this state about; and in the end all receive its consequences. Hence such men as *K*ih the robber, Ȝăng Shăn, and Shih Ȝhûi ought not to be found in a well-governed age. But those who governed the world went on to distinguish between the good and the bad, and occupied themselves with rewarding and punishing. When they wished men to rest in the requirements of their nature, was it not difficult for them to realise the wish?

And how much more was it so when they went on in addition to insist on acute hearing and clear vision, on benevolence, righteousness, ceremonies, music, sageness, and knowledge (par. 2)! They did not know that these eight things were certainly of no use to the world, but injurious to it. Led astray by them, and not perceiving this, they continued to practise them, and to do this every day more and more. This is what we see indeed in the ordinary men of the world, but not what we should have expected from superior men. The Superior man does nothing, and rests in the instincts of his nature. He values and loves his own person, which fits him to be entrusted with the charge of the world, and thereupon we see things becoming transformed of themselves. Yes, we see indeed that men's minds are not to be interfered with (par. 3).

Let me try to attest this from (the example of) the ancient Tîs and Kings. These in their interference with the minds of men, began with their inculcation of benevolence and righteousness, proceeded to their distinctions of what was right and wrong, and ended with their punishments and penalties. Their government of the world ended with the disordering of it. And the result can be seen, the Literati and the Mohists still thinking how they can remedy them.

But let us ask who it really was that brought things to this pass. The answer is supplied to us in the words of Lâo Tan (see T. T. *K*., ch. 19), 'Abolish sageness and cast away wisdom, and the world will be brought to a state of good order.' But the issue does not commence with the state of the world. When Kwang *Kh*ăng-ʒze replied to Hwang-Tî's questions, he said (par. 4), 'Watch over your body, and increase the vigour of things. Maintain the unity, and dwell in the harmony.' What he said, about the rain descending before the clouds collected, about the trees shedding their leaves before they were yellow, about the light (of the sun and moon) hastening to extinction, about Hwang-Tî's mind being that of a flatterer of which he would make no account, and about how he should do nothing but rest in the instincts of his nature, and not interfere with the minds of men:—all these are expressions bearing on the value and love which should be given to the body. And the lesson in his words does not end with the watching over the body.

There are the words addressed by Hung Mung to Yün

*K*iang, 'Nourish in your mind a great agreement (with the primal ether). (Things) return to their root, and do not know (that they are doing so). As to what you say, that "the mysterious operations of Heaven are not accomplished, that the birds all sing at night, that vegetation withers under calamity, and that insects are all overtaken by disaster:—about all these things there is no occasion for anxiety." While you do nothing, rest in the promptings of your human nature, and do not interfere with the minds of men;—such is the genial influence that attracts and gathers all things round itself (par. 2).'

But the Superior man's letting the world have its own course in this generous way;—this is what the ordinary men of the world cannot fathom. When such men speak about governing, they examine carefully between others and themselves, and are very earnest to distinguish between differing and agreeing. Their only quest is to find how they may overcome others, and the end is that they are always overcome by others. They do not know that in order to reduce others to the level of things, there must be those who cannot be reduced by others to that level. Those are said to be the sole possessors of the power (par. 6).

The teaching of the Great man, however, is not of this nature. He responds to others according to their qualities, without any selfish purpose. Although he is the sole possessor of the power, that power comes to be nothing in his view. Between having and not having there is to him no difference in the use. Doing nothing, and yet sometimes obliged to act, he forthwith does so; when he acts, yet no one sees that he has acted, and it is the same as if he did not act. So it is according to the Tâo; but therein there are both the Heavenly and the Human elements. In accordance with this there are (in actual government) the Lord and the Minister (par. 7). When one discerns this, and knows which element is to be preferred, convinced that it is doing nothing which is valuable, what difficulty has he in governing the world?

The thread of connexion running through this Book is 'Doing Nothing.' Whether it speaks of the promptings of the nature or of the minds of men, it shows how in regard to both there must be this 'doing nothing.' In the end, with much repetition it distinguishes and discusses, showing that what doing there may be in doing nothing need not trouble us, and is not the same as the 'Extinction' of the Buddhists. There is not much difference between the teaching of this Book, and what we read in the Confucian Analects, 'He did nothing and yet governed efficiently (Bk. XV, ch. iv).' This is an instance of the light thrown by our 'old *K*wang' on the *K*ing, and shows how an understanding may take place between him and our Literati.

In the style there are so many changes and transformations, so many pauses and rests as in music, conflicting discussions, and subtle disquisitions, the pencil's point now hidden in smoke and now among the clouds, the author's mind teeming with his creations, that no one who has not made himself familiar with a myriad volumes should presume to look and pronounce on this Book.

BOOK XX.

The afflictions of men in the world are great, because their attainments in the Tâo and Its Attributes are shallow. The Tâo with Its Attributes is the Author of all things. To follow It in Its transformings according to the time is not like occupying one's self with the qualities of things, and with the practice and teaching of the human relations, which only serve to bring on disaster and blame. He who seeks his enjoyment in It, however, must begin by emptying himself. Hence we have, 'Rip your skin from your body, cleanse your heart, and put away your desires (par. 2);' then afterwards 'you can enjoy yourself in the land of Great Vacuity.' In this way one attains to the status represented by coming across 'an empty vessel' and escapes 'the evils which the close-furred fox and the elegantly-spotted leopard' are preparing for themselves.

These are the ideas in the paragraph about Î-liâo of

Shih-nan which may help to illustrate, and receive illustration from, what *K*wang-ȝze says (par. 1) that 'he would prefer to be in a position between being fit to be useful and wanting that fitness.'

In the case of Pei-kung Shê collecting taxes for the making of a peal of bells, we have only the exercise of a small art (par. 3). He could, however, put away all thought of self, and act as the time required. He was 'as a child who has no knowledge,' so slow was he and hesitating in this respect; there escorting those who went, here welcoming those who came. But from all this we may know how far he had advanced (in the knowledge of the Tâo).

But on consideration I think it was only Confucius of whom this could be spoken. Did not he receive a great share of the world's afflictions (par. 4)? When Thâi-kung *Z*ăn spoke to him of 'putting away the ideas of merit and fame, and placing himself on the level of the masses of men,' he forthwith put away the idea of himself and complied with the requirements of the time. This was the art by which he enjoyed himself in the Tâo and Its attributes, and escaped the troubles of the world.

He could put away the idea of self in responding to the world, but he could not do so in determining his associations. In consequence of this, more distant acquaintances did not come to lay further afflictions on him, and his nearer friends perhaps came to cast him off because of those afflictions. What was he to do in these circumstances?

If one be able to comply with the requirements of the time in his relations with men, but cannot do so in his relations to Heaven, then in the world he will indeed do nothing to others contrary to what is right, but he will himself receive treatment contrary to it; and what is to be done in such a case? Ȝze-sang Hû saw the difficulty here and provided for it. What he said about 'a union of Heaven's appointment,' and about 'the intercourse of superior men being tasteless as water,' shows how well he knew the old lessons about a connexion growing out of external circumstances and one founded in inward feeling. When one has divested himself of the idea of self, there will not again be such an experience as that of Confucius, when his intimate associates were removed from him more and more, and his followers and friends were more and more dispersed.

And Confucius himself spoke of such a case. What he said about its being 'easy not to receive (as evils) the inflictions of Heaven,' and 'difficult not to receive as benefits the favours of men (par. 7),' shows how truly he perceived the connexion between the Heavenly and the Human (in man's constitution), and between 'the beginning and end' of experiences. When one acts entirely according to the requirements of the time, the more he enlarges himself the greater he becomes, and the more he loves himself the more sorrow he incurs. If he do not do so, then we have the case of him who in the prospect of gain forgets the true instinct of his preservation, as shown in the strange bird of the park of Tiâo-ling (par. 8), and the case of the Beauty of the lodging-house, who by her attempts to show off her superiority made herself contemned. How could such parties so represented occupy themselves with the Tâo and Its attributes so as to escape the calamities of life?

This Book sets forth the principles which contribute to the preservation of the body, and keeping harm far off, and may supplement what still needed to be said on this subject in Book IV. The Tâo and Its attributes occupy the principal place in it; the emptying of Self, and conforming to the time, are things required by them. The exquisite reasonings and deep meaning of the Book supply excellent rules for getting through the world. Only the sixth paragraph is despicable and unworthy of its place. It is evidently a forgery, and I cannot but blame Kwo Ȝze-hsüan for allowing it to remain as the production of *K*wang-ȝze.

Book XXII.

The Tâo made Its appearance before Heaven and Earth. It made things what they are and was Itself no THING, being what is called their Root and Origin (par. 2). If we consider It something existing, It was not such; if we consider It as something non-existing, that does not fully express the idea of it. The 'I know it (of Hwang-Tî)' is an addition of 'Knowledge' to the idea of it, and (his) 'I will tell you' is the addition of a description of it (par. 1). Therefore he who would embody the Tâo can only employ the names of 'Do Nothing' and 'Returning to the Root,' and then go forward to the region of the Unknown and the Indescribable.

Now the Tâo originally was a Unity. The collection of the breath, constituting life, and its dispersion, which we call death, proceed naturally. The denominations of the former as 'spirit-like and wonderful' and of the latter as 'foetor and putridity' are the work of man. But those of 'Non-action' and 'Returning to the Root' are intended to do honour to the Unity. Knowledge, Heedless Bluster, and Hwang-Tî, all perceived this, but they also went on to reason about it, showing how not to know is better than to know, and not to talk better than to talk.

As it is said in par. 2, 'the beautiful operations of Heaven and Earth, and the distinctive constitutions of all things,' from the oldest time to the present day, go on and continue without any difference. But who is it that makes them to be what they are? And what expression of doubt or speculation on the point has ever been heard from them? It is plain that the doctrine of the Tâo originated with man.

When Phei-î (par. 3) told Nieh *K*hüeh, 'Keep your body as it should be; look only at the One thing; call in your knowledge; make your measures uniform:'—all this was saying to him that we are to do nothing, and turn to (the Tâo as) our Root. When he further says to him, 'You should have the simple look of a new-born calf; and not ask about the cause of your being what you are:'—this is in effect saying that knowledge is in not knowing, and that speech does not require the use of words.

If you suddenly (like Shun in par. 4) think that the Tâo

is yours to hold, not only do you not know what the Tâo is, but you do not know yourself. How is this? You are but a thing in the Tâo. If your life came to you without its being produced by the Tâo, you would yourself be a life-producer. But whether one lives to old age or dies prematurely he comes equally to an end. Your life properly was not from yourself, nor is your death your own act. You did not resist (the coming of your life); you do not keep it (against the coming of death); you are about to return to your original source. This simply is what is meant by the Sage's 'Do nothing, and return to your Root.' As to 'the bodily frame coming from incorporeity and its returning to the same (par. 5),' that certainly is a subject beyond the reach of our seeing and hearing; and how can any one say that the Tâo is his to hold?

What Lâo-ȝze (says to Confucius in par. 5), and what *Kh*ăng tells Shun (in par. 4), have not two meanings; but notwithstanding, it should not be said that the Tâo is not to be found anywhere (par. 6). Speaking broadly, we may say that its presence is to be seen in an ant, a stalk of panic grass, an earthenware tile, and in excrement. Seeking for it in what is more delicate and recondite, let us take the ideas of fulness and emptiness, of withering and decay, of beginning and end, of accumulation and dispersion. These are all ideas, and not the names of things; and (the Tâo) which makes things what they are has not the limit which belongs to things. No wonder that Tung-kwo Ȝze should have been so perplexed as he was!

Those who think that the Tâo has no positive existence (par. 7), speak of it as 'The Mysterious and Obscure,' and then it would seem to be equivalent to the name 'Mystery,' which cannot be rightly applied to it. And those who think that it has a positive existence speak of it as being considered now noble and now mean, now bound and compressed, now dispersed and diffused, and what is One is divided into the noble and the mean, the compressed and the dispersed;—a mode of dealing with it, of which the Tâo will not admit. Better is it to say with No-beginning, 'There should be no asking about the Tâo; any question about it should not be replied to.' The opposite of this would imply a knowledge of what is not known, and the use of words which should not be spoken. In accordance with this, when Star-light puts his question to Non-entity, and it is added, 'To conceive the ideas of Existence and Non-existence is not so difficult as to conceive of a Non-existing non-existence,' this is an advance on speaking of (the Tâo) as Non-existent; and when the forger of Swords says to the Minister of War that by long practice he came to the exercise of his art as if he took no thought about it (par. 9), this is an advance on speaking of (the Tâo) as existent.

The substance of what we know is to this effect:—The Tâo was produced before heaven and earth. It made things what they are and is not itself a thing. It cannot be considered as of ancient origin or of recent, standing as it does in no relation to time. It had no beginning and will have no end. Life and death, death and life equally proceed from It. To speak of It as existing or as non-existing is a one-sided presentation of It. Those who have embodied It, amid all external changes, do not change internally. They welcome and meet all men and things, and none can do them any injury (par. 11). Whatever they do not know and are unequal to, they simply let alone. This is the meaning of 'Doing nothing, and turning in everything to the Root.' Where the want of knowledge and of language is the most complete, Žăn *Kh*iû (par. 10) and Yen-ʒze (par. 11) apply to *K*ung-nî for his judgment in the case, and the consideration of it comes to an end.

In this Book the mysteries of the Tâo are brought to light; one slight turn of expression after another reveals their successive depths, beyond the reach of Reasoning. Lû Fang-hû says, 'Master this Book, and the Mahâyâna of the Tripi*t*aka will open to you at the first application of your knife.'—Well does he express himself!

Book XXVI.

Those who practise the Tâo know that what is external to themselves cannot be relied on, and that what is internal and belonging to themselves, does not receive any injury (par. 1). They are therefore able to enjoy themselves in the world, emptying their minds of all which would interfere with their pursuing their natural course.

What men can themselves control are their minds; external things are all subject to the requirements and commands of the world. Good and evil cannot be prevented from both coming to men, and loyalty and filial duty may find it hard to obtain their proper recompense. From of old it has been so; and the men of the world are often startled to incessant activity with their minds between the thoughts of profit and injury, and are not able to overcome them (par. 1). But do they know that among the enemies (of their serenity) there are none greater than the Yin and Yang? The water and fire of men's minds produce irregularity in their action, and then again overcome it; but after the harmony of the mind has been consumed, there remains in them no more trace of the action of the Tâo.

On this account, when *K*ung-nî was obstinately regardless of a myriad generations (in the future), Lâo Lâi-ȝze still warned him to have done with his self-conceit (par. 5). His reason for doing so was that wisdom had its perils, and even spirit-like intelligence does not reach to everything (par. 6). It was so with the marvellous tortoise, and not with it only. The sage is full of anxiety and indecision (par. 5), and thereby is successful in his undertakings; the man of the greatest knowledge puts away (the idea of) skill, and without any effort shows his skill:—they can both look on what seems to have no use and pronounce it useful, and allow their nature while it is able to enjoy itself to take its course without being anxious about its issue in advantage or injury (par. 1).

And moreover, it is not necessary that they should leave

the world in order to enjoy themselves. There are the distinctions of antiquity and the present day indelibly exhibited in the course of time (par. 8). The way in which the Perfect man enjoys himself is by his passing through the world of men without leaving any trace of himself. His way is free and encounters no obstruction (par. 9); his mind has its spontaneous and enjoyable movements, and so his spirit is sure to overcome all external obstructions. Very different is this from the way of him who is bent on concealing himself, and on extinguishing all traces of his course (par. 8). He will seek his enjoyment in the great forest with its heights and hills, and not be able to endure the trouble of desiring fame, having recourse also to violence, laying plans, seeking to discharge the duties of office so as to secure general approval.

Thus the Perfect man obtains the harmony of his Heaven (-given nature), and his satisfactions spring up, he knows not how, as when the growing grain in spring has been laid by the rains (par. 9). As to the arts of curing illness, giving rest to old age, and restraining hasty measures to remedy the effects of errors, he can put them on one side, and not discuss them; thus playing the part of one who has apprehended the ideas and then forgets the words in which they were conveyed (par. 11). Let him who occupies himself with the Tâo beware of 'seeking the fish-baskets and hare-snares,' and falling into such mistakes as are instanced in the cases of emaciation to death, or suicide by drowning.

This Book points out the true form of substances, and gave rise to the talk in subsequent ages about the Khân and Lî hexagrams, and about the lead and quicksilver. Nearly the whole of it has been called in question, and the second, third, and fourth paragraphs are so marked by the shallowness of their style, and the eccentricity of their sentiments, that it may be doubted if they are genuine. I suspect they were written and introduced by some imitator of *K*wang-ȝze, and therefore call attention to them and cast them out of my analysis.

Book XXXII.

Lin Hsî-*k*ung omits Books XXVIII, XXIX, XXX, and XXXI from his edition of *K*wang-ȝze's Writings. Our Book XXXII, the Lieh Yü-khâu, is with him Book XXVIII. He explains and comments on its various paragraphs as he does in the case of all the previous Books. Instead of subjoining an Analysis and Summary of the Contents in his usual way, he contents himself with the following note:—

In the Notice given by Sû Ȝze-*k*an[1] of the Sacrificial Hall to *K*wang-ȝze, he says that after reading the last paragraph of Book XXVII (the Yü Yen, or 'Metaphorical Words'), about Yang Ȝze-*k*ü, and how (when he left the inn) the other visitors would have striven with him about the places for their mats, he forthwith discarded the four Books that followed,—the *Z*ang Wang, the Tâo *K*ih, the Yüeh *K*ien, and the Yü-fû; making the Lieh Yü-khâu immediately follow that paragraph. Having done so, he fully saw the wisdom of what he had done, and said with a laugh, 'Yes, they do indeed belong to one chapter!'

So did the old scholar see what other eyes for a thousand years had failed to see. No subsequent editor and commentator, however, ventured to take it on him to change the order of the several Books which had been established, following therein the Critical Canon laid down by Confucius about putting aside subjects concerning which doubts are entertained[2]; but we ought not to pass the question by without remark.

The subject of the last paragraph of the Lieh Yü-khâu is *K*wang-ȝze, 'when he was about to die.' It clearly

---

[1] Sû Shih (蘇軾), styled Ȝze-*k*an (子瞻) and also, and more frequently, Tung-pho (東坡), one of the most celebrated statesmen and scholars of the eleventh century (1036–1101). The notice of the Sacrificial Hall of *K*wang-ȝze was written in 1078. See Appendix viii.

[2] See the Confucian Analects II, xviii:—'Learn much and put aside the points of which you stand in doubt, while you speak cautiously at the same time of the others.'

intimates how he, the man of *Kh*î-yüan, from that time ceased to use his pencil, just as the appearance of the Lin (in the Ȝo-*k*wan) did in the case of Confucius. Not a single character therefore should appear as from him after this. We have no occasion therefore to enter into any argument about the Thien Hsiâ (Book XXXIII). We may be sure that it was made, not by *K*wang-ȝze, but by some editor of his writings. Later writers, indeed, contend vehemently for *K*wang-ȝze's own authorship of it. We can only say, Great is the difficulty in treating of the different views of Scholars [1]!

[1] The arguments both of Sû Shih and Lin Hsî-*k*ung as set forth in this note are far from conclusive.

APPENDIX VI.

List of Narratives, Apologues, and Stories of various kinds in the Writings of *K*wang-ʒze.

Book I.

Paragraph 1. The enjoyment of the Tâo by such vast creatures as the Khwăn and the Phăng.

2. The enjoyment and foolish judgments of smaller creatures. Big trees and Phăng 3û.

3. Questions put by Thang to *K*î. The Tâo in different men:—Yung-ʒze; Lieh-ʒze; and an ideal Tâoist. The Perfect man, the Spirit-like man, and the Sagely-minded man.

4. Yâo wishing to resign the throne to Hsü Yû.

5. *K*ien Wû and Lien Shû on the ideal Tâoist.

6. A cap-seller of Sung. Yâo after visiting the four Perfect ones.

7. Hui-ʒze and *K*wang-ʒze:—the great calabashes; the hand-protecting salve; and the great Ailantus tree.

Book II.

Par. 1. Nan-kwo 3ze-*kh*î in a trance, and his disciple. The notes of heaven, earth, and man.

4. 'In the morning three:'—the monkeys and their acorns.

7. Yâo and Shun,—on the wish of the former to smite some small states.

9. Lî *K*î before and after her marriage.

10. The penumbra and the shadow. *K*wang-ʒze's dream that he was a butterfly.

Book III.

Par. 2. King Wăn-hui and his cook;—how the latter cut up his oxen.

3. Kung-wăn Hsien and the Master of the Left who had only one foot.

4. The death of Lâo-ȝze; and adverse judgment on his life.

Book IV.

Pars. 1, 2. Yen Hui and Confucius;—on the proposal of the former to go and convert the ruler of Wei.

3, 4. Ȝze-kâo and Confucius;—on the mission of the former from *Kh*û to *Kh*î.

5. Yen Ho and *K*ü Po-yü;—on the former's undertaking to be tutor to the wayward son of duke Ling of Wei.

6. The master-mechanic and the great tree;—so large and old through its uselessness.

7. Nan-po Ȝze-*kh*î and the great tree, preserved by its uselessness. Trees of Sung cut down because of their good timber. Peculiarities exempting from death as sacrificial victims.

8. The deformed object Shû and his worth.

9. Rencontre between Confucius and the madman of *Kh*û.

Book V.

Par. 1. Confucius explains the influence of the cripple Wang Thâi over the people of Lû.

2. The fellow-students Ȝze-*kh*ân and the cripple Shăn-thû *K*iâ.

3. Confucius and Toeless of Shû-shan. Judgment of Toeless and Lâo-ȝze on Confucius.

4. Duke Âi of Lû and Confucius;—on the ugly but most able and fascinating man, Âi-thâi Tho. Admiration for Confucius of duke Âi.

5. The deformed favourites of duke Ling of Wei and duke Hwan of *Kh*î. Argument between *K*wang-ȝze and Hui-ȝze, growing out of the former's account of them.

Book VI.

Par. 8. Nan-po Ȝze-khwei and the long-lived Nü Yü. How Pû-liang Î learned the Tâo.

9. Four Tâoists, and the submission of Ȝze-yü, one of them, a poor deformed hunchback, to his lot, when he was very ill.

10. The submission of Ȝze-lâi, another of the four, as his life was ebbing away.

11. Three Tâoists, and the ways of two of them on the death of the third. Conversation on the subject between Confucius and Ȝze-kung.

12. Confucius and Yen Hui on the mourning of Măng-sun Ȝhâi.

13. Î-*r* Ȝze and Hsü Yû. How the Tâo will remove the injuries of error, and regenerate the mind.

14. Confucius and Yen Hui. The growth of the latter in Tâoism.

15. Ȝze-yü and Ȝze-sang. The penury of the latter and submission to his fate.

Book VII.

Par. 1. Nieh *Kh*üeh, Wang Î, and Phû-î-ȝze. That Shun was inferior in his Tâoistic attainments to the more ancient sovereign, Thâi.

2. *K*ien Wû and the recluse *Kh*ieh-yü;—on the ideal of government.

3. Thien Kăn and a nameless man;—that non-action is the way to govern the world.

4. Yang Ȝze-*k*ü and Lâo Tan on the nameless government of the Intelligent Kings.

5. Lieh-ȝze and his master Hû-ȝze. How the latter defeated the wizard of *K*ăng.

6. The end of Chaos, wrought by the gods of the southern and northern seas.

Book VIII.

Par. 4. How two shepherd slaves lose their sheep in

different ways. The corresponding cases of the righteous Po-î and the robber *K*ih.

Book X.

Par. 1. Murder of the ruler of *Kh*î by Thien *Kh*ăng-ȝze, and his usurpation of the State.

2. How the best and ablest of men, such as Lung-făng, Pî-kan, *Kh*ang Hung, and Ȝze-hsü, may come to a disastrous end, and only seem to have served the purposes of such men as the robber *K*ih.

3. Evils resulting from such able men as Ȝăng Shăn, Shih *Kh*iû, Yang *K*û, Mo Tî, Shih Khwang, *Kh*ui, and Lî *K*û.

4. Character of the age of Perfect Virtue, and sovereigns who flourished in it in contrast with the time of *K*wang-ȝze.

Book XI.

Par. 3. Ȝhui *Kh*ü and Lâo-ȝze. The latter denounces the meddling with the mind which began with Hwang-Tî, and the spread of knowledge, as productive of all evil.

4. Hwang-Tî and Kwang *Kh*ăng-ȝze, his master, who discourses on the mystery of the Tâo, and how it promotes long life.

5. Yün *K*iang and Hung Mung, or the Leader of the Clouds and the Great Ether;—the wish of the former to nourish all things, and how they would be transformed by his doing nothing.

Book XII.

Par. 4. The loss and recovery by Yâo of his dark-coloured Pearl;—the Tâo.

5. Hsü Yû's reply to Yâo on the character of Nieh *Kh*üeh and his unfitness to take the place of Sovereign.

6. Yâo rejects the good wishes for him of the Border-warden of Hwâ.

7. Yü and Po-*kh*ăng Ȝze-kâo. The latter vindicates his resignation of dignity and taking to farming.

9. Confucius and Lâo-ȝze;—on the attitude to the Tâo of a great sage and ruler.

10. *K*iang-lü Mien and *K*î *Kh*êh ;—on the counsel which the former had given to the ruler of Lû.

11. 3ze-kung and the old gardener ;—argument of the latter in favour of the primitive simplicity, and remarks thereon by Confucius.

12. *K*un Mâng and Yüan Fung ;—on the government of the sage ; of the virtuous and kindly man ; and of the spirit-like man.

13. Măn Wû-kwei and *Kh*ih-*k*ang Man-*kh*î ;—that there had been confusion and disorder before the time of Shun ; and the character of the age of Perfect Virtue.

BOOK XIII.

Par. 6. Yâo and Shun ;—on the former's method of government.

7. Confucius, wishing to deposit some writings in the royal Library, is repulsed by Lâo-3ze. Argument between them on Benevolence and Righteousness in relation to the nature of man.

8. Shih-*kh*ăng *Kh*î and Lâo-3ze ;—the strange conferences between them, and the charges brought by the one against the other.

10. Duke Hwan and the wheelwright Phien ;—that the knack of an art cannot be conveyed to another, and the spirit of thought cannot be fully expressed in writing.

BOOK XIV.

Par. 2. Tang, a minister of Shang, and *K*wang-3ze on the nature of Benevolence.

3. Pei-măn *Kh*ăng and Hwang-Tî ;—a description of Hwang-Tî's music, the Hsien-*kh*ih.

4. Yen Yüan and *K*in, the music-master of Lû, on the course of Confucius ;—the opinion of the latter that it had been unsuccessful and was verging to entire failure.

5. Confucius and Lâo-3ze. The former has not yet got the Tâo, and Lâo-3ze explains the reason.

6. Confucius and Lâo-3ze. Confucius talks of Benevolence

and Righteousness; and how the tables are turned on him. He is deeply impressed by the other.

7. Ȝze-kung, in consequence of the Master's report of his interview, goes also to see Lâo-ȝze; and is nonplussed and lectured by him.

8. Confucius sees Lâo-ȝze again, and tells him how he has profited from his instructions. The other expresses his satisfaction with him.

Book XVI.

Par. 2. The state of Perfect Unity, and its gradual Decay.

Book XVII.

Pars. 1–7. The Spirit-earl of the Ho and *Z*o of the Northern Sea;—on various metaphysical questions growing out of the doctrine of the Tâo.

8. The khwei, the millipede, the serpent, the wind, the eye, and the mind;—how they had their several powers, but did not know how.

9. Confucius in peril in Khwang is yet serene and hopeful.

10. Kung-sun Lung and Mâu of Wei. The Frog of the dilapidated well, and the Turtle of the Eastern Sea. The greatness of *K*wang-ȝze's teachings.

11. *K*wang-ȝze refuses the invitation of the king of *Kh*û to take office. The wonderful tortoise-shell of the king.

12. Hui-ȝze and *K*wang-ȝze. The young phoenix and the owl.

13. Hui-ȝze and *K*wang-ȝze;—how *K*wang-ȝze understood the enjoyment of fishes.

Book XVIII.

Par. 2. Hui-ȝze and *K*wang-ȝze;—vindication by the latter of his behaviour on the death of his wife.

3. Mr. Deformed and Mr. One-foot;—their submission under pain and in prospect of death.

4. *K*wang-ȝze and the skull;—what he said to it, and its appearance to him at night in a dream.

5. The sadness of Confucius on the departure of Yen Hui for *Kh*î; and his defence of it to 3ze-kung. The appearance of a strange bird in Lû, and his moralizings on it.

6. Lieh-ȝze and the skull. The transmutations of things.

Book XIX.

Par. 2. Lieh-ȝze and Kwan Yin;—on the capabilities of the Perfect man.

3. Confucius and the hunchback, who was skilful at catching cicadas with his rod.

4. The boatman on the gulf of *Kh*ang-shăn, and his skill.

5. Thien Khâi-*k*ih and duke Wei of *K*âu;—on the best way to nourish the higher life. How it was illustrated by Thien's master, and how enforced by Confucius.

6. The officer of sacrifice and his pigs to be sacrificed.

7. Duke Hwan gets ill from seeing a ghostly sprite, and how he was cured.

8. The training of a fighting-cock.

9. Confucius and the swimmer in the gorge of Lü.

10. *Kh*ing, the worker in rottlera wood, and the bell-frame;—how he succeeded in making it as he did.

11. Tung-yê *K*î and his chariot-driving;—how his horses broke down.

12. The skill of the artisan Shui.

14. The weakling Sun Hsiû and the Master 3ze-pien *Kh*ing-ȝze, with his disciples.

Book XX.

Par. 1. *K*wang-ȝze and his disciples;—the great tree that was of no use, and the goose that could not cackle.

2. Î-liâo of Shih-nan and the marquis of Lû;—how the former presses it on the marquis to go to an Utopia of Tâoism in the south, to escape from his trouble and sorrow.

3. Pei-kung Shê and prince *Kh*ing-*k*î;—how the former collected taxes and made a peal of bells.

4. How the Thâi-kung *Z*ăn condoled with Confucius on his distresses, and tried to convert him to Tâoism.

5. Confucius and Ȝze-sang Hû. The Tâoistic effect of their conversation on the former. The dying charge of Shun to Yü.

6. *K*wang-ȝze in rags before the king of Wei. The apologue of the climbing monkey.

7. Confucius and Yen Hui;—on occasion of the perilous situation between *Kh*ăn and Ȝhâi. Confucius expounds the principles that supported him.

8. *K*wang-ȝze's experiences in the park of Tiâo-ling;—has the character of an apologue.

9. The Innkeeper's two concubines;—the beauty disliked and the ugly one honoured.

Book XXI.

Par. 1. Thien Ȝze-fang and the marquis Wăn of Wei.

2. Wăn-po Hsüeh-ȝze and the scholars of the Middle States.

3. Confucius and Yen Hui;—on the incomprehensibleness to the latter of the Master's course.

4. Conversation between Confucius and Lâo-ȝze on the beginning of things.

5. *K*wang-ȝze and duke Âi of Lû;—on the dress of the scholar.

6. Pâi-lî Hsî.

7. The duke of Sung and his map-drawers.

8. King Wăn and the old fisherman of Ȝang. Confucius and Yen Hui on king Wăn's dream about the fisherman.

9. The archery of Lieh-ȝze and Po-hwăn Wû-ȝăn.

10. *K*ien Wû, and Sun Shû-âo, the True man. Confucius's account of the True man. The king of *Kh*û and the ruler of Fan.

Book XXII.

Par. 1. Knowledge, Dumb Inaction, Head-strong Stammerer, and Hwang-Tî on the Tâo.

3. Nieh *Kh*üeh questioning Phei-î about the Tâo.

4. Shun and his minister *Kh*ăng;—that man is not his own.

5. Confucius and Lâo Tan;—on the Perfect Tâo.

6. Tung-kwo 3ze's question to *K*wang-ȝze about where the Tâo was to be found, and the reply.

7. Â-ho Kan, Shăn Năng, Lâo-lung *K*î, Yen Kang;—Grand Purity, Infinitude, Do-nothing, and No-beginning:—on what the Tâo is.

8. Star-light and Non-entity.

9. The Minister of War and his forger of swords.

10. *Z*ăn *Kh*iû and Confucius;—how it was before heaven and earth.

11. Confucius and Yen Hui:—No demonstration to welcome, no movement to meet.

Book XXIII.

Par. 1. Kăng-sang *Kh*û and the people about Wei-lêi hill.

2. Kăng-sang *Kh*û and his disciples. He repudiates being likened by them to Yâo and Shun.

3. Kăng-sang *Kh*û and the disciple Nan-yung *Kh*û.

4–12. Lâo-ȝze lessoning Nan-yung *Kh*û on the principles of Tâoism.

Book XXIV.

Pars. 1, 2. Hsü Wû-kwei, Nü Shang, and the marquis Wû of Wei:—Hsü's discourses to the marquis.

3. Hwang-Tî, with six attending sages, in quest of the Tâo, meets with a wise boy herding horses.

5. Debate between *K*wang-ȝze and Hui-ȝze, illustrating the sophistry of the latter.

6. The artisan Shih cleans the nose of a statue with the wind of his axe; but declines to try his ability on a living subject.

7. Advice of Kwan *K*ung on his death-bed to duke Hwan of *Kh*î about his choice of a successor to himself.

8. The king of Wû and the crafty monkey. His lesson from its death to Yen Pû-î.

9. Nan-po 3ze-*kh*î and his attendant Yen *Kh*ăng-ȝze.

The trance is the highest result of the Tâo. Practical lesson to be drawn from it.

10. Confucius at the court of *Kh*û along with Sun Shû-âo and Î-liâo.

11. Ȝze-*kh*î, and his eight sons, with the physiognomist *K*iû-fang Yăn.

12. Nieh *Kh*üeh meets Hsü Yû fleeing from the court of Yâo.

BOOK XXV.

Par. 1. Ȝeh-yang seeking an introduction to the king of *Kh*û. Î *K*ieh, Wang Kwo, and the recluse Kung-yüeh Hsiû.

3. The ancient sovereign *Z*ăn-hsiang; Thang, the founder of the Shang dynasty; Confucius; and Yung-*kh*ăng Ȝze.

4. King Yung of Wei and his counsellors:—on his desire and schemes to be revenged on Thien Mâu of *Kh*î. Tâi Ȝin-*z*ăn and his apologue about the horns of a snail.

5. Confucius and the Recluse at Ant-hill in *Kh*û.

6. The Border-warden of *Kh*ang-wû's lessons to Ȝze-lâo. *K*wang-ȝze's enforcement of them.

7. Lâo-ȝze and his disciple Po *K*ü:—that the prohibitions of Law provoke to transgression.

8. The conversion to Tâoism of *K*ü Po-yü.

9. Confucius and the historiographers;—about the honorary title of duke Ling of Wei.

10. Little Knowledge and the Correct Harmonizer:—on the Talk of the Hamlets and Villages.

11. On the namelessness of the Tâo; and that Tâo is but a borrowed or metaphorical name.

BOOK XXVI.

Par. 2. Against delaying to do good when it is in one's power to do it. The apologue of *K*wang-ȝze meeting with a goby on the road.

3. The big fish caught by the son of the duke of *Z*ăn.

4. The Resurrectionist Students.

5. How Lâo Lâi-ȝze admonished Confucius.

6. The dream of the ruler Yüan of Sung about a tortoise.

7. Hui-ȝze and *K*wang-ȝze;—on the use of being useless.

11. Illustrations of the evil accruing from going to excess in action, or too suddenly taking action.

Book XXVII.

Par. 2. *K*wang-ȝze and Hui-ȝze on Confucius;—did he change his views in his sixtieth year?

3. Confucius and his other disciples:—on Ȝăng-ȝze and his twice taking office with different moods of mind.

4. Yen *Kh*ăng Ȝze-yû tells his Master Tung-kwo Ȝze-*kh*î of his gradual attainments.

5. The penumbrae and the shadows.

6. Lâo-ȝze's lessoning of Yang Ȝze-*k*ü, and its effects on him.

Book XXVIII.

Par. 1. Yâo's proffers of the throne to Hsü Yû and Ȝze-*k*âu *K*ih-fû. Shun's proffers of it to Ȝze-*k*âu *K*ih-po, to Shan *K*üan, and to the farmer of Shih-hû. Thâi-wang Than-fû and the northern tribes. Prince Sâu of Yüeh.

2. Counsel of Ȝze-hwâ Ȝze to the marquis *K*âo of Han.

3. The ruler of Lû and the Tâoist Yen Ho, who hides himself from the advances of the other.

4. Lieh-ȝze and his wife, on his declining a gift from the ruler of *K*ăng.

5. The high-minded and resolute sheep-butcher Yüeh, and king *K*âo of *Kh*û.

6. The poor Yüan Hsien and the wealthy Ȝze-kung. Ȝăng-ȝze, in extreme poverty, maintaining his high and independent spirit. The satisfaction of Confucius in Yen Hui refusing, though poor, to take any official post.

7. Prince Mâu of *K*ung-shan, living in retirement, was not far from the Tâo.

8. Confucius and the disciples Yen Hui, Ȝze-lû, and Ȝze-kung, during the perilous time between *Kh*ăn and Ȝhâi.

9. Shun and the northerner Wû-*k*âi who refuses the throne. Thang, and Pien Sui and Wû Kwang, who both refused it.

10. The case of the brothers Po-î and Shû-*kh*î, who refused the proffers of king Wû.

Book XXIX.

Par. 1. The visit of Confucius to the robber *K*ih, and interview between them.

2. Ȝze-*k*ang and Mân Kâu-teh (Mr. Full of Gain-recklessly-got) on the pursuit of wealth.

3. Mr. Dissatisfied and Mr. Know-the-Mean; — on the pursuit and effect of riches.

Book XXX.

How *K*wang-ȝze dealt with the king of *K*âo and his swordsmen, curing the king of his love of the sword-fight. The three Swords.

Book XXXI.

Confucius and the Old Fisherman;—including the story of the man who tried to run away from his shadow.

Book XXXII.

Par. 1. Lieh-ȝze and the effect of his over-manifestation of his attractive qualities. Failure of the warnings of his master.

2. The sad fate of Hwan of *K*ăng, a Confucianist, who resented his father's taking part with his Mohist brother.

5. *K*û Phing-man and his slaughtering the dragon.

8. *K*wang-ȝze's rebuke of Ȝhâo Shang for pandering to the king of Sung, and thereby getting gifts from him.

9. Description to duke Âi of Lû of Confucius by Yen Ho as unfit to be entrusted with the government.

11. Khâo-fû the Correct, and his humility.

12. *K*wang-ȝze's rebuke of the man who boasted of having received chariots from the king of Sung, and comparison of him to the boy who stole a pearl from under the chin of the Black Dragon when he was asleep.

13. *K*wang-ȝze declines the offer of official dignity. The apologue of the sacrificial ox.

14. *K*wang-ȝze, about to die, opposes the wish of his disciples to give him a grand burial. His own description of what his burial should be.

Book XXXIII.

Par. 1. The method of the Tâo down to the time of Confucius.

2. The method of Mo Tî and his immediate followers.

3, 4. The method of Mo's later followers.

5. The method of Kwan Yin and Lâo-ȝze.

6. The method of *K*wang-ȝze.

7. The ways of Hui Shih, Kung-sun Lung, and other sophists.

APPENDIX VII.

I.

THE STONE TABLET IN THE TEMPLE OF LÂO-ȜZE. BY HSIEH TÂO-HĂNG OF THE SUI DYNASTY[1].

1. After the Thâi *K*î (or Primal Ether) commenced its action, the earliest period of time began to be unfolded.

---

[1] Hsieh Tâo-hăng 薛道衡, called also Hsüan-*kh*ing (玄卿), was one of the most famous scholars and able ministers of the Sui dynasty (581–618), and also an eloquent writer. His biography is given at considerable length in the fifty-seventh chapter of the Books of Sui.

For about 200 years after the end of the Ȝin dynasty, the empire had been in a very divided and distracted state. The period is known as the epoch of 'The Southern and Northern Dynasties,' no fewer than nine or ten of which co-existed, none of them able to assert a universal sway till the rise of Sui. The most powerful of them towards the end of the time was 'The Northern *K*âu,' in connexion with the Wû-*kh*ăng (武成) reign of which (558–561) the name of our Hsieh first appears. In the Wû-phing (武平) reign of 'The Northern *Kh*î (570–576),' we find him member of a committee for revising the rules of 'The Five Classes of Ceremonial Observances,' and gaining distinction as a poet.

When the emperor Wăn (文帝), by name Yang *K*ien (楊監), a scion of the ruling House of Sui, a small principality in the present Hû-pei, and founder of the dynasty so called, had succeeded in putting down the various conflicting dynasties, and claimed the sovereignty of the empire in 581, Hsieh freely yielded his allegiance to him, and was employed in the conduct of various affairs. The important paper, of the translation of the greater part of which a translation is here attempted, was the outcome of one of them. Wăn Tî regularly observed the Confucian worship of God, but also kept up the ceremonies of Buddhism and Tâoism. Having repaired the dilapidated temple of Lâo-ȝze at his birth-place, he required from Hsieh an inscription for the commemorative tablet in it, the composition of which is referred to the year 586, 'the sixth year of Sui's rule over all beneath the sky.'

Hsieh appears to have been a favourite with the emperor Wăn, but when Wăn was succeeded in 605 by his son, known as Yang Tî (煬帝), his relations with

The curtain of the sky was displayed, and the sun and moon were suspended in it; the four-cornered earth was established, and the mountains and streams found their places in it. Then the subtle influences (of the Ether) operated like the heaving of the breath, now subsiding and again expanding; the work of production went on in its seasons above and below; all things were formed as from materials, and were matured and maintained. There were the (multitudes of the) people; there were their rulers and superiors.

2. As to the august sovereigns of the highest antiquity, living as in nests on trees in summer, and in caves in winter, silently and spirit-like they exercised their wisdom. Dwelling like quails, and drinking (the rain and dew) like newly-hatched birds, they had their great ceremonies like the great terms of heaven and earth, not requiring to be regulated by the dishes and stands; and (also) their great music corresponding to the common harmonies of heaven and earth, not needing the guidance of bells and drums.

3. By and by there came the loss of the Tâo, when its Characteristics took its place. They in their turn were lost, and then came Benevolence. Under the Sovereigns and Kings that followed, now more slowly and anon more rapidly, the manners of the people, from being good and simple, became bad and mean. Thereupon came the Literati and the Mohists with their confused contentions; names and

---

the throne became less happy. Offended by a memorial which Hsieh presented, and the ground of offence in which we entirely fail to perceive, the emperor ordered him to put an end to himself. Hsieh was surprised by the sentence, and hesitated to comply with it, on which an executioner was sent to strangle him. Thus ended the life of Hsieh Tâo-hăng in his seventieth year. His death was regretted and resented, we are told, by the people generally. A collection of his writings was made in seventy chapters, and was widely read. I do not know to what extent these have been preserved; if many of them have been lost, and the paper, here in part submitted to the reader, were a fair specimen of the others, the loss must be pronounced to be great. Of this paper I have had two copies before me in translating it. One of them is in Ȝiâo Hung's 'Wings to Lâo-ȝze;' the other is in 'The Complete Works of the Ten Philosophers.' Errors of the Text occur now in the one copy, now in the other. From the two combined a Text, which must be exactly correct or nearly so, is made out.

rules were everywhere diffused. The 300 rules[1] of ceremony could not control men's natures; the 3000 rules[1] of punishment were not sufficient to put a stop to their treacherous villanies. But he who knows how to cleanse the current of a stream begins by clearing out its source, and he who would straighten the end of a process must commence with making its beginning correct. Is not the Great Tâo the Grand Source and the Grand Origin of all things?

4. The Master Lâo was conceived under the influence of a star. Whence he received the breath (of life) we cannot fathom, but he pointed to the (plum-) tree (under which he was born), and adopted it as his surname[2]; we do not understand[2] whence came the musical sounds (that were heard), but he kept his marvellous powers concealed in the womb for more than seventy years. When he was born, the hair on his head was already white, and he took the designation of 'The Old Boy' (or Lâo-ȝze). In his person, three gateways and two (bony) pillars formed the distinctive marks of his ears and eyes; two of the symbols for five, and ten brilliant marks were left by the wonderful tread of his feet and the grasp of his hands. From the time of Fû-hsî down to that of the *K*âu dynasty, in uninterrupted succession, dynasty after dynasty, his person appeared, but with changed names. In the times of kings Wăn and Wû he discharged the duties, (first), of Curator of the Royal Library[3], and (next), of the Recorder under the Pillar[3]. Later on in that dynasty he filled different offices, but did

---

[1] Compare vol. xxviii, p. 323, par. 38.

[2] Lî (李), a plum-tree. For this and many of the other prodigies mentioned by Hsieh, see what Julien calls 'The Fabulous Legend of Lâo-ȝze,' and has translated in the Introduction to his version of the Tâo Teh *K*ing. Others of them are found in the Historical, or rather Legendary, Introduction in the 'Collection of Tâoist Treatises,' edited by Lû Yü in 1877.

[3] The meaning of the former of these offices may be considered as settled;—see the note in Wang *K*ăn-*k*âi's edition of the 'Historical Records (1870),' under the Biography of Lâo-ȝze. The nature of the second office is not so clearly ascertained. It was, I apprehend, more of a literary character than the curatorship.

not change his appearance. As soon as Hsüan Nî[1] saw him, he sighed over him as 'the Dragon,' whose powers are difficult to be known[2]. Yin (Hsî), keeper of the (frontier) gate, keeping his eyes directed to every quarter, recognised 'the True Man' as he was hastening into retirement. (By Yin Hsî he was prevailed on) to put forth his extraordinary ability, and write his Book in two Parts[3],—to lead the nature (of man) back to the Tâo, and celebrating the usefulness of 'doing nothing.' The style of it is very condensed, and its reasoning deep and far-reaching. The hexagram which is made up of the 'dragons on the wing[4]' is not to be compared with it in exquisite subtlety. (The 3o *K*wan) which ends with the capture of the Lin, does not match it in its brightness and obscurity. If employed to regulate the person, the spirit becomes clear and the will is still. If employed to govern the state, the people return to simplicity, and become sincere and good. When one goes on to refine his body in accordance with it, the traces of material things are rolled away from it; in rainbow-hued robes and mounted on a stork he goes forwards and backwards to the purple palace; on its juice of gold and wine of jade[5] he feasts in the beautiful and pure capital. He is lustrous as the sun and moon; his ending and beginning are those of heaven and earth. He who crosses its stream, drives away the dust and noise of the world; he who finds its gate, mounts prancing up on the misty clouds. It is not for the ephemeral fly to know the fading and luxuriance of the Tâ-*kh*un[6], or for a Făng-î[7] to fathom the depth of an Arm of the sea. Vast indeed (is the Tâo)! words are not sufficient to describe its excellence and powers!

5. *K*wang *K*âu tells us, that, 'when Lâo Tan died,

---

[1] Confucius, who was styled after the beginning of our era for several centuries 'Duke Nî, the Illustrious.'

[2] See vol. xxxix, pp. 34, 35.

[3] See vol. xxxix, p. 35.

[4] The *Kh*ien or first of all the hexagrams of the Yî *K*ing; but the sentence is to be understood of all the hexagrams,—of the Yî as a whole.

[5] Compare Pope's line, 'The juice nectareous, and the balmy dew.'

[6] Vol. xxxix, p. 166.

[7] Vol. xxxix, p. 244.

*Kh*in Shih went to condole (with his son), but after crying out three times, immediately left the house[1].' This was what is called the punishment for his neglecting his Heaven (-implanted nature), and although it appears as one of the metaphorical illustrations of the supercilious officer, yet there is some little indication in the passage of the reappearance of the snake after casting its exuviae[2].

[At this point the author leaves the subject of the Tâo and its prophet, and enters on a long panegyric of the founder of the Sui dynasty and his achievements. This sovereign was the emperor Wăn (文帝), the founder of Sui (隋高祖), originally Yang *K*ien, a scion of the House of Sui, a principality whose name remains in Sui-*k*âu, of the department Teh-an in Hû Pei. He was certainly the ablest man in the China of his day, and deserves a portion of the praise with which Mr. Hsieh celebrates him after his extravagant fashion. He claimed the throne from the year 581. While doing honour to Confucianism, he did not neglect the other two religions in the empire, Tâoism and Buddhism; and having caused the old temple of Lâo-ȝze to be repaired in grand style in 586, he commissioned Hsieh Tâo-hăng to superintend the setting up in it a commemorative Tablet of stone.

I pass over all this, which is related at great length, and proceed to give the inscription. It occupies no fewer than 352 characters in 88 lines, each consisting of four characters. The lines are arranged in what we may call eleven stanzas of equal length, the second, fourth, sixth, and eighth lines of each rhyming together. There is a good deal of art in the metrical composition. In the first six stanzas the rhyming finals are in the even tone and one of the deflected tones alternately. In the last five stanzas this arrangement is reversed. The rhymes in 7, 9, and 11 are deflected, and in 8 and 10 even. The measure of four characters is the most common in the Shih *K*ing or Ancient Book of Poetry.

[1] Vol. xxxix, p. 201.

[2] Referring, I suppose, to the illustration of the fire and the faggots.

It continued to be a favourite down to the Thang dynasty, after which it fell very much into disuse. Through the many assonances of the Chinese characters, and the attention paid to the tones, we have in Chinese composition much of the art of rhyming, but comparatively little of the genius of poetry.]

II.

The Inscription.

St. 1. Back in the depths of ancient time;
Remote, before the Tîs began;
Four equal sides defined the earth,
And pillars eight the heaven sustained.
All living things in classes came,
The valleys wide, and mighty streams.
The Perfect Tâo, with movement wise,
Unseen, Its work did naturally.

St. 2. Its power the elements[1] all felt;
The incipient germs of things[2] appeared.
Shepherd and Lord established were,
And in their hands the ivory bonds[3].
The Tîs must blush before the Hwangs[4];
The Wangs must blush before the Tîs[4].
More distant grew Tâo's highest gifts,
And simple ways more rare became.

St. 3. The still placidity was gone,
And all the old harmonious ways.
Men talents prized, and varnished wit;
The laws displayed proved but a net.

---

[1] 'The five essences;' meaning, I think, the subtle power and operation of the five elements.

[2] So Williams, under Wei (微). See also the Khang-hsî Thesaurus under the phrase 三微.

[3] 'Bonds' with written characters on them superseded the 'knotted cords' of the primitive age. That the material of the bonds should be, as here represented, slips of ivory, would seem to anticipate the progress of society.

[4] The Hwangs (皇) preceded the Tîs in the Tâoistic genesis of history; and as being more simple were Tâoistically superior to them; so it was with the Tîs and the Wangs or Kings.

Wine-cups and stands the board adorned,
And shields and spears the country filled.
The close-meshed nets the fishes scared:
And numerous bows the birds alarmed.

St. 4. Then did the True Man[1] get his birth,
As 'neath the Bear the star shone down[2].
All dragon gifts his person graced;
Like the stork's plumage was his hair.
The complicated he resolved[3], the sharp made blunt[3],
The mean rejected, and the generous chose;
In brightness like the sun and moon,
And lasting as the heaven and earth[3].

St. 5. Small to him seemed the mountains five[4],
And narrow seemed the regions nine[4];
About he went with lofty tread,
And in short time he rambled far.
In carriage by black oxen drawn[5],
Around the purple air was bright.
Grottoes then oped to him their sombre gates,
And thence, unseen, his spirit power flowed forth.

St. 6. The village near the stream of Ko[6]
Traces of him will still retain[6];
But now, as in the days of old,
With changèd times the world is changed.

---

[1] This of course was Lâo-ȝze. [2] See above, p. 313, par. 4.

[3] In the Tâo Teh *K*ing, p. 50, par. 2, and p. 52, par. 1. The reading of line 7 is different in my two authorities: — in the one 日角月角; in the other 乃前月角. I suppose the correct reading should be— 日前月角, and have given what I think is the meaning.

[4] Two well-known numerical categories. See Mayers's Manual, pp. 320, 321, and p. 340.

[5] So it was, according to the story, that Lâo-ȝze drew near to the barrier gate, when he wished to leave China.

[6] The Ko is a river flowing from Ho-nan into An-hui, and falling into the Hwâi, not far from the district city of Hwâi-yüan. It enters the one province from the other in the small department of Po (亳州), in which, according to a Chinese map in my possession, Lâo-ȝze was born. The Khang-hsî Thesaurus also gives a passage to the effect that the temple of his mother was hereabouts, at a bend in the Ko.

His stately temple fell to ruin;
His altar empty was and still;
By the nine wells dryandras grew [1],
And the twin tablets were but heaps of stone.

St. 7. But when our emperor was called to rule,
All spirit-like and sage was he.
Earth's bells reverberated loud,
And light fell on the heavenly mirror down.
The universe in brightness shone,
And portents all were swept away;
(All souls), or bright or dark [2], revered,
And spirits came to take from him their law.

St. 8. From desert sands [3] and where the great trees grow [3],
From phoenix caves, and from the dragon woods,
All different creatures came sincere;
Men of all regions gave their hearts to him.
Their largest vessels brought their gifts,
And kings their rarest things described;
Black clouds a thousand notes sent forth;
And in the fragrant winds were citherns heard [4].

St. 9. Through his transforming power, the tripods were made sure;
And families became polite and courteous.

---

[1] The nine wells, or bubbling springs, near the village where Lâo was born, are mentioned by various writers; but I fail to see how the growth of the trees about them indicated the ruin of his temple.

[2] I have introduced the 'all souls' in this line, because of the 鬼 in the second character. Williams defines the first character, yao (曜), as 'the effulgence of the sun,' and of 'heavenly bodies generally;' the second (魄) is well known as meaning 'the animal soul,' and 'the dark disk of the moon.' The Thesaurus, however, explains the two characters together as a name for the pole star (北 辰; see Analects I, i); and perhaps I had better have followed this meaning.

[3] The 'desert sands' were, no doubt, what we call 'the desert of Gobi.' The trees referred to were 'in the extreme East.' The combination phan-mû is not described more particularly.

[4] This and the three preceding lines are not a little dark.

Ever kept he in mind (the sage) beneath the Pillar[1],
Still emulous of the sovereigns most ancient[2].
So has he built this pure temple,
And planned its stately structure;
Pleasant, with hills and meadows around,
And lofty pavilion with its distant prospect.

St. 10. Its beams are of plum-tree, its ridge-pole of cassia;
A balustrade winds round it; many are its pillars;
About them spreads and rolls the fragrant smoke[3];
Cool and pure are the breezes and mists.
The Immortal officers come to their places[4];
The Plumaged guests are found in its court[4],
Numerous and at their ease,
They send down blessing, bright and efficacious.

St. 11. Most spirit-like, unfathomable,
(Tâo's) principles abide, with their symbolism attached[5].
Loud is Its note, but never sound emits[6],
Yet always it awakes the highest echoes.
From far and near men praise It;
In the shades, and in the realms of light, they look up for Its aid;
Reverently have we graven and gilt this stone
And made our lasting proclamation thereby to heaven and earth.

---

[1] 'The (sage) beneath the Pillar' must be Lâo-ȝze. See above in the Introductory notice, p. 313.

[2] See the note on the meaning of the epithet 太上, vol. xxxix, p. 40.

[3] 'The smoke,' I suppose, 'of the incense, and from the offerings.'

[4] Tâoist monks are called 'Plumaged or Feathered Scholars (羽士),' from the idea that by their discipline and pills, they can emancipate themselves from the trammels of the material body, and ascend (fly up) to heaven. Arrived there, as Immortals or Hsien (仙), it further appears they were constituted into a hierarchy or society, of which some of them were 'officers,' higher in rank than others.

[5] An allusion to the text of the hexagrams of the Yî *K*ing, where the explanations of them by king Wăn,—his thwan, are followed by the symbolism of their different lines by the duke of *K*âu,—his hsiang.

[6] See the Tâo Teh *K*ing, ch. xli, par. 2.

APPENDIX VIII.

RECORD FOR THE SACRIFICIAL HALL OF *K*WANG-ƷZE. BY SÛ SHIH[1].

1. *K*wang-ʒze was a native (of the territory) of Măng and an officer in (the city of) *Kh*î-yüan. He had been dead for more than a thousand years, and no one had up to this time sacrificed to him in Măng. It was Wang *K*ing, the assistant Secretary of the Prefect, who superintended the erection of a Sacrificial Hall (to *K*wang-ʒze), and (when the building was finished) he applied to me for

---

[1] The elder of two brothers, both famous as scholars, poets, and administrators in the history of their country, and sons of a father hardly less distinguished. The father (A. D. 1009–1066) was named Sû Hsün (蘇洵), with the designation of Ming-yun (明允), and the two names of locality, Lâo-*kh*wan (老泉) and Mei-shân (眉山). Of the two brothers the elder (1036–1101), author of the notice here adduced, was the more celebrated. His name was Shih (軾), and his designation Ʒze-*k*ân (子瞻); but he is more frequently styled Tung-pho (東坡), from the situation of a house which he occupied at one time. His life was marked by several vicissitudes of the imperial favour which was shown to him and of the disgrace to which he was repeatedly subjected. He was versed in all Chinese literature, but the sincerity of his Confucianism has not been called in question. His brother (1039–1112), by name *K*eh (轍), by designation Ʒze-yû (子由), and by locality Ying-pin (潁濱), has left us a commentary on the Tâo Teh *K*ing, nearly the whole of which is given by Ʒiâo Hung, under the several chapters. It seems to have been *K*eh's object to find a substantial unity under the different forms of Confucian, Buddhistic, and Tâoist thought.

The short essay, for it is more an essay than 'a record,' which is here translated is appended by Ʒiâo Hung to his 'Wings to *K*wang-ʒze.' It is hardly worthy of Shih's reputation.

a composition which might serve as a record of the event; (which I made as follows):—

2. According to the Historical Records (of Sze-mâ *Kh*ien), *K*wang-ȝze lived in the time of the kings Hui of Liang (B.C. 370–333 [?])[1] and Hsüan of *Kh*î (B.C. 332–314). There was no subject of study to which he did not direct his attention, but his preference was for the views of Lâo-ȝze; and thus it was that of the books which he wrote, containing in all more than ten myriad characters, the greater part are metaphorical illustrations of those views. He made 'The Old Fisherman,' 'The Robber *K*ih,' and 'The Cutting Open Satchels,' to deride the followers of Confucius, and to set forth the principles of Lâo-ȝze. (So writes Sze-mâ *Kh*ien, but) his view is that of one who had only a superficial knowledge of *K*wang-ȝze. My idea is that *K*wang wished to support the principles of Khung-ȝze, though we must not imitate him in the method which he took to do so. (I will illustrate my meaning by a case of a different kind):—A prince of *Kh*û[2] was once hurrying away from the city in disguise[2], when the gate-keeper refused to let him pass through. On this his servant threatened the prince with a switch, and reviled him, saying, 'Slave, you have no strength!' On seeing this, the gate-keeper allowed them to go out. The thing certainly took place in an irregular way, and the prince escaped by an inversion of what was right;—he seemed openly to put himself in opposition, while he was secretly maintaining and supporting. If we think that his servant did not love the prince, our judgment will be wrong; if we think that his action was a model for imitation in serving a prince, in that also we shall be wrong. In the same way the words of *K*wang-ȝze are thrown out in a contradictory manner, with which the tenor of his writing does not agree. The correct interpre-

[1] Compare vol. xxxix, pp. 36, 37, 39. Sze-mâ *Kh*ien enters king Hui's death in this year. The 'Bamboo Books' place it sixteen years later, see 'The General Mirror of History,' under the thirty-fifth year of king Hsien of *K*âu.

[2] I suppose this incident is an invention of Sû Shih's own. I have not met with it anywhere else. In Ȝiâo's text for the 'in disguise' of the translation, however, there is an error. He gives 徽服 instead of 微服.

tation of them shows them to be far from any wish to defame Khung-ȝze.

3. And there is that in the style which slightly indicates his real meaning. (In his last Book for instance), when discussing the historical phases of Tâoism, he exhibits them from Mo Tî, *Kh*in Hwâ-lî, Phăng Măng, Shăn Tâo, Thien Pien, Kwan Yin, and Lâo Tan, down even to himself, and brings them all together as constituting one school, but Confucius is not among them [1]. So great and peculiar is the honour which he does to him!

4. I have had my doubts, however, about 'The Robber *K*ih (Bk. XXIX),' and 'The Old Fisherman (Bk. XXXI),' for they do seem to be really defamatory of Confucius. And as to 'The Kings who have wished to Resign the Throne (Bk. XXVIII)' and 'The Delight in the Sword-fight (Bk. XXX);' they are written in a low and vulgar style, and have nothing to do with the doctrine of the Tâo. Looking at the thing and reflecting on it, there occurred to me the paragraph at the end of Book XXVII ('Metaphorical Language'). It tells us that 'when Yang Ȝze-*k*ü had gone as far as *Kh*in, he met with Lâo-ȝze, who said to him, "Your eyes are lofty, and you stare; who would live with you? The purest carries himself as if he were defiled, and the most virtuous seems to feel himself defective." Yang Ȝze-*k*ü looked abashed and changed countenance. When he first went to his lodging-house, the people in it met him and went before him. The master of it carried his mat for him, and the mistress brought to him the towel and comb. The lodgers left their mats and the cook his fire-place, as he went past them. When he went away, the others in the house would have striven with him about (the places for) their mats.'

After reading this paragraph, I passed over the four intermediate Books,—the *Z*ang Wang, the Yüeh *K*ien, the Yü Fû, and the Tâo *K*ih, and joined it on to the first paragraph of the Lieh Yü-khâu (Book XXXII). I then read how Lieh-ȝze had started to go to *Kh*î but came back

[1] See Book XXXIII, pars. 2, 3, 4, 5, 6.

when he had got half-way to it. (When asked why he had done so), he replied, 'I was frightened, I went into ten soup-shops to get a meal, and in five of them the soup was set before me before I had paid for it.' Comparing this with the paragraph about Yang Ȝze-*k*ü, the light flashed on me. I laughed and said, 'They certainly belong to one chapter!'

The words of *K*wang-ȝze were not ended; and some other stupid person copied in (these other four Books) of his own among them. We should have our wits about us, and mark the difference between them. The division of paragraphs and the titles of the Books did not proceed from *K*wang-ȝze himself, but were introduced by custom in the course of time[1].

Recorded on the 19th day of the 11th month of the first year of the period Yüan Făng (1078–1085).

---

[1] Few of my readers, I apprehend, will appreciate this article, which is to me more a jeu d'esprit than 'a record.' It is strange that so slight and fantastic a piece should have had the effect attributed to it of making the four Books which they call in question be generally held by scholars of the present dynasty to be apocryphal, but still Sû Shih avows in it his belief in Book XXXIII. Compare the quotation from Lin Hsî-*k*ung on pp. 296, 297.

INDEX

TO

VOLUMES XXXIX (i), XL (ii).

TRANSLITERATION OF ORIENTAL ALPHABETS ADOPTED FOR THE TRANSLATIONS OF THE SACRED BOOKS OF THE EAST.

CONSONANTS.	MISSIONARY ALPHABET.			Sanskrit.	Zend.	Pehlevi.	Persian.	Arabic.	Hebrew.	Chinese.
	I Class.	II Class.	III Class.							
Gutturales.										
1 Tenuis	k	...	....	क	𐬐	[illegible]	ک	ک	כּ	k
2 ,, aspirata	kh	...	....	ख	𐬑	[illegible]	...	...	כ	kh
3 Media	g	...	....	ग	𐬔	[illegible]	گ	...	גּ	...
4 ,, aspirata	gh	...	....	घ	𐬖	[illegible]	...	...	ג	...
5 Gutturo-labialis	q	...	....	...	....	...	ق	ق	ק	...
6 Nasalis	ṅ (ng)	...	....	ङ	{[illegible] (ng) / [illegible] (N)}	...	...	...	...	...
7 Spiritus asper	h	...	....	ह	𐬵 ([illegible] *hv*)	[illegible]	ه	ه	ה	h, hs
8 ,, lenis	'	...	....	...	....	...	ا	ا	א	...
9 ,, asper faucalis	ʽh	...	....	...	....	...	ح	ح	ח	...
10 ,, lenis faucalis	ʼh	...	....	...	....	...	ع	ع	ע	...
11 ,, asper fricatus	...	*ʽh*	....	...	....	...	خ	خ	ח	...
12 ,, lenis fricatus	...	*ʼh*	....	...	....	...	...	...	...	...
Gutturales modificatae (palatales, &c.)										
13 Tenuis	...	*k*	....	च	𐬗	[illegible]	چ	...	...	*k*
14 ,, aspirata	...	*kh*	....	छ	....	...	...	...	...	*kh*
15 Media	...	*g*	....	ज	𐬘	[illegible]	ج	ج	...	...
16 ,, aspirata	...	*gh*	....	झ	....	...	غ	غ	...	...
17 ,, Nasalis	...	*ñ*	....	ञ	....	...	...	...	...	...

CONSONANTS (*continued*).	MISSIONARY ALPHABET. I Class.	II Class.	III Class.	Sanskrit.	Zend.	Pehlevi.	Persian.	Arabic.	Hebrew.	Chinese.
18 Semivocalis	y	...	...	य	𐬫, [illegible] init.	[illegible]	ي	ي	י	y
19 Spiritus asper	...	(ẏ)	...	...	...	...	...	...	...	...
20 ,, lenis	...	(ẏ)	...	...	...	...	...	...	...	...
21 ,, asper assibilatus	...	*s*	...	श	𐬱	[illegible]	ش	ش	...	...
22 ,, lenis assibilatus	...	*z*	...	...	𐬲	[illegible]	ژ	...	...	*z*
Dentales.										
23 Tenuis	t	...	...	त	𐬙	[illegible]	ت	ت	תּ	t
24 ,, aspirata	th	...	...	थ	𐬚	...	...	...	ת	th
25 ,, assibilata	...	...	TH	...	...	...	ث	ث	...	...
26 Media	d	...	...	द	𐬛	[illegible]	د	د	דּ	...
27 ,, aspirata	dh	...	...	ध	𐬜	...	...	...	ד	...
28 ,, assibilata	...	...	DH	...	...	...	ذ	ذ	...	...
29 Nasalis	n	...	...	न	𐬥	[illegible]	ن	ن	נ	n
30 Semivocalis	l	...	...	ल	...	[illegible]	ل	ل	ל	l
31 ,, mollis 1	...	*l*	...	ळ	...	...	...	...	...	...
32 ,, mollis 2	...	...	L	...	...	...	...	...	...	...
33 Spiritus asper 1	s	...	...	स	𐬯	[illegible]	س (ث)	س	שׂ	s
34 ,, asper 2	...	...	s (ʃ)	...	...	...	...	...	ס	...
35 ,, lenis	z	...	...	...	𐬰	[illegible]	ز (ذ)	ز	ז	z
36 ,, asperrimus 1	...	...	z (ʒ)	...	...	...	ص	ص	צ	ʒ, ʒh
37 ,, asperrimus 2	...	...	ẓ (ʒ̣)	...	...	...	ض	...	...	...

	Column 1	Column 2	Column 3	Column 4	Column 5	Column 6	Column 7	Column 8	Column 9	Column 10
Dentales modificatae (linguales, &c.)										
38 Tenuis	...	*t*	....	ट	....	...	ط	ط	ט	...
39 „ aspirata	...	*th*	....	ठ	....	...	ظ	ظ	...	...
40 Media	...	*d*	....	ड	[illegible]	[illegible]	...	...	...	...
41 „ aspirata	...	*dh*	....	ढ	....	...	...	ض	...	...
42 Nasalis	...	*n*	....	ण	[illegible]	...	...	...	...	...
43 Semivocalis	r	...	....	र	[illegible]	[illegible]	ر	ر	ר	...
44 „ fricata	...	*r*	....	...	....	...	...	...	...	*r*
45 „ diacritica	...	...	R	...	....	...	...	...	...	...
46 Spiritus asper	sh	...	....	ष	[illegible]	[illegible]	...	...	...	sh
47 „ lenis	zh	...	....	...	....	...	...	...	...	...
Labiales.										
48 Tenuis	p	...	....	प	[illegible]	[illegible]	پ	...	פּ	p
49 „ aspirata	ph	...	....	फ	....	...	...	...	פ	ph
50 Media	b	...	....	ब	[illegible]	[illegible]	ب	ب	בּ	...
51 „ aspirata	bh	...	....	भ	....	...	...	...	ב	...
52 Tenuissima	...	*p*	....	...	....	...	...	...	...	...
53 Nasalis	m	...	....	म	[illegible]	[illegible]	م	م	מ	m
54 Semivocalis	w	...	....	...	[illegible]	...	...	...	...	w
55 „ aspirata	hw	...	....	...	....	...	...	...	...	...
56 Spiritus asper	f	...	....	...	[illegible]	[illegible]	ف	ف	...	f
57 „ lenis	v	...	....	व	»	[illegible]	و	و	ו	...
58 Anusvâra	...	*m*	....	अं	[illegible] ã	...	...	...	...	...
59 Visarga	...	*h*	....	अः	....	...	...	...	...	...

VOWELS.	MISSIONARY ALPHABET. I Class.	II Class.	III Class.	Sanskrit.	Zend.	Pehlevi.	Persian.	Arabic.	Hebrew.	Chinese.
1 Neutralis	0	...	....	...	....	...	...	...	ְ	ǎ
2 Laryngo-palatalis	ĕ	...	....	...	....	...	...	...	...	...
3 „ labialis	ŏ	...	....	...	....	𐭠 fin.	...	...	...	...
4 Gutturalis brevis	a	...	....	अ	𐬀	𐭠 init.	َ	َ	ַ	a
5 „ longa	â	(a)	....	आ	𐬁	𐭠	ـَا	ـَا	ָ	â
6 Palatalis brevis	i	...	....	इ	𐬌	...	ِ	ِ	ִ	i
7 „ longa	î	(i)	....	ई	𐬍	𐭩	ـِي	ـِي	ִי	î
8 Dentalis brevis	*li*	...	....	ऌ	....	...	...	...	...	...
9 „ longa	*lî*	...	....	ॡ	....	...	...	...	...	...
10 Lingualis brevis	*ri*	...	....	ऋ	....	...	...	...	...	...
11 „ longa	*rî*	...	....	ॠ	....	...	...	...	...	...
12 Labialis brevis	u	...	....	उ	𐬎	...	ُ	ُ	ֻ	u
13 „ longa	û	(u)	....	ऊ	𐬏	𐭥	ـُو	ـُو	וּ	û
14 Gutturo-palatalis brevis	e	...	....	...	𐬆(e) 𐬈(e)	...	...	...	ֶ	e
15 „ longa	ê (ai)	(e)	....	ए	𐬉, 𐬇	𐭩	ـَیْ	ـَیْ	ֵ	ê
16 Diphthongus gutturo-palatalis	âi	(ai)	....	ऐ	....	...	ـَیْ	ـَیْ	...	âi
17 „ „	ei (ĕi)	...	....	...	....	...	...	...	...	ei, êi
18 „ „	oi (ŏu)	...	....	...	....	...	...	...	...	...
19 Gutturo-labialis brevis	o	...	....	...	𐬊	...	...	...	ָ	o
20 „ longa	ô (au)	(o)	....	ओ	𐬋	𐭥	ـَوْ	ـَوْ	וֹ	...
21 Diphthongus gutturo-labialis	âu	(au)	....	औ	𐬁𐬎 (*au*)	...	ـَوْ	ـَوْ	...	âu
22 „ „	eu (ĕu)	...	....	...	....	...	...	...	...	...
23 „ „	ou (ŏu)	...	....	...	....	...	...	...	...	...
24 Gutturalis fracta	ä	...	....	...	....	...	...	...	...	...
25 Palatalis fracta	ï	...	....	...	....	...	...	...	...	...
26 Labialis fracta	ü	...	....	...	....	...	...	...	...	ü
27 Gutturo-labialis fracta	ö	...	....	...	....	...	...	...	...	...

SACRED BOOKS OF THE EAST

TRANSLATED BY

VARIOUS ORIENTAL SCHOLARS

AND EDITED BY

F. MAX MÜLLER

*** *This Series is published with the sanction and co-operation of the Secretary of State for India in Council.*

REPORT presented to the ACADÉMIE DES INSCRIPTIONS, May 11, 1883, by M. ERNEST RENAN.

'M. Renan présente trois nouveaux volumes de la grande collection des "Livres sacrés de l'Orient" (Sacred Books of the East), que dirige à Oxford, avec une si vaste érudition et une critique si sûre, le savant associé de l'Académie des Inscriptions, M. Max Müller. . . . La première série de ce beau recueil, composée de 24 volumes, est presque achevée. M. Max Müller se propose d'en publier une seconde, dont l'intérêt historique et religieux ne sera pas moindre. M. Max Müller a su se procurer la collaboration des savans les plus éminens d'Europe et d'Asie. L'Université d'Oxford, que cette grande publication honore au plus haut degré, doit tenir à continuer dans les plus larges proportions une œuvre aussi philosophiquement conçue que savamment exécutée.'

EXTRACT from the QUARTERLY REVIEW.

'We rejoice to notice that a second series of these translations has been announced and has actually begun to appear. The stones, at least, out of which a stately edifice may hereafter arise, are here being brought together. Prof. Max Müller has deserved well of scientific history. Not a few minds owe to his enticing words their first attraction to this branch of study. But no work of his, not even the great edition of the Rig-Veda, can compare in importance or in usefulness with this English translation of the Sacred Books of the East, which has been devised by his foresight, successfully brought so far by his persuasive and organising power, and will, we trust, by the assistance of the distinguished scholars he has gathered round him, be carried in due time to a happy completion.'

Professor E. HARDY, Inaugural Lecture in the University of Freiburg, 1887.

'Die allgemeine vergleichende Religionswissenschaft datirt von jenem grossartigen, in seiner Art einzig dastehenden Unternehmen, zu welchem auf Anregung Max Müllers im Jahre 1874 auf dem internationalen Orientalistencongress in London der Grundstein gelegt worden war, die Übersetzung der heiligen Bücher des Ostens' (*the Sacred Books of the East*).

Oxford

AT THE CLARENDON PRESS

LONDON: HENRY FROWDE

OXFORD UNIVERSITY PRESS WAREHOUSE, AMEN CORNER, E.C.

FIRST SERIES.

VOL. I. The Upanishads.

Translated by F. MAX MÜLLER. Part I. The *Kh*ândogya-upanishad, The Talavakâra-upanishad, The Aitareya-âra*n*yaka, The Kaushîtaki-brâhma*n*a-upanishad, and The Vâgasaneyi-sa*m*hitâ-upanishad. 8vo, cloth, 10*s*. 6*d*.

The Upanishads contain the philosophy of the Veda. They have become the foundation of the later Vedânta doctrines, and indirectly of Buddhism. Schopenhauer, speaking of the Upanishads, says: 'In the whole world there is no study so beneficial and so elevating as that of the Upanishads. It has been the solace of my life, it will be the solace of my death.'

[See also Vol. XV.]

VOL. II. The Sacred Laws of the Âryas,

As taught in the Schools of Âpastamba, Gautama, Vâsish*th*a, and Baudhâyana. Translated by GEORG BÜHLER. Part I. Âpastamba and Gautama. 8vo, cloth, 10*s*. 6*d*.

The Sacred Laws of the Âryas contain the original treatises on which the Laws of Manu and other lawgivers were founded.

[See also Vol. XIV.]

VOL. III. The Sacred Books of China.

The Texts of Confucianism. Translated by JAMES LEGGE. Part I. The Shû King, The Religious Portions of the Shih King, and The Hsiâo King. 8vo, cloth, 12*s*. 6*d*.

Confucius was a collector of ancient traditions, not the founder of a new religion. As he lived in the sixth and fifth centuries B.C. his works are of unique interest for the study of Ethology.

[See also Vols. XVI, XXVII, XXVIII, XXXIX, and XL.]

VOL. IV. The Zend-Avesta.

Translated by JAMES DARMESTETER. Part I. The Vendîdâd. 8vo, cloth, 10*s*. 6*d*.

The Zend-Avesta contains the relics of what was the religion of Cyrus, Darius, and Xerxes, and, but for the battle of Marathon, might have become the religion of Europe. It forms to the present day the sacred book of the Parsis, the so-called fire-worshippers. Two more volumes will complete the translation of all that is left us of Zoroaster's religion.

[See also Vols. XXIII and XXXI.]

VOL. V. Pahlavi Texts.

Translated by E. W. WEST. Part I. The Bundahis, Bahman Yast, and Shâyast lâ-shâyast. 8vo, cloth, 12*s*. 6*d*.

The Pahlavi Texts comprise the theological literature of the revival of Zoroaster's religion, beginning with the Sassanian dynasty. They are important for a study of Gnosticism.

VOLS. VI AND IX. The Qur'ân.

Parts I and II. Translated by E. H. PALMER. 8vo, cloth, 21*s*.

This translation, carried out according to his own peculiar views of the origin of the Qur'ân, was the last great work of E. H. Palmer, before he was murdered in Egypt.

VOL. VII. The Institutes of Vish*n*u.

Translated by JULIUS JOLLY. 8vo, cloth, 10*s*. 6*d*.

A collection of legal aphorisms, closely connected with one of the oldest Vedic schools, the Kathas, *but considerably added to in later time. Of importance for a critical study of the Laws of Manu.*

VOL. VIII. The Bhagavadgîtâ, with The Sanatsu*g*âtîya, and The Anugîtâ.

Translated by KÂSHINÂTH TRIMBAK TELANG. 8vo, cloth, 10*s*. 6*d*.

The earliest philosophical and religious poem of India. It has been paraphrased in Arnold's 'Song Celestial.'

VOL. X. The Dhammapada,

Translated from Pâli by F. MAX MÜLLER; and

The Sutta-Nipâta,

Translated from Pâli by V. FAUSBÖLL; being Canonical Books of the Buddhists. 8vo, cloth, 10*s*. 6*d*.

The Dhammapada contains the quintessence of Buddhist morality. The Sutta-Nipâta gives the authentic teaching of Buddha on some of the fundamental principles of religion.

VOL. XI. Buddhist Suttas.

Translated from Pâli by T. W. RHYS DAVIDS. 1. The Mahâparinibbâna Suttanta; 2. The Dhamma-*k*akka-ppavattana Sutta. 3. The Tevigga Suttanta; 4. The Âkaṅkheyya Sutta; 5. The *K*etokhila Sutta; 6. The Mahâ-sudassana Suttanta; 7. The Sabbâsava Sutta. 8vo, cloth, 10*s*. 6*d*.

A collection of the most important religious, moral, and philosophical discourses taken from the sacred canon of the Buddhists.

VOL. XII. The *S*atapatha-Brâhma*n*a, according to the Text of the Mâdhyandina School.

Translated by JULIUS EGGELING. Part I. Books I and II. 8vo, cloth, 12*s*. 6*d*.

A minute account of the sacrificial ceremonies of the Vedic age. It contains the earliest account of the Deluge in India.

[See also Vol. XXVI.]

VOL. XIII. Vinaya Texts.

Translated from the Pâli by T. W. RHYS DAVIDS and HERMANN OLDENBERG. Part I. The Pâtimokkha. The Mahâvagga, I–IV. 8vo, cloth, 10*s*. 6*d*.

The Vinaya Texts give for the first time a translation of the moral code of the Buddhist religion as settled in the third century B.C.

[See also Vols. XVII and XX.]

VOL. XIV. The Sacred Laws of the Âryas,

As taught in the Schools of Âpastamba, Gautama, Vâsish*th*a, and Baudhâyana. Translated by GEORG BÜHLER. Part II. Vasish*th*a and Baudhâyana. 8vo, cloth, 10*s*. 6*d*.

VOL. XV. The Upanishads.

Translated by F. MAX MÜLLER. Part II. The Ka*th*a-upanishad, The Mu*nd*aka-upanishad, The Taittirîyaka-upanishad, The B*ri*hadâra*n*yaka-upanishad, The *S*vetâ*s*vatara-upanishad, The Pra*sñ*a-upanishad, and The Maitrâya*n*a-brâhma*n*a-upanishad. 8vo, cloth, 10*s*. 6*d*.

VOL. XVI. The Sacred Books of China.

The Texts of Confucianism. Translated by JAMES LEGGE. Part II. The Yî King. 8vo, cloth, 10*s*. 6*d*.

VOL. XVII. Vinaya Texts.

Translated from the Pâli by T. W. RHYS DAVIDS and HERMANN OLDENBERG. Part II. The Mahâvagga V–X. The *K*ullavagga, I–III. 8vo, cloth, 10*s*. 6*d*.

VOL. XVIII. Pahlavi Texts.

Translated by E. W. WEST. Part II. The Dâ*d*istân-î Dînîk and The Epistles of Mânû*sk*îhar. 8vo, cloth, 12*s*. 6*d*.

VOL. XIX. The Fo-sho-hing-tsan-king.

A Life of Buddha by A*s*vaghosha Bodhisattva, translated from Sanskrit into Chinese by Dharmaraksha, A.D. 420, and from Chinese into English by SAMUEL BEAL. 8vo, cloth, 10*s*. 6*d*.

This life of Buddha was translated from Sanskrit into Chinese, A.D. 420. It contains many legends, some of which show a certain similarity to the Evangelium infantiae, etc.

VOL. XX. Vinaya Texts.

Translated from the Pâli by T. W. RHYS DAVIDS and HERMANN OLDENBERG. Part III. The *K*ullavagga, IV–XII. 8vo, cloth, 10*s*. 6*d*.

VOL. XXI. The Saddharma-pu*nd*arîka; or, The Lotus of the True Law.

Translated by H. KERN. 8vo, cloth, 12*s*. 6*d*.

'The Lotus of the true Law,' a canonical book of the Northern Buddhists, translated from Sanskrit. There is a Chinese translation of this book which was finished as early as the year 286 *A.D.*

VOL. XXII. *G*aina-Sûtras.

Translated from Prâkrit by HERMANN JACOBI. Part I. The Â*k*ârâṅga-Sûtra and The Kalpa-Sûtra. 8vo, cloth, 10*s*. 6*d*.

The religion of the Gainas *was founded by a contemporary of Buddha. It still counts numerous adherents in India, while there are no Buddhists left in India proper.*

VOL. XXIII. The Zend-Avesta.

Translated by JAMES DARMESTETER. Part II. The Sîrôzahs, Ya*s*ts, and Nyâyi*s*. 8vo, cloth, 10*s*. 6*d*.

VOL. XXIV. Pahlavi Texts.

Translated by E. W. WEST. Part III. Dînâ-î Maînôg-î Khira*d*, *S*ikand-gûmânîk Vigâr, and Sad Dar. 8vo, cloth, 10*s*. 6*d*.

SECOND SERIES.

VOL. XXV. Manu.

Translated by GEORG BÜHLER. 8vo, cloth, 21*s*.

This translation is founded on that of Sir William Jones, which has been carefully revised and corrected with the help of seven native Commentaries. An Appendix contains all the quotations from Manu which are found in the Hindu Law-books, translated for the use of the Law Courts in India. Another Appendix gives a synopsis of parallel passages from the six Dharma-sûtras, the other Sm*ri*tis, the Upanishads, the Mahâbhârata, etc.

VOL. XXVI. The *S*atapatha-Brâhma*n*a.

Translated by JULIUS EGGELING. Part II. Books III and IV. 8vo, cloth, 12*s*. 6*d*.

VOLS. XXVII AND XXVIII. The Sacred Books of China.

The Texts of Confucianism. Translated by JAMES LEGGE. Parts III and IV. The Lî *K*î, or Collection of Treatises on the Rules of Propriety, or Ceremonial Usages. 8vo, cloth, 12*s*. 6*d*. each.

VOL. XXIX. The G*ri*hya-Sûtras, Rules of Vedic Domestic Ceremonies.

Part I. *S*âṅkhâyana, Â*s*valâyana, Pâraskara, Khâdira. Translated by HERMANN OLDENBERG. 8vo, cloth, 12*s*. 6*d*.

These rules of Domestic Ceremonies describe the home life of the ancient Âryas with a completeness and accuracy unmatched in any other literature. Some of these rules have been incorporated in the ancient Law-books.

VOL. XXX. The G*ri*hya-Sûtras. Part II. [*In the Press.*]

VOL. XXXI. The Zend-Avesta.

Part III. The Yasna, Visparad, Âfrînagân, Gâhs, and Miscellaneous Fragments. Translated by L. H. MILLS. 8vo, cloth, 12*s*. 6*d*.

VOL. XXXII. Vedic Hymns.

Translated by F. MAX MÜLLER. Part I. [*In the Press.*]

VOL. XXXIII. The Minor Law-books.

Translated by JULIUS JOLLY. Part I. Nârada, B*ri*haspati. 8vo, cloth, 10*s*. 6*d*.

VOL. XXXIV. The Vedânta-Sûtras, with the Commentary by *S*aṅkarâ*k*ârya.

Translated by G. THIBAUT. 8vo, cloth, 12*s*. 6*d*.

VOL. XXXV. The Questions of King Milinda. Translated from the Pâli by T. W. RHYS DAVIDS. 8vo, cloth, 10*s*. 6*d*.

VOL. XXXVII. The Contents of the Nasks, as stated in the Eighth and Ninth Books of the Dînka*rd*. Translated by E. W. WEST. [*In the Press.*]

VOLS. XXXIX AND XL. The Sacred Books of China. The Texts of Taoism. Translated by JAMES LEGGE. [*In the Press.*]

*** **The Second Series will consist of Twenty-four Volumes in all.**

SOME ORIENTAL WORKS

RECENTLY PUBLISHED BY THE CLARENDON PRESS.

A Practical Arabic Grammar. Part I.

Compiled by A. O. GREEN, Brigade Major, Royal Engineers. *Second Edition, Enlarged.* Crown 8vo, 7*s.* 6*d.*

A Catalogue of the Chinese Translation of the Buddhist Tripiṭaka, *the Sacred Canon of the Buddhists in China and Japan.*

Compiled by order of the Secretary of State for India by BUNYIU NANJIO, Priest of the Temple, Eastern Hongwanzi, Japan; Member of the Royal Asiatic Society. 4to, 32*s.* 6*d.*

'An immense service rendered to Oriental scholarship.'—*Saturday Review.*

The Chinese Classics: with a Translation, Critical and Exegetical Notes, Prolegomena, and Copious Indexes. By JAMES LEGGE, D.D., LL.D. In Seven Volumes. Royal 8vo.

Vol. I. *Confucian Analects, &c.* [*Out of print.*]

Vol. II. *The Works of Mencius.* 1*l.* 10*s.*

Vol. III. *The Shoo-King, or the Book of Historical Documents.* In two Parts. 1*l.* 10*s.* each.

Vol. IV. *The She-King, or the Book of Poetry.* In two Parts. 1*l.* 10*s.* each.

Vol. V. *The Ch'un Ts'ew, with the Tso Chuen.* In two Parts. 1*l.* 10*s.* each.

The Nestorian Monument of Hsî-an Fû in Shen-hsî, China, relating to the Diffusion of Christianity in China in the Seventh and Eighth Centuries. By JAMES LEGGE, D.D., LL.D. *Paper covers,* 2*s.* 6*d.*

Record of Buddhistic Kingdoms; being an Account by the Chinese Monk FÂ-HIEN of his Travels in India and Ceylon (A.D. 399–414) in search of the Buddhist Books of Discipline. Translated and annotated, with a Corean recension of the Chinese Text, by JAMES LEGGE, M.A., LL.D. Crown 4to, boards, 10*s.* 6*d.*

Catalogue of the Hebrew Manuscripts in the Bodleian Library and in the College Libraries of Oxford.

Compiled by AD. NEUBAUER, M.A. *With* 40 *Facsimiles.* cloth, 5*l.* 5*s.*

Also separately:

The Catalogue. 3*l.* 13*s.* 6*d.* The Facsimiles. 2*l.* 12*s.* 6*d.*

Anecdota Oxoniensia.

ARYAN SERIES.

Buddhist Texts from Japan. I. Vagrakkhedikâ; *The Diamond-Cutter.*

Edited by F. MAX MÜLLER, M.A. Small 4to, 3*s.* 6*d.*

One of the most famous metaphysical treatises of the Mahâyâna Buddhists.

Buddhist Texts from Japan. II. Sukhâvatî-Vyûha: *Description of Sukhâvatî, the Land of Bliss.*

Edited by F. MAX MÜLLER, M.A., and BUNYIU NANJIO. With two Appendices: (1) Text and Translation of Saṅghavarman's Chinese Version of the Poetical Portions of the Sukhâvatî-Vyûha; (2) Sanskrit Text of the Smaller Sukhâvatî-Vyûha. Small 4to, 7*s.* 6*d.*

The *editio princeps* of the Sacred Book of one of the largest and most influential sects of Buddhism, numbering more than ten millions of followers in Japan alone.

Buddhist Texts from Japan. III. *The Ancient Palm-Leaves containing the* Pragñâ-Pâramitâ-H*ri*daya-Sûtra *and the* Ush*n*îsha-Vigaya-Dhâra*n*î.

Edited by F. MAX MÜLLER, M.A., and BUNYIU NANJIO, M.A. With an Appendix by G. BÜHLER, C.I.E. With many Plates. Small 4to, 10*s.*

Contains facsimiles of the oldest Sanskrit MS. at present known.

Dharma-Sa*m*graha, *an Ancient Collection of Buddhist Technical Terms.*

Prepared for publication by KENJIU KASAWARA, a Buddhist Priest from Japan, and, after his death, edited by F. MAX MÜLLER and H. WENZEL. Small 4to, 7*s.* 6*d.*

Kâtâyana's Sarvânukrama*n*î of the *Ri*gveda.

With Extracts from Sha*d*guru*s*ishya's Commentary entitled Vedârthadîpikâ. Edited by A. A. MACDONELL, M.A., Ph.D. 16*s.*

Oxford

AT THE CLARENDON PRESS

LONDON: HENRY FROWDE

OXFORD UNIVERSITY PRESS WAREHOUSE, AMEN CORNER, E.C.